War Torn

Manchester, its Newspapers and the Luftwaffe's Christmas Blitz of 1940

War Torn

Manchester, its Newspapers and the Luftwaffe's Christmas Blitz of 1940

By Guy Hodgson

University of Chester Press

First published 2015
by University of Chester Press
University of Chester
Parkgate Road
Chester CH1 4BJ

Printed and bound in the UK by the
LIS Print Unit
University of Chester
Cover designed by the
LIS Graphics Team
University of Chester

© Guy Hodgson, 2015

Wartime images
© The Greater Manchester Police
Museum & Archives

All Rights Reserved
No part of this publication may be reproduced, stored in a retrieval system or transmitted in any form or by any means without the prior permission of the copyright owner, other than as permitted by current UK copyright legislation or under the terms and conditions of a recognised copyright licensing scheme

A catalogue record for this book is available from the British Library

ISBN 978-1-908258-16-8

For Sheila, Josie and Alexandra

CONTENTS

List of Illustrations	x
Preface	xi
Acknowledgements	xiv
Introduction	1

PART I
Chapter One: Historical Perspective
1. 'A jumbled-up nondescript place'	7
2. The Christmas Blitz	10

Chapter Two: The Press and the Mythology of the Blitz
1. 'Harlots of democracy'	19
2. Creation of the Myth	24

Chapter Three: Methodology
1. Approaching the Sources	31
2. Newspaper Production	33
3. Dissemination	35
4. The Audience	46
5. The Limits of the Research	47

PART II
Chapter Four: The Newspapers
1. Putting on the Battle Dress	51
2. The Editors	54
3. 'Serious again in the morning'	63

Chapter Five: Censorship
1. A Barrage of D-Notices — 72
2. 'Any use to us?' — 75
3. Guidance to Editors — 84
4. Fit to Print: Censorship and the Manchester Blitz — 89
5. Self-Censorship at the *Manchester Guardian* — 98

Chapter Six: Propaganda and the Management of Opinion
1. The First World War Model — 105
2. Before the Manchester Blitz
   2.1 *Manchester Guardian* — 109
   2.2 *Manchester Evening News* — 111
   2.3 *Evening Chronicle* — 113
3. The Blitz Editions
   3.1 *Manchester Guardian* — 115
   3.2 *Manchester Evening News* — 121
   3.3 *Evening Chronicle* — 124
4. The Post-Blitz Editions
   4.1 *Manchester Guardian* — 129
   4.2 *Manchester Evening News* — 132
   4.3 *Evening Chronicle* — 134
5. 'No one dare report the tears' — 136

Chapter Seven: All in This Together?
1. The Social Divide — 146
2. Crime and Newspaper Coverage of the Courts — 154
3. Letters to the Editor — 159
4. A Template of Cheerfulness — 164

Contents

Chapter Eight: The Aftermath of Christmas 1940
1. Observing the Masses — 167
2. Report on Manchester and Liverpool — 177
3. Contemporary Reaction — 185
4. Looking Back on Manchester's Blitz — 188
5. Lingering Suspicion and Rumours — 190

Chapter Nine: Escape and the Moving News Agenda
1. Satisfying the Audience? — 194
2. Entertaining the Masses — 196
3. War and Non-War News — 203
4. Piccadilly, Manchester, or Piccadilly London? — 209
5. *The Times*, the *Daily Mirror* and the *Salford City Reporter* — 217

Chapter Ten: 'Useless to Buy Newspapers'
1. The Front Line — 226
2. Final Word — 231

Appendices
Appendix 1: Newspaper Circulations — 235
Appendix 2: National Newspapers Printed in Manchester in 1940 — 236

Bibliography — 238

LIST OF ILLUSTRATIONS

Cover picture: Miller Street and Shude Hill from the corner of Swan Street and Rochdale Road (courtesy of The Greater Manchester Police Museum & Archives).

Plate 1: Oxford Road at war (courtesy of The Greater Manchester Police Museum & Archives). — 139

Plate 2: Inspecting the wreckage of the Free Trade Hall (courtesy of The Greater Manchester Police Museum & Archives). — 140

Plate 3: Manchester Piccadilly in the Blitz (courtesy of The Greater Manchester Police Museum & Archives). — 141

Plate 4: Manchester Christmas Blitz 1940 (courtesy of The Greater Manchester Police Museum & Archives). — 142

Plate 5: Surveying the damage in Piccadilly Gardens (courtesy of The Greater Manchester Police Museum & Archives). — 143

Plate 6: Rising from the destruction on Miller Street and Shude Hill (courtesy of The Greater Manchester Police Museum & Achives). — 144

Plate 7: Echoes of the past at the Manchester Printworks. — 145

Plate 8: The Fire Window in Manchester Cathedral. — 146

PREFACE

The role of the British press in the Second World War is frequently overlooked, which is a surprising omission given that, from the outset, newspapers were the main form of communication between the government and its people – a position that would be matched by radio during the conflict.[1] Furthermore, Anderson has argued that the printing press was one of the key factors in the creation of nationhood as an 'imagined community', an essential prerequisite in the conducting of war on an industrial and national scale.[2] He wrote:

> Regardless of the actual inequality and exploitation that may prevail in each, the nation is always conceived as a horizontal comradeship. Ultimately it is this fraternity that makes it possible, over the past two centuries, for so many millions of people, not so much to kill, as willingly to die for such limited imaginings.[3]

In more recent times, Gillespie argued that the earliest newspapers connected dispersed people to national discourses and the 'mass ritual and ceremony of newspaper reading' contributed to the construction of ideas of national community.[4]

The mythology of 1939–45 was either invented by Fleet Street or considerably advanced by it: the 'triumph' of Dunkirk was born in newspaper offices; the 'few' of the Battle

---

[1] Martin Conboy, *Journalism in Britain: A Historical Introduction* (London: Sage, 2011), p. 26.
[2] Benedict Anderson, *Imagined Communities*, 3rd edn (London: Verso, 2006), pp. 5–7.
[3] Ibid., p. 7.
[4] Marie Gillespie, 'Transnational Communications and Diaspora Communities' in Simon Cottle, ed., *Ethnic Minorities and the Media* (Buckingham: Open University Press, 2000), p. 167.

of Britain and the Blitz Spirit were pieces of Churchillian rhetoric that were embellished and given impetus by news pages. Yet, as Bingham observed: 'Historians have, in fact, generally been reluctant to examine the press for insights into the past.'[5] This book seeks to partly redress the balance by analysing Manchester's newspapers before and after the city's Christmas Blitz of 1940. This is predominantly a qualitative study, which has taken an interpretative and contextual approach to the newspaper headlines and copy, involving analysis of all sections, including news and non-news pages, editorials and readers' letters. Quantitative methods have not been entirely neglected, however, and they are used to measure the proportion of war against non-war reports, the amount of coverage given to lighter items such as entertainment and sport, and to monitor news agendas.

War, generally, is good news for newspapers. What is being reported has an increased significance, readers have a greater stake in what appears in print and, correspondingly, circulations rise, as they did for national and local newspapers between 1939 and 1945. Boyd-Barrett wrote:

> Classic warfare is the epitome of a 'good story', high in tension and drama, with complex main plots and sub-plots played out within traditional binary oppositions of aggressor and victim, winner and loser. While expensive to cover, warfare is commercially rewarding for the media, since its threat and unfolding ignite insatiable audience appetite for news.[6]

---

[5] Adrian Bingham, *Gender, Modernity and the Popular Press in Inter-War Britain* (Oxford: Clarendon, 2004), p. 1.
[6] Oliver Boyd-Barrett, 'Understanding the Second Casualty', in S. Allan and B. Zelizer, eds, *Reporting War: Journalism in Wartime* (London: Routledge, 2004), p. 26.

Preface

The effect of war on journalism, rather than the economics of journalism, is more complex. Webster stated that the media are needed for more than reporting acceptable news from the battlefield: 'They are also central players in justifying war itself … especially so in democratic regimes.'[7] The role of marshalling and maintaining morale on one's own side, and attacking the opponent's, 'munitions of the mind' ensured that journalists faced a dilemma in the Second World War if they wished to observe the military in action and record the first draft of history.[8] Knightley asked:

> If doing that as objectively and as truthfully as possible means writing and broadcasting stories damaging to their nation's war effort, what are correspondents to do? Does the journalist within the correspondent prevail? Or the patriot? And what if reporting patriotically involves telling lies? Is that journalism or propaganda?[9]

This is a question that is fundamental to this book: was the imperative for journalists between 1939 and 1945 to support the war effort in a 'deliberate and systematic attempt to shape opinions' or to hold the authorities to account?[10] And if they did the latter, would they be helping or hindering the fight against Adolf Hitler? This book will examine how Manchester's newspapers came to terms with that dilemma, even if it was never resolved.

---

[7] Frank Webster, 'Information Warfare in an Age of Globalization' in Daya Kishan Thussu and Des Freedman, eds, *War and the Media* (London: Sage, 2003), p. 65.

[8] Susan L. Carruthers, *The Media At War* (London: Macmillan, 2000), p. 55.

[9] Phillip Knightley, *The First Casualty: The War Correspondent as Hero and Myth-Maker from the Crimea to Iraq*, 5th edn (Baltimore, MD: Johns Hopkins University Press, 2004), p. xi.

[10] Garth S. Jowett and Victoria O'Donnell, *Propaganda and Persuasion*, 5th edn (London: Sage, 2012), p. 289.

ACKNOWLEDGEMENTS

This book owes its roots to a PhD studied at the University of Chester between 2008 and 2013.

With thanks to my supervisors, Dr Michael Huggins and Professor Peter Gaunt, colleagues Michael Nally, Brendan O'Sullivan, Bernard Pratt, Dr Simon Roberts, Dr Vera Slavtcheva-Petkova, and the staff of Manchester Central and John Rylands Libraries.

INTRODUCTION

The author John Steinbeck was not complimentary when he reviewed the work of journalists in the Second World War. 'We were all part of the war effort', he wrote. 'We went along with it, and not only that, we abetted it.' He added: 'I don't mean the correspondents were liars ... It is in the things not mentioned that the untruth lies.'[1] Steinbeck was a war correspondent for the *New York Herald Tribune* from June to December 1943 and in this relatively short time, his work followed that of other reporters in avoiding writing about the reality of war and, instead, he subscribed to an idealised view of the Allied war effort in which 'our' people were eternally stoic, 'our' soldiers impeccably brave and 'our' bombers unerringly accurate. British journalists were in the vanguard of that effort and several academics, such as Calder, Knightley, Curran and Seaton, noted that the writing of the myth of the war against Hitler began from the moment Prime Minister Neville Chamberlain formally announced the opening of hostilities on BBC radio on 3 September 1939.[2] It encompassed, among what appear often to be other rose-tinted visions, Dunkirk, 'we're all in this together', the 'few' of the Battle of Britain, genial Uncle Joe Stalin and, perhaps the most potent of all, the Blitz Spirit.

This book will help bring a further understanding of the British press and the experience of bombing during the Second World War. It will examine the myth of that Blitz Spirit that

---

[1] John Steinbeck, *Once There was a War* (New York: Viking, 1958), cited in Paul Fussell, *Wartime: Understanding and Behaviour in the Second World War* (Oxford: Oxford University Press, 1989), p. 285.
[2] Angus Calder, *The Myth of the Blitz*, (London: Jonathan Cape, 1991); Knightley, *The First Casualty*; J. Curran and J. Seaton, *Power Without Responsibility: Press, Broadcasting and the Internet in Britain*, 6th edn (London: Routledge, 2003).

has become so engrained in the UK's popular perception that, 75 years on, it is used as a metaphor of first resort for politicians and the media whenever the nation is under threat, be it from war, natural extremes such as floods, sharp economic down-turns, or attacks by terrorists. It will study the role of newspapers in the Second World War, with a particular reference to Manchester, which was Britain's second newspaper centre at the time and would have become the principal one in the event of irreparable damage to Fleet Street.

The first bomb to land on the city was dropped on 8 August 1940 and it was attacked throughout the Second World War, but Manchester's Blitz, concentrated and prolonged bombing, lasted only two nights, 22/23 and 23/24 December 1940, when nearly 1,000 people were killed and 3,500 injured.[3] In excess of 50,000 homes in the area were damaged along with the cathedral and other important public buildings.[4] 'Manchester will remember the horrors of that attack as long as the heart of the north continues to beat', a contemporary Co-operative Wholesale Society newsreel reported, before adding the eulogy typical of the reporting in 1940 and 1941, 'but she will remember its glories too.'[5] The newsreel glossed over the fact that troops were filmed with their bayonets attached to their rifles, which may have been an embellishment for the cameras or an over-reaction by the authorities, but, more likely, an indication of the undercurrent of lawlessness in a city with its infrastructure in ruins and its

---

[3] Stuart Hylton, *A History of Manchester*, 2nd edn (Andover: Phillimore, 2010), p. 253.
[4] Clive Hardy, Ian Cooper and Henry Hochland, *Manchester at War* (Bowdon: Archive, 1986), p. 44.
[5] Co-operative Wholesale Society, *The Manchester Blitz: Manchester Took it Too* (Imperial War Museum) <http://www.youtube.com/watch?v=Fte9DpZRfwo> [accessed 3 January 2012].

Introduction

population struggling to cope with, in Manchester's experience, unprecedented levels of destruction.

There has been much research into London's Blitz, but relatively little about cities elsewhere in the UK, an imbalance that can be justified by the capital's suffering nearly 50 per cent of the British deaths caused by the Luftwaffe's bombing, 29,890 to 30,705. The narrative of the irrepressible East Ender has become pervasive, however, so that provincial tales have been overwhelmed.[6] Maconie wrote that South Shields, in the north east of England, suffered 200 air raids in the Second World War:

> One direct hit on the marketplace killed more than 40 people sheltering in tunnels below the square. These are statistics to remember next time you watch a programme about the Blitz. It will be about London as always and feature Piccadilly Circus in flames and cheery Cockneys making their way to Tube stations. If you trusted the London media you could be forgiven for thinking that the south won the war single-handed and that northern England was as quiet as Switzerland. It wasn't, as the people in South Shields will testify.[7]

This book focuses on the region to which Maconie was referring, the north of England. It will ask three principal questions. Firstly, did the Manchester press submit its coverage to self-imposed censorship as it strived to achieve a difficult balance between journalists' traditional belief that they were obliged to report 'facts' and government exhortations that popular morale had to be maintained and information useful to the enemy edited out? Second, were there reasons, other than self and official censorship, for the editorialising of news of the war? Third, did the reporting of

---

[6] T. H. O'Brien, *Civil Defence* (London: HMSO, 1955), p. 677.
[7] Stuart Maconie, *Pies and Prejudice: In Search of the North* (London: Ebury, 2007), p. 303.

the war impact negatively on the reputation of Manchester's newspapers?

The book is divided into two parts: context and research. Three chapters comprise the context section, the first of which explores Manchester's place in the UK newspaper industry in the Second World War and the Blitz that struck the city in December 1940. The second chapter examines myth and its application to the Second World War and the third shows how the study was conducted in methodological terms, why the newspapers, 144 editions of the *Manchester Guardian*, the *Manchester Evening News* and the *Evening Chronicle,* were selected and how their influence and audience reach met the requirements for the aims of this study. The second part consists of chapters focusing on a specific set of themes and so provides the analysed core of this book. Each chapter, typically, is organised into two main sections, the first providing a national or theoretical background before the second studies the specific newspapers. The press, censorship and propaganda are examined before these themes are drawn together to explore the alleged unity of purpose and equality of suffering. Chapter Eight assesses the reliability of what was published in Manchester's newspapers by comparing the press to the contemporary accounts in the archives of Mass Observation, Home Intelligence and Stockport Library. Quantitative analysis is then conducted to examine how much emphasis Manchester newspapers gave to escapist elements in their columns and how quickly the Manchester Blitz fell down the news agenda. To assess whether Manchester's newspapers were exceptions to the norm, these findings are compared to similar research into two national publications, *The Times* and the *Daily Mirror,* and a local weekly, the *Salford City Reporter.*

Traditional news values, Randall asserted, insist that a newspaper's role is to 'find out fresh information on matters of public interest and to relay it as quickly and as accurately as

Introduction

possible to readers in an honest and balanced way'.[8] This book will explore whether the press, Manchester and national, fell short of those self-proclaimed standards, or whether they met these ideals of speed, accuracy, and balance only when there was good news to spread.

---

[8] David Randall, *The Universal Journalist*, 2nd edn (London: Pluto, 2000), p. 22.

PART I

CHAPTER ONE
HISTORICAL PERSPECTIVE

1. 'A jumbled-up nondescript place'

Manchester and Salford had a combined population of more than a million at the start of the Second World War, the 1931 census counting 766,378 and 223,438 people respectively.[1] These figures grew in the 1930s and 1940s and in 1949 the Royal Commission on the Press estimated the population of greater Manchester as 1.5 million, rising to 2.25 million if the outlying Bolton, Oldham, Stockport, Bury and Rochdale were included.[2] There was a significant Catholic minority, amounting to 130,000 or 13 per cent in 1931, including approximately 800 Italians in the inner-city area of Ancoats, and Williams estimated there was a 40,000-strong Jewish community in Manchester in 1933, a figure boosted before the war as 8,000 refugees, most of them Jews, fled to the city to escape the Nazis in Germany, Austria and Czechoslovakia.[3]

The city, according to Hayes in the mid nineteenth century, was attractive to immigrants, because of its tolerance:

---

[1] Steven J. Fielding, 'The Irish Catholics of Manchester and Salford: Aspects of Their Religious and Political History, 1890–1939', (unpublished doctoral thesis, University of Warwick, 1988), p. 347. No census was undertaken in 1941 because of the hostilities.

[2] HMSO, *Royal Commission on the Press 1947–1949* (London: HMSO, 1949), p. 10.

[3] Fielding, 'Irish Catholics', p. 52; Paul Di Felice, 'Reconstructing Manchester's Little Italy', *Manchester Region History Review*, 12 (1998), 54–65 (p. 56); Bill Williams, *Jews and Other Foreigners: Manchester and the Rescue of the Victims of European Fascism, 1933–40* (Manchester: Manchester University Press, 2011), pp. 11, 435.

> Our foreign trade brings us into contact with most nationalities, and makes us probably more cosmopolitan in our views ... Manchester makes no distinction as to creed or race. She opens her portals and offers an equal chance to all those who wish to settle here to trade and get gain.[4]

This may have been the case in 1840, but 90 years later the membership of the British Union of Fascists was so large in Manchester that Sir Oswald Mosley considered moving its headquarters from London to the city.[5] The support for the BUF disappeared at the outbreak of war and a change of mood might be detected in that riots broke out in Little Italy, Ancoats, in 1940 when Mussolini allied with Germany and invaded France.[6] Most of the city's Italian males in a community described by Williams as 'subsisting largely as itinerant ice-cream sellers, barrel organists and manual workers' in Ancoats and academics, lawyers and entrepreneurs dotted elsewhere in the city, were interned in Bury and many died when the *Arandora Star* was sunk the following month.[7] The book will return to this subject in Chapter Seven.

The view of 1940s Manchester by Home Intelligence, an organisation reporting on civilian morale to the Ministry of Information (MOI), was less than flattering.[8] When its observers visited the city in January 1941, immediately after the Christmas Blitz, they found spirits to be low, but their criticism extended beyond the immediate difficulties to pre-war attitudes. Describing Manchester as an 'uncoordinated,

---

[4] Louis M. Hayes, *Reminiscences of Manchester and Some of its Surroundings from the Year 1840* (Manchester: 1905), cited in Williams, *Jews*, p. 2.
[5] Ibid., p. 394.
[6] Ibid., p. 396.
[7] Ibid.
[8] University of Sussex, Mass Observation Archive, FR 538, *Liverpool and Manchester*, January 1941.

topographically incoherent, overlapping, jumbled-up nondescript place', their report continued: 'Even at the best of times Manchester feeling and a positive Manchester outlook are liable to be lacking.'[9] The inspectors added:

> Long before the war competent *observers* were saying that there was a noticeable strain of selfishness and strict utilitarianism in Manchester. And in the last few months several people have pointed out the tendency for Manchester people to stop work at the slightest siren, sleep all night in shelters long before the Blitz, etc.[10]

While Home Intelligence may have been less than impressed, the city's significance in the British newspaper industry was undeniable. The roots of Manchester's position as Britain's second print centre began growing from 1821 when the *Manchester Guardian* was published for the first time, to be followed by the *Manchester Courier* four years later.[11] The *Manchester Evening News* and the *Evening Chronicle* were established in 1868 and 1897 respectively and the city started printing a national newspaper on 3 February 1900 when a northern edition of the *Daily Mail* was launched in Gorton.[12] It was a landmark moment because, of the national daily titles, only *The Times* and the *Financial Times* declined to establish print centres in the city. Manchester's distribution area embraced England north of Birmingham, Scotland for those newspapers not published in Glasgow or Edinburgh, North Wales and all of Ireland. This provided a market for regional and provincial publications as well as national newspapers and by the start of the Second World War the *Sunday Empire*

---

[9] Ibid.
[10] Ibid.
[11] Robert Waterhouse, *The Other Fleet Street* (Altrincham: First Edition, 2004), p. 16.
[12] Ibid.

News, the *Daily Dispatch*, the *Chronicle Mid-Day* and the *Sporting Chronicle* were printed exclusively in the city.[13] Waterhouse wrote:

> For the best part of the twentieth century Manchester was the other Fleet Street, publishing between a quarter and a third of all newspapers consumed in the British Isles ... Manchester was the means by which national newspapers became truly national.[14]

It was a city so important for the national and provincial press in Britain that when the Berry brothers, Lords Camrose and Kemsley, formed Allied Northern Newspapers in 1924, its Withy Grove site was described as Europe's largest single print hub, employing 3,000 people.[15] 'Manchester is far and away the largest newspaper centre outside London', Camrose wrote. 'Indeed, it closely rivals the metropolis itself.'[16] During the war Manchester was the natural choice as an emergency centre of publication should Fleet Street be put out of action by the Luftwaffe and, although this scenario never materialised, transport problems meant many southern editions had to be printed in the city.[17]

2. The Christmas Blitz

The concentrated bombing raid on Coventry on 14 and 15 November 1940 – *The Times* described it as 'butchery' – highlighted a change in tactics by the Luftwaffe as it extended its bombing of London to Britain's provincial centres.[18]

---

[13] HMSO, *Royal Commission*, p. 185.
[14] Waterhouse, *Other Fleet Street*, p. 7.
[15] Ibid., p. 9.
[16] Viscount Camrose, *British Newspapers and their Controllers* (London: Cassell, 1947), p. 116.
[17] Waterhouse, *Other Fleet Street*, p. 9.
[18] 'The Butchery of Coventry', *The Times*, 18 November 1940, p. 4; Fussell, *Wartime*, p. 148.

Historical Perspective

Birmingham was attacked on 25 October, and Glasgow, Plymouth, Coventry, Bristol, Southampton, Merseyside, Manchester and Sheffield followed.[19] The Germans began the war directing bombers by a radio device named the *Knickebein*, but when the British jammed the beams, they revised their methods and pathfinder forces were sent out to light the way for the heavy bombers with incendiaries.[20] Coventry was the first city to be attacked using the new method.

The first raid of the Manchester Blitz occurred on 22–23 December 1940, a Sunday night and Monday morning, when 149 aircraft of *Luftflotte 3* and 121 of *Luftflotte 2* dropped 272 tons of high-explosive bombs and 37,152 incendiaries.[21] The attacks, lasting from 7.45 pm to 6.55 am, concentrated on the western side of the city, the docks and industrial areas of Trafford Park and Salford and such was the glare from the more than 400 fires, it could be seen by crews flying over London.[22] More than 100 of these fires were serious and the problems for the emergency services were exacerbated by a shortage of staff, many of whom had been sent to help in Liverpool the previous day.[23] Both the city's main railway

---

[19] Calder, *The Myth of the Blitz*, p. 36.
[20] W. Ramsey, ed., *The Blitz Then And Now*, II, (London: Battle of Britain, 1988), p. 628; R. V. Jones, *Most Secret War: British Scientific Intelligence, 1939–1945* (London: Coronet, 1979), p. 177.
[21] It is also known locally as the Christmas Blitz (see Chris Perkins and Martin Dodge, 'Mapping the Imagined Future: The Roles of Visual Representation in the 1945 City of Manchester Plan', *Professional Geographer*, 59, 1 (2007): p. 31; Ramsey, *Blitz Then and Now*, p. 351.
[22] Ramsey, *Blitz Then and Now*, p. 351.
[23] Manchester sent 200 fire fighters to Liverpool to deal with aftermath of the bombing on 20 and 21 December (Hylton, *A History*, p. 253).

stations, Central and London Road (now Manchester Piccadilly), and the main bus station were hit. Fletcher wrote:

> At times another Coventry seemed to be threatened and people living near Withy Grove [where the *Evening Chronicle* was based] risked death by deserting their own surface and Anderson shelters to seek greater protection afforded them beneath the largest of all provincial newspaper offices. Difficult as conditions were, none could be refused shelter that night and the refugees crowded on to the benches while the cramped sub-editors went about their job preparing for the morning's newspapers.[24]

The following night, 23–24 December, 171 aircraft of *Luftflotte 3* dropped 195 tons of high explosive and 7,020 incendiary bombs between 7.15 pm and midnight bringing the casualty list in Manchester alone to an estimated 684 people dead and 2,364 wounded.[25] Within a mile of Albert Square, 31.3 acres were in ruins and many important buildings were severely damaged, including the Free Trade Hall, Cross Street Chapel, Manchester Cathedral, Chetham's Hospital, the Corn Exchange, St Anne's Church, City Hall, Smithfield Market and the Gaiety Theatre.[26] Salford, the city separated from Manchester only by the River Irwell, suffered 215 deaths and 910 wounded, while Stretford, the domestic area closest to the factories and warehouses of Old Trafford and Trafford Park, suffered an estimated 73 deaths.[27] The human cost was also reflected in the numbers of homeless people: 6,000 in

---

[24] Leonard Fletcher, *They Never Failed: The Story of the Provincial Press in Wartime* (London: Newspaper Society, 1946), p. 62.
[25] Ramsey, *Blitz Then and Now*, p. 352; Imperial War Museum North, *Manchester Blitz* <http://www.iwm.org.uk/server/show/ConWebDoc.2790> [accessed 3 July 2010].
[26] Hardy, Cooper and Hochland, *Manchester at War*, p. 44.
[27] Vicki Masterton and Karen Cliff, *Stretford: An Illustrated History* (Derby: Breedon, 2002), p. 156.

Historical Perspective

Manchester; 5,000 in Salford; and 4,000 in Stretford.[28] These figures, confused by the destruction of burial and crematorium records in Barlow Moor Road, south of the city, during the same two nights of bombing, were depressing enough given that they represent nearly one in 60 of every UK civilians killed in the Second World War, but many believed they were an underestimate. Freethy, for example, summed up the confusion over the number of casualties when he stated:

> Records show that between the 22 and 25 of December 1,005 people were killed and many more injured. This compares to the 4,100 people who were killed in Liverpool between 1940 and 1941 and the 1,236 poor folk who were killed in Coventry.[29]

None of these figures correlates with statistics supplied by the Imperial War Museum, but there was widespread suspicion in 1940 and 1941 that the published figures did not match the reality. Joyce Kilshaw, of Sale, four miles south west of Manchester, recalled:

> One of my vivid memories of the war was looking at the lists, which were pinned up informing the neighbourhood who had been killed in the various air raids. However, I am now sure that these lists didn't give quite a full picture of those who lost their lives and most certainly the numbers had been well and truly censored.[30]

She articulated the common fear of people emerging from their shelters not knowing whether their house had survived the air raid intact:

---

[28] Hardy, Cooper and Hochland, *Manchester at War*, p. 44.
[29] Ron Freethy, *Lancashire v Hitler: Civilians at War* (Newbury: Countryside, 2006), p. 16.
[30] Ron Freethy, *Lancashire 1939–1945. The Secret War* (Newbury: Countryside, 2005), p. 14.

Sometimes news of homes that had been bombed filtered through to the shelter but the ARP wardens were told not to give any information to stop people going out of the shelters whilst the raids were still going on to rescue their belongings. The ARP wardens had to write detailed reports and they were also censored.[31]

The fact that people were concerned about their possessions is indicative of the prevalence, or fear, of looters.[32]

Although Manchester was bombed throughout the war, it endured only one further major raid, in June 1941, leaving it relatively lightly touched compared, for example, to nearby Liverpool which, according to official figures, suffered 2,716 casualties between 1939 and 1945 (and a further 1,173 in neighbouring areas).[33] Liverpool endured 16 heavy raids in 1940 and 1941, and 50 of varying degrees of severity between August and Christmas 1940, including two bombardments that killed 365 people on 20/21 and 21/22 December, the two nights immediately before the Manchester Blitz, yet Home Intelligence inspectors, as this book will examine, observed that morale suffered far more in the latter than it did in Merseyside.[34] There were reasons for this, partly economic. Liverpool boomed during the Second World War, largely because of imports from the United States and Canada which reversed the trend of growth in trade to ports in the south of England, particularly London, during the previous two

---

[31] Ibid., pp. 14–16.
[32] Juliet Gardiner, *The Blitz. The British Under Attack* (London: Harper, 2010), p. 324.
[33] E. Chambré Hardman Archive, Liverpool.
[34] Tom Harrisson, *Living Through the Blitz*, 2nd edn (London: Penguin, 1990), p. 234; Merseyside Maritime Museum, *Spirit of the Blitz* (2003) <http://www.liverpoolmuseums.org.uk/maritime/exhibitions/blitz/blitz.asp> [accessed 17 February 2012]; Mass Observation, FR 538.

decades.[35] As in the First World War, trade concentrated on the North Atlantic and by 1947, 35 per cent of the city's labour force was employed in shipping and other dependent industries.[36] Manchester did not have an equivalent commercial boom to balance the effects of the bombing, but, irrespective of economic factors, Calder stated that often it was those cities and towns that were less used to bombing that suffered most psychologically. 'The effect on popular attitudes of even a single sharp raid should not be underestimated.'[37] Manchester, too, lacked an advantage of London because of its size. If a grocer's shop was bombed, another would be within walking distance, so the capital could absorb the strain of continuous bombing. In smaller cities the quality of life could be severely reduced by the loss of utilities and amenities. Also, when the centre of a smaller city was razed, the symbols and buildings of local pride and the centres of local pleasure were destroyed with it. Beaven and Thoms noted that Manchester suffered disproportionately in this respect, stating that Manchester's Blitz-scale attacks were concentrated on the heart of the city, seriously affecting key institutions such as 'public houses, cinemas, and public utilities, along with transport systems which linked Manchester's centre with its suburban areas'.[38]

Calder argued: 'Small raids were interspersed unpredictably with periods of lull and fierce Blitzes, and no

---

[35] Richard Lawton and Catherine M. Cunningham, eds, *Merseyside: Social and Economic Studies*, (Harlow: Longman, 1970), p. 69.
[36] Ibid.
[37] Angus Calder, *The People's War: Britain 1939–45* (London: Jonathan Cape, 1969), p, 220.
[38] B. Beaven and D. Thoms, 'The Blitz and Civilian Morale in Three Northern Cities, 1940–1942', *Northern History,* 32 (1996), p. 199.

"even tenor" could be established.'[39] After Leicester was bombed relatively lightly for eight hours on 19 November 1940 at a cost of 108 deaths, a special constable wrote: 'Many fantastic tales swept through the city about the damage, the hundreds, some said, even thousands that had been killed.'[40] That raid brought a residue of fear that lasted for several months. 'There was nothing but the incessant drone of enemy planes and the constant vigil', the same man wrote, describing the 20-minute spells of severe anxiety as people braced themselves for the noise of bombs exploding. Only when they did not arrive did relief come with: 'Well, they're not coming for us, this time.'[41] Calder stated it was the lack of regular bombings, the uncertainty, that frayed the nerves:

> The worst feature of morale, as the Mass Observers saw it, was the feeling of helplessness which emerged as the weight of remembered and anticipated fear, and of present inconvenience, sank down on the shoulders of populations which did not, like London's, have the stimulus to adaption [sic] provided by nightly raids.[42]

The Manchester Blitz appears to have had an effect out of proportion to its destruction, but perhaps that was because the bombing came as such a shock, both in its occurrence and its timing as the city prepared to enjoy its Christmas break. Freethy stated that while it was relatively easy at the start of the war to censor the armed forces, and even newspapers, it was more of a problem to convince civilians in the north of England that careless talk could cost lives: 'The people of

---

[39] Calder, *The People's War*, p. 205.
[40] George Harold Ingles, *When the War Came to Leicester: The Account of the Air Raids on this Great Midland City*, (Leicester: Brooks, 1945), pp. 19–20.
[41] Ibid.
[42] Calder, *The People's War*, pp. 218–19.

Historical Perspective

Lancashire needed even more persuading than most because, initially, they felt themselves remote from danger, unlike those in the southern counties.'[43] To many Mancunians the most obvious signs that Britain was at war were minor inconveniences. All Ordnance Survey maps were removed from sale, for fear of being acquired by enemy agents, milestones and signposts were removed – even the Cross Street building of the *Manchester Guardian* and *Manchester Evening News* had all traces of the word 'Manchester' removed from its exterior – and the names of railway stations were painted over.[44] Even train timetables were pulped to avoid revealing lists of stations in the correct order.[45]

Donald Read, born in 1930, was a schoolboy in Burnage, a suburb of Manchester three miles from the centre, when the war began and his initial experience was typical of many. He was among 72,000 children from the Manchester area who were evacuated to safer areas, going to Kirkham, in Lancashire, when the war started and then to Bollington, Cheshire, 18 miles south of the city. He was back home by the end of September 1939, however, when the expected bombing did not materialise immediately. Read's recollection of the Manchester Blitz was of a city caught unawares. 'Many voluntary workers in Manchester social services had taken Christmas week off, leaving the city's rest centres and other emergency systems short of staff just when help was most needed.'[46] That, as subsequent chapters will show, added to

---

[43] Freethy, *Lancashire 1939–45*, p. 9.
[44] Ibid., p. 14; Denis Thorpe, ed., *A Long Exposure: Pictures from 100 Years of Guardian Photography in Manchester 1908–2008*, (Manchester: Axis, 2008).
[45] Freethy, *Lancashire 1939–45*, p. 14.
[46] Donald Read, *A Manchester Boyhood in the Thirties and Forties: Growing up in War and Peace* (Lampeter: Mellen, 2003), p. 78.

War Torn

the confusion and lack of preparedness that afflicted the city in the aftermath of its Blitz.

CHAPTER TWO

THE PRESS AND THE MYTHOLOGY OF THE BLITZ

1. 'Harlots of democracy'

British newspapers began the Second World War in a paradoxical position. Gannon argued that, in terms of circulation and influence, they were at their zenith, yet there are counter arguments that readers were losing trust in the press.[1] There was also criticism that newspapers were too hostile to Germany, most notably from Sir Nevile Henderson, British Ambassador to Berlin, who wrote on 16 August 1939, less than three weeks before Britain declared war: 'History will judge the press, generally to have been the principal cause of war.'[2] He was writing from an exceptional position, from the political crucible that was Berlin in 1939, but there was also criticism closer to home and 15 days earlier the *Manchester Guardian* reported a speech in Parliament by Arnold Wilson, the Conservative MP for Hitchin. In it he said: 'I would seriously suggest the time has come to consider whether we should not take voluntary powers to enable the press to control itself – at least the headlines.'[3] Interestingly in respect of this book, he added: 'We would do so without the smallest hesitation on the outbreak of war. Is it not better to do it now?'

---

[1] Franklin R. Gannon, *The British Press and Germany 1936–9* (Oxford: Clarendon, 1971), p. 1; Anthony Adamthwaite, 'The British Government and the Media 1937–1938', *Journal of Contemporary History*, 18 (1983), 281–97.
[2] Henderson to Strang, 16 August 1939, *Documents on British Foreign Policy 1919–1939*. Third Series, VII, No. 37 (London: HMSO, 1953).
[3] 'Premier and the Moscow Negotiations', *Manchester Guardian*, 1 August 1939, p. 12.

These comments reflect Fleet Street's position as the primary provider of news in Britain in the 1930s. The BBC gave limited bulletins on its fledgling radio service (which would improve dramatically during the war), but, that outlet apart, the only sources of news outside the press came in the form of out-of-date newsreels – many of which were owned by newspaper groups – shown at the cinema. Gannon wrote: 'The late 1930s … were the golden age of newspapers in Great Britain. More newspapers reached more people than ever before, or than anywhere else in the world.'[4] To meet the public's eagerness for news there were, in 1938, 52 morning newspapers in Great Britain, 85 evening, and 18 Sundays, yet, despite this potential power, historians have argued that newspapers failed in two fundamentals of journalism: in holding the government to account in its foreign relations and in reflecting public opinion in the build-up to the Second World War.[5] Price stated: 'When Downing Street sought the help of the press to reassure the public and downplay the threat to Britain too many editors and proprietors were willing to comply.'[6]

Much of this criticism has focused on the response of the British press to the Munich Agreement in that it failed properly to reflect public opinion. Bingham and Conboy have argued that by the summer of 1938 the *Daily Mirror* was

---

[4] Gannon, *The British Press*, p. 1.
[5] Political and Economic Planning, *Report on the British Press: A Survey of its Current Operations and Problems with Special Reference to National Newspapers and their Part in Public Affairs* (London: PEP, 1938), pp. 3, 47; Adamthwaite, 'The British Government', pp. 281–82, R. Cockett, *Twilight of Truth: Chamberlain, Appeasement and the Manipulation of the Press* (London: Palgrave Macmillan, 1989), and Stephen Koss, *The Rise And Fall of the Political Press in Britain* (London: Hamilton, 1984).
[6] Lance Price, *Where Power Lies: Prime Ministers v the Media* (London: Simon & Schuster, 2010), p. 94.

'already articulating a vigorous populist critique of appeasement', but Fleet Street's and the public's reaction to Chamberlain's accord with Hitler, agreed in September 1938, was initially favourable.[7] An opinion poll taken almost immediately afterwards showed 51 per cent of the public were 'satisfied' by the settlement, with 39 per cent 'not satisfied', while an analysis of 50 British newspapers showed they were virtually unanimous in praising the Prime Minister for preserving peace.[8] Yet, while the press lauded Chamberlain, indicators of an alternative public mood emerged elsewhere. Alfred Duff Cooper, the First Lord of the Admiralty, resigned from the Cabinet over Czechoslovakia and Chamberlain and the Conservatives surrendered voting share in seven by-elections held in October and November 1938, losing Dartford to Labour on 7 November and Bridgwater to an independent candidate 10 days later.[9] The press did not reflect this opposition and, with the cajoling of Downing Street, was largely supportive of the Prime Minister throughout the winter of 1938–39 until Hitler marched into Prague the following spring.[10] In doing so, Adamthwaite argued, newspapers failed to reflect a significant body of opinion critical of British foreign policy:

> It used to be thought, that Hitler's Prague coup produced a sudden and lasting change in British opinion to Germany.

---

[7] Adrian Bingham and Martin Conboy, 'The *Daily Mirror* and the Creation of a Commercial Popular Language', *Journalism Studies*, 10, 5 (2009), 639–54, (p. 650).

[8] P. M. H. Bell, *The Origins of the Second World War in Europe*, 2nd edn (London: Longman, 1997), p. 86; W. W. Hadley, *Munich: Before and After* (London: Cassell, 1944), p. 93.

[9] Roger Eatwell, 'Munich, Public Opinion and Popular Front', *Journal of Contemporary History*, 6, 4 (1971), p. 123.

[10] A. J. P. Taylor, *The Origins of the Second World War*, 2nd edn (London: Penguin, 1991), p. 25.

Now it is conceded that this change was underway in the winter of 1938-39. The evidence of deeply divided opinion in the spring and summer of 1938 warrants the conclusion that a reappraisal had begun *before* Munich.[11]

The inability of the press at large to reflect this opinion was principally because of the overbearing presence of the government. Whereas the owners of the *Daily Express* and *Daily Mail*, Lords Beaverbrook and Rothermere respectively, had campaigned for Baldwin's removal as Conservative leader in 1931, Chamberlain was seen in a more favourable light. The Prime Minister allied that approval to personal friendships with leading newspaper figures so that he did not use compulsion, but rather influence on the men who mattered, the opinion makers such as press barons, leading journalists and the BBC. This, Richard Cockett argued, allowed Chamberlain 'to mask the real divisions that lay within the government and society', the main consequence of which was:

> No alternative policy to appeasement as pursued by Chamberlain could ever be consistently articulated in the British press, nor were the facts and figures that might have supported such an alternative policy ever put in front of the majority of the British public.[12]

A study of newspapers in the four weeks before the start of the Second World War suggests that either by accident or by design, the growing crisis in Europe was not given its due attention until after the announcement of the signing of the Nazi-Soviet Pact on 21 August 1939 when war was considered inevitable. On 15 August the *Daily Mail* reported that the 'Danzig question will be settled without a conflict' and it

---

[11] Adamthwaite, 'The British Government', p. 292.
[12] Cockett, *Twilight of Truth*, pp. 83, 188.

believed that there were 'far bigger matters to be discussed'.[13] A day later *The Times* wrote that the German and Italian governments were putting into shape their own ideas of a settlement in Europe: 'Its first object is, manifestly, to prevent a war.'[14] On 19 August the *Daily Mirror* reported that an American dancer, Miriam Verne, might be romantically linked to Hitler, following it up with a reported quote: 'I think Herr Hitler's absolutely the nicest man I know.'[15] Beaverbrook's *Daily Express* mocked the 'jitter-mongers' who had long predicted that 15 August would be 'crisis day', noting that England had enjoyed a day in the sun.[16] Three days later its front page carried the benign headline: 'Hitler the joker', over an interview with Verne. 'When Hitler goes to a party "he's great fun"', it reported.[17]

The optimism dimmed rapidly with the announcement of the Nazi-Soviet Pact. 'We have done our best to preserve peace', the *Daily Mail* commented, 'and are ready now for whatever may befall.'[18] An editorial in *The Times* on 2 September 1939, the day before the declaration of war, read: 'This nation has never in its history been so unanimous in support of any decision taken by its leaders as it is now.'[19] The *Manchester Guardian*, on the same day, wrote that it was for 'the overthrow of this dictator [Hitler] and his system of

---

[13] 'Axis Hard at Work on "Peace Plan"', *Daily Mail*, 15 August 1939, p. 9.
[14] 'The Whole Peace Front', *The Times*, 16 August 1939, p. 11.
[15] 'Hitler is Charming', *Daily Mirror*, 19 August 1939, p. 5; 'Cassandra', *Daily Mirror*, 21 August 1939, p. 13.
[16] 'Did You Remember Yesterday was to be a Crisis Day?', *Daily Express*, 16 August 1939, p. 2.
[17] 'Hitler the Joker', *Daily Express*, 19 August 1939, p. 1.
[18] 'Hitler Must Decide', *Daily Mail*, 25 August 1939, p. 8.
[19] 'One Man's Crime' *The Times*, 2 September 1939, p. 11.

government that we enter the war.'[20] The mood had changed from meek collusion with government policy to reluctant resignation that war was inevitable, but Cockett argued it was too late: 'By September 1939, the press had become not so much the watchdog of democracy as the harlots of democracy.'[21]

2. Creation of the Myth

Fleet Street had not held the government to account in the two years before the war when they had the freedom to do so; once the hostilities began the restrictions on the press were quickly imposed and newspapers had lost the opportunity. Academics, including Curran, Seaton and Williams, noted that newspapers consciously sought to boost morale at the expense of objective reporting: 'Most of the British press responded to government overtures, abandoning their role of acting as a watchdog on behalf of the public and adopting a partisan role in favour of government policy.'[22] This, according to Herman and Chomsky, conformed to the normal model of media coverage of wars, which is notable for the unquestioning reporting of official sources, government and military, and the ignoring of ideological alternatives. As a consequence, the media provide propaganda rather than 'disinterested' journalism. [23] Herman and Chomsky were writing about the Vietnam War but this book will show that their assertions also

---

[20] 'War', *Manchester Guardian*, 2 September 1939, p. 8.
[21] Cockett, *Twilight of Truth*, p. 187.
[22] Curran and Seaton, *Power Without Responsibility*, p. 62; Kevin Williams, *Get Me a Murder a Day!: A History of Media and Communication in Britain*, 2nd edn (London: Bloomsbury, 2010), p. 119.
[23] Edward S. Herman and Noam Chomsky, *Manufacturing Consent: The Political Economy of the Mass Media* (New York: Pantheon, 1988), p. 252.

pertained to the period between 1939 and 1945, and this relationship between newspapers and Britain's leaders led to the creation of many myths and semi-truths that have obscured 'the way Britain survived and the other stirring events'.[24]

In place of a critical reflection of the war effort, journalists helped build a myth of fortitude under fire. Myth, Barthes stated, is 'a system of communication … a message', one of the ways that nations establish their values and their morality, and, with the large UK cities being bombarded on a nightly basis, the government was fearful that those values might disappear as the population sought an end to its suffering.[25] Myth also reinforces sets of beliefs, 'usually put forward as a narrative, held by a community about itself', and the ongoing narrative of the Blitz of Britain was given its definition on 4 June 1940.[26] On that day the Prime Minister Winston Churchill addressed Parliament with a speech that has become the oral shorthand for Britain's boldness against Hitler:

> We shall go on to the end, we shall fight in France, and we shall fight on the seas and oceans, we shall fight with growing confidence and growing strength in the air, we shall defend our island, whatever the cost may be, we shall fight on the beaches, we shall fight on the landing grounds, we shall fight in the fields and in the streets, we shall fight in the hills; we shall never surrender.[27]

---

[24] Clive Ponting, *1940: Myth and Reality* (London: Sphere, 1990), p. 1.
[25] Roland Barthes, *Roland Barthes: Mythologies*, trans. by Annette Laves (London, Vintage, 1993), p. 109.
[26] George Schopflin, 'The Functions of Myth and a Taxonomy of Myths' in Geoffrey Hosking and George Schopflin, eds, *Myths and Nationhood*, (London: Hurst, 1997), p. 19.
[27] Winston Churchill, 4 June 1940, cited by Lewis Broad, *Winston Churchill* (London: Hutchinson, 1956), p. 289.

The BBC recorded that, when Churchill spoke on the radio, 70 per cent of the population listened, and in doing so they became witnesses to one of the great mythical constructions.[28] Churchill's rhetoric was wishful thinking as Britain's army was defeated and short of weapons, and only the Royal Navy and the RAF stood in the way of invasion.[29] As Ponting put it, the choice looming for Britain was to 'become a dependency of the United States or it would have to seek peace from a victorious Germany'.[30]

The creation of the myth of unwavering resilience by Britain's civilian population in the Second World War was borne out of an anxiety that had, in terms of powered flight, a comparatively long pedigree. As early as 1908 H. G. Wells had predicted the effects of blanket bombing in *The War in the Air*, writing: 'No place is safe, no place is at peace ... People go out in the morning and see air-fleets passing overhead – dripping death – dripping death!'[31] Newsreels from the Spanish Civil War and subsequent writing had intensified fears that had derived initially from fiction and had been articulated by the leader of the Conservative Party Stanley Baldwin in 1932: 'I think it is well ... for the man in the street to realise that there is no power on earth that can prevent him from being bombed. Whatever people may tell him, the bomber will always get

---

[28] R. J. E. Silvey, 'Some Recent Trends in Listening', in *BBC Year Book 1946*, pp. 28–29, cited in Anthony Aldgate and Jeffrey Richards, *Britain Can Take It*, 2nd edn (Edinburgh: Edinburgh University Press, 1994), p. 49.

[29] Peter Clarke, *Hope and Glory: Britain 1900–1990* (London: Penguin, 1997), pp. 196-97.

[30] Ponting, *1940*, p. 4.

[31] H. G. Wells *The War in the Air* (Whitefish, MT: Kessinger, 2004), p. 154.

through.'[32] In 1937 British experts predicted 60 days of bombing if war broke out with Germany, with 600,000 people killed and twice that number injured.[33] Dilks wrote: 'If ministers took literally all that was recommended to them by the best expert opinion, they would have had to expect from concentrated air bombardment something like the effects which we should now anticipate from limited nuclear warfare.'[34] As a consequence, the British entered the war in a climate of extreme fear, an anxiety that declared itself in a mass evacuation of the big cities within days. Around 827,000 children were taken from threatened areas, including Donald Read, a Manchester schoolboy, who wrote:

> Two years earlier, the bombing of Guernica during the Spanish Civil War and of Canton by the Japanese in China had been reported in the British press with great alarm. The widely held impression was that cities could now be destroyed from the air almost at will.[35]

The Blitz, the sustained bombing of Britain, is commonly considered to have started on the night of 7/8 September 1940 when London was bombed for the first of 58 consecutive nights before the Luftwaffe switched its attention mainly to

---

[32] See J. B. S. Haldane, *ARP* (London: Gollancz, 1938) and J. Thornburn Muirhead, *Air Attack on Cities: The Broader Aspects of the Problem* (London: Allen and Unwin, 1938); *Hansard*, HC Debate, 10 November 1932, 270 (London: HMSO, 1932), cols 630–41.
[33] Calder, *The Myth of the Blitz*, p. 60.
[34] D. Dilks, 'The Unnecessary War? Military Advice and Foreign Policy in Great Britain, 1931–1939', in Adrian Preston, ed., *General Staffs and Diplomacy before the Second World War* (London: Croom Helm, 1978), p. 117.
[35] Calder, *The Myth of the Blitz*, p. 60; Read, *A Manchester Boyhood*, p. 72.

industrial centres in the provinces.[36] Over the entire war, according to British official figures, more than 60,000 civilians were killed, 86,182 people were admitted to hospital, most of them seriously injured, and 150,833 were recorded as 'slightly injured'.[37] Wood and Dempster stated that, of five aims for the attacks listed by Hermann Goering, Air Minister and commander in chief of the Luftwaffe, the fourth was demoralisation of the civilian population.[38] To counter this, the British press, under concerted pressure from the government, facilitated what Temple described as 'the creation of "necessary myths" which helped boost morale and unify the nation'.[39] This propaganda had it that the nation rallied behind Churchill and calmly endured the horrors inflicted on the population by Hitler's bombers. It is a myth that endures, so that the 'Blitz Spirit' has become an expression used, lazily, to describe any signs of British fortitude. For example, in recent times Prime Minister Gordon Brown invoked it to rally the population to overcome the country's economic problems; it was utilised when the West Country was flooded in 2007; and more bizarrely, David Lloyd tried to resurrect it when he played recordings of Churchill's speeches to inspire greater efforts from the England cricket team when he was the national coach during the 1990s.[40]

---

[36] A. J. P. Taylor, *English History 1914–1945* (Oxford: Oxford University Press, 1988), p. 501.

[37] O'Brien, *Civil Defence*, p. 677.

[38] D. Wood and D. Dempster, *The Narrow Margin: The Definitive Story of the Battle of Britain* (London: Arrow, 1969), p. 255.

[39] Mick Temple, *The British Press* (Maidenhead: Open University Press, 2008), p. 41.

[40] Michael Lea, 'Brown: the Blitz Spirit will Save Us', *Daily Mail*, 29 December 2008, p. 4; Laura Clout, 'Shrugging Off the Hardships with a Little Blitz Spirit', *The Daily Telegraph*, 25 July

The Press and the Blitz Mythology

The establishment of that myth began with the word Blitz itself. The *Oxford English Dictionary* definition is: 'an attack or offensive launched suddenly with great violence with the object of reducing the defences immediately', which overstates what happened even at the height of the Luftwaffe's action.[41] London and Coventry were damaged but were not reduced to rubble and if 'Blitz' could be applied to any bombing operations it would be to Hamburg in July 1943, that killed an estimated 42,000, and Dresden in February 1945, when British and American aircrews destroyed 13 square miles of the city and killed, by conservative estimates, at least 35,000.[42] Britain escaped lightly when set in this context. The word Blitz had been appropriated from the word *Blitzkrieg*, lightning war, applied by the world's press to Germany's rapid conquest of Poland, and was used in anticipation of Hitler's attempt to bomb Britain out of the war. Taylor pointed out that a nine-month bombardment was the very opposite of lightning war but O'Brien stated 'as heavy bombing began in the late summer [of 1940], Blitz became almost overnight a British colloquialism for an air raid'.[43] Calder argued that from the first 'Blitz' meant more than that – 'It was instantaneously and spontaneously "mythologised"' – and it allowed the British to draw a line with another myth from the First World War when literature and folklore found ways to make everyone in the

---

    2007, p. 7; Derek Pringle, 'The Man Who Has Brought the Smile Back to English Cricket', *The Independent,* 1 July 1996, p. S1.

[41] *Oxford English Dictionary* <http://www.oed.com> [accessed 4 December 2012].

[42] Noble Frankland and Charles Webster, *The Strategic Air Offensive Against Germany, 1939–1945,* II, *Endeavour* (London: HMSO, 1961), pp. 260–61.

[43] Taylor, *English History 1914–1945,* p. 501; O'Brien, *Civil Defence,* p. 386.

armed services heroic.[44] This, he wrote, set a precedent in the 1940s for those wishing to eulogise the entire British population, who, apart from a few areas of London and, briefly, in other places like Manchester, suffered an experience far less extreme than that of the soldiers a quarter of a century earlier.[45]

But, contrary to the relentlessly positivist version of events, the effects of the Blitz on London, and other parts of Britain, were varied. Academics such as Calder, Ponting and Gardiner, have reported that contemporary memoirs and documents testify to 'panic, to horrified revulsion, to post-raid depression, to antisocial behaviour', and these variations to the mythologised story should be acknowledged.[46] Curran and Seaton wrote that the mythology has encouraged the belief that the British people closed ranks behind the unchallenged leadership of Churchill, but this has hidden less palatable truths:

> A significantly named Home Morale Emergency Committee of the Ministry of Information reported in June 1940 on 'fear, confusion, suspicion, class feeling and defeatism'. Even the Ministry's parliamentary secretary, Harold Nicolson, confided in his diary during this period: 'It will now be almost impossible to beat the Germans'. For at least the first two and a half years of the war, the relationship between the authorities and the press was dominated by a constant and probably misplaced concern about the state of public morale.[47]

---

[44] Calder, *The Myth of the Blitz*, p. 2.
[45] Ibid., p. 18.
[46] Ibid., p. 120.
[47] Curran and Seaton, *Power Without Responsibility*, p. 55.

CHAPTER THREE
METHODOLOGY

1. Approaching the Sources

The cultural studies scholar Stuart Hall's encoding/decoding communication model offered a theoretical approach to how media messages are produced, disseminated and interpreted, arguing that audiences translate these messages in different ways depending on their cultural background, economic means, and personal experiences.[1] An advertisement, for example, can mean different things to different people, some decoding the message as it was encoded, others either rejecting it entirely or negotiating a position where individual elements are accepted or rejected. This theory was developed in the 1970s and was first applied to television, but it has been adopted and applied across the media by theorists and provides a suitable model for the 1940s newspapers. Three types of primary source were used in this book, representing in terms of that model, the production of the newspapers (encoding), the dissemination (reports and headlines), and the audience (decoding).

For the empirical part of the research the focus of the attention was on three newspapers: the *Manchester Guardian,* the *Manchester Evening News* and the *Evening Chronicle.* They were chosen because they dominated the market of the daily regional press in Manchester during the Second World War, in terms of influence, circulation and style, and all three were parts of national newspaper groups, the *Manchester Guardian* and *Manchester Evening News* being owned by the Scott Trust,

---

[1] Stuart Hall, 'Encoding/Decoding', in Paul Marris and Sue Thornham, eds, *Media Studies: A Reader,* 2nd edn (New York, NY: New York University Press, 2000), pp. 51–61.

and the *Evening Chronicle* being printed by Kemsley Newspapers, who also owned the *Sunday Times* the *Daily Dispatch* and other national and regional newspapers. The three sampled newspapers represent different deadlines, and different publication pressures, with a national morning newspaper (the *Manchester Guardian*) and two evening publications.

Other local newspapers were considered but none had the influence, the central Manchester base nor the geographical reach of the chosen titles. The *Manchester Guardian*'s circulation was modest (51,000 in 1939, rising to 140,000 in 1951), but its influence was far greater and in 1947 Lord Camrose described it as 'one of the famous papers of the world' and 'the widest distribution of any provincial daily'.[2] Its editor, William Percival Crozier, met Churchill on a regular basis, Lord Halifax, the Foreign Secretary from February 1938 until December 1940, said he read the *Manchester Guardian* every day and the *Manchester Guardian Weekly*, an abridged version of the newspaper, gained the *Guardian* an enhanced reputation in the United States.[3] The German edition of the same publication, printed in Berlin, had such an influence that Alexander Werth, the newspaper's foreign correspondent, wrote that the '*Guardian* here counts for more than any other

---

[2] 1910–1939 figures taken from T. B. Browne's Advertiser's ABC 1910–40; 1951 figures from the Audit Bureau of Circulations, both cited in David Butler and Anne Sloman, *British Political Facts 1900–1975*, 5th edn (London: Macmillan, 1975), p. 452; Camrose, *British Newspapers*, p. 116.

[3] Crozier listed 16 meetings with Churchill between October 1939 and October 1943 (W. P. Crozier, *Off The Record, Political Interviews 1939–45* (London: Hutchinson, 1973), pp. xii–xiii; John Rylands Library, University of Manchester, *The Guardian* Archive, Papers and Correspondence 1821–1970s, Crozier to Voigt, 28 July 1938; Gannon, *The British Press*, p. 75.

Methodology

English paper', but it became such an irritant to the Nazi hierarchy that it was suppressed, along with many other newspapers, in 1933.[4] The profits of the *Manchester Evening News* sustained the loss-making *Manchester Guardian* and perhaps that is a reason why the former did not submit circulation numbers before the Second World War.[5] Its audited figure for 1945 was 250,000, a suspiciously rounded number, but it justifiably described itself as 'the oldest established and leading evening journal in Manchester'.[6] The *Evening Chronicle*, its title page proclaiming 'the largest evening sale in the provinces', sold more than 200,000 copies a day in the build-up to the war and in 1945 was licensed as selling 224,000.[7]

2. Newspaper Production

Interviews with senior journalists of the time were impossible because the nature of the call-up meant that only those who were older than fighting age or unfit for service remained in the UK to make the key decisions concerning newspaper content.[8] In terms of the *Manchester Guardian* and *Manchester Evening News* there is access to the memos and correspondence for leading editorial figures, however, albeit in a limited form, in *The Guardian* Archive at the University of Manchester's John Rylands Library. Paper shortages imposed by war rationing may have contributed to the relatively few memos that were

---

[4] John Rylands Library, *The Guardian* Archive, Werth to Crozier, 27 January 1933; Gannon, *The British Press*, p. 75.
[5] Ibid. (Profits were never large but the *Manchester Guardian* had sufficient reserves to buy the *Manchester Evening News* in 1924. The *Guardian* ran at a loss throughout the 1930s).
[6] Colin Seymour-Ure, *The British Press and Broadcasting Since 1945*, 2nd edn (Oxford: Blackwell, 1997), pp. 274–76.
[7] Ibid.
[8] Calder, *The People's War*, p. 505.

available, but the distinctive editorial structure, in UK national newspaper terms, of the *Manchester Guardian* where decisions had to be relayed between Cross Street, Manchester, and the London office meant there was important correspondence.[9] As Crozier was the editor in chief of the *Guardian* and set editorial policy, memos to and from him and his responses to readers' letters were examined in detail. *The Guardian* Archive has his correspondence from 1932 to his death in 1944 but as the focus of this study is the period from December 1940 to February 1941 and the censorship framework was erected from the moment war was declared, greatest attention was paid to the period from the beginning of 1939 to the end of 1941. In addition to Crozier's correspondence, the memos of the London editor James Bone and the newspaper's war correspondent Evelyn Montague, were studied, representing the most important actors in the *Manchester Guardian*'s coverage of the war in 1940 and 1941. These are limited sources – there is only one surviving memo from Bone to Crozier written during the war – and there were similar restrictions regarding Haley's correspondence. Although he was editor of the *Manchester Evening News,* his appointment as general manager for the newspaper group meant his memos largely related to logistics rather than editorial policy. There are no similar primary documents available for the *Evening Chronicle.*

The memos, etc., in *The Guardian* Archive were complemented by the diaries of Crozier and the editor of the *Manchester Evening News*, William Haley, although neither is extensive. Crozier's diary runs from October 1940 to February 1941, but is not intimate and was not intended for publication. Ayerst wrote:

> The formless jumble of entries, including a few snatches in Latin and Greek, chronicle the progress of his roses, the hunt

---

[9] John Rylands Library, *The Guardian* Archive.

Methodology

for cigarettes for his wife and daughter, office rows, university business, the planning of a novel, illness, anxiety over the war, and the time spent in the shelters.[10]

Ayerst concluded that the artlessness of the entries 'reveals the writer' and the no-nonsense brevity of Haley's diary also is an insight into the man. His summary of the war position in July 1940 was: 'Worlds have happened in the last two months. Holland, Belgium and France have all gone. Now Great Britain feverishly prepares for invasion.'[11] But that was extensive compared to 1943, the entry for which amounted to half an A4 page.

3. Dissemination

This comprised a study of reports and headlines in the newspapers from 16 December 1940 to 10 February 1941, a total of 144 editions. In the six-page *Evening Chronicle* of 17 December 1940, which was a typical edition, there were 33 war-based reports and 34 non-war items although only one story related to local incidents. Even six days later, the first edition of the *Chronicle* after the Manchester Blitz, there were only two reports and an editorial on the city's bombing, again a typical number. These were lengthy, but the relatively low number allowed for extensive scrutiny of every article and for other related items such as official notices and readers' letters. The study period allowed critical reflection on press reports in the week before the Manchester Blitz and for seven weeks afterwards, monitoring whether there was a change in the reporting before and after the bombings of 22/23 and 23/24 December. The newspapers after the Blitz also provided

---

[10] David Ayerst, *The Manchester Guardian: Biography of a Newspaper* (London: *The Guardian*, 1971), p. 536.
[11] Churchill Archives Centre, University of Cambridge, Sir William John Haley, Diaries and Correspondence 1922–1986, 10 July 1940.

evidence of the local press's willingness to investigate any national and local authority shortcomings exposed by the extreme circumstances brought about by severe bombing. Manchester also suffered another night's bombing during this seven weeks. The study period also coincides with the suppression of the *Daily Worker*, an important moment in the evolving relationship between the government and the press.

Critical discourse analysis was applied to study the 'interpretations of the meanings of texts rather than just quantifying textual features and deriving meaning from this'.[12] What is printed in newspapers needs to be judged against what else was in the news that day; where and how reports appear in the newspaper; and what other lines of inquiry were ignored or under-exploited. Journalism, according to Richardson, is inescapably connected to the social, political and cultural context in which it is written and consumed. A typical application could be used on the front page of the late night edition in August 1944 of *The Star*, a London evening newspaper in competition with the *Evening Standard* and *Evening News*. There were only five reports and each concentrated on foreign news, including the second lead headlined 'Nazis race for Seine "Dunkirk".'[13] There are a number of discourses in operation here, some of them contradictory. As British newspapers had used Dunkirk as a metaphor for snatching victory from defeat in 1940 was the reader to conclude that the Germans were staging an unexpected rally? Or, was *The Star* making assumptions that its target audience had grown to question, or never properly subscribed to, the 'Bloody Marvellous' narrative being peddled in the *Daily*

---

[12] John E. Richardson, *Analysing Newspapers. An Approach from Critical Discourse Analysis* (Basingstoke: Palgrave Macmillan, 2007), p. 15.
[13] 'Nazis race for Seine "Dunkirk"', *The Star,* 23 August 1944, p. 1.

Methodology

Mirror and elsewhere in Fleet Street four years previously and had 'Dunkirk' become a convenient label to signify a serious military reverse?[14] The quotation marks around Dunkirk, albeit derived from a non-attributed phrase in the copy, signalled a potential deviation from the previously accepted meaning of the word and the sub-headline – 'Their retreat is now a rout' – removed all doubt. Below the headlines the copy read:

> The Seventh German Army has completely collapsed as a fighting force, and we are all out in pursuit of what remains of this once formidable army as the Germans race for the Seine, where hurried preparations have been made for an 'inland Dunkirk'.

The 'their' in the headline and the 'we' in the copy underline the abandonment of objectivity and the 'othering' in the report, but there is another, more subtle, sign of bias. The reporter (the above 'we' suggested the journalist was with the pursuing forces) wrote that the German army was not just retreating, it had 'completely collapsed' to the point the reporter could write dismissively of 'what remains' and 'hurried preparations' for a retreat. An alternative report could have used the word 'regrouping' and, as the Seventh Army would play a role in the major German offensive, the Battle of the Bulge, four months later, it would possibly have been the more accurate description.[15]

All reports in the Manchester newspapers during the study period were examined in this manner to see if they abandoned reporting norms, although particular attention was paid to the editions of 23 to 27 December 1940. These were the first three after the first Manchester Blitz, when the

---

[14] 'Bloody Marvellous', *Daily Mirror*, 1 June 1940, p. 7.
[15] Hugh M. Cole, *The Ardennes: The Official History of the Battle of the Bulge* (St Petersburg, FL: Red and Black, 2011).

Luftwaffe was still targeting the city and strains on reporting would have been at their greatest, but when news could be gathered from just outside the newspapers' front doors (production of the *Manchester Guardian* was disrupted when the office was hit by incendiary bombs).[16] Journalists were not just using news agencies, subject to the gate-keeping of the censor, but also would have had direct access to eye-witness accounts.

The standard format for news reports is the inverted pyramid 'which places the most important information at the head of the story and uses the lead paragraph to answer the five 'W questions': Who? What? Why? Where? and When?'[17] Harold Lasswell is credited with developing the five Ws model of communication in 1948 but, even though his work was published after the period of study, war and non-war reports in the Manchester newspapers generally followed the journalistic convention that White described as the 'order of meaning'. A typical example was printed in the *Manchester Evening News* on 17 December 1940:

> Another German spy **[WHO]** was executed **[WHAT]** in London **[WHERE]** today **[WHEN]**. He was associated with Waldberg and Meier, the two spies who were hanged in Pentonville a week ago. Like them he was equipped with a wireless set **[WHY]**.[18]

There are other forms of news construction, such as the delayed drop or more literary forms of newspaper journalism, but they were not common in news reports in the 1940s, and any deviation from the normal 'order of meaning' is an

---

[16] Ayerst, *The Manchester Guardian*, p. 541.
[17] Bob Franklin, Martin Hamer, Mark Hanna, Marie Kinsey and John E. Richardson, *Key Concepts in Journalism Studies* (London: Sage, 2005), p. 122.
[18] 'Third Nazi Spy Executed', *Manchester Evening News*, 17 December 1940, p. 1.

indicator of unusual pressures on, or priorities of, the reporter or sub-editor.[19] Emphasis on the bravery of the fire fighters placed high in a story about Blitz deaths would be a typical example. What failed to appear in reports, casualty figures for example, is also significant, particularly in the context of wartime rationing of newsprint that reduced newspapers to between four and 10 pages in length.[20]

An important element of this book is news values and whether the coverage of 1940 can be judged by twenty-first century criteria. News values are the benchmarks by which journalists measure the worth of stories and are used to prioritise the collection and production of news, and, although they 'may not be written down or codified by news organisations … they exist in the daily practice and in knowledge gained on the job'.[21] Certainly, a Manchester reporter covering the Second World War was not short of advice in terms of the function of his trade or what made news. In 1852 *The Times* defined the role of journalism: 'The first duty of the press is to obtain the earliest and most correct intelligence of the events of the time and instantly, by disclosing them, to make them the common property of the nation.'[22] It added that the journalist should seek out 'the truth as near as he can attain it'. More

---

[19] A. Blundy, *The Bad News Bible* (London: Review, 2004), p. 181; Richardson, *Analysing Newspapers*, p. 72.
[20] T. A. Van Dijk, *Discourse Studies*, 5 vols (London: Sage, 2007), cited in Ruth Wodak and Michael Meyer, eds, *Methods of Critical Discourse Analysis* (London: Sage, 2009), p. 2; Kurt Lang and Gladys Engel Lang, 'Personal Influence and the New Paradigm: Some Inadvertent Consequences' in *The Annals of the American Academy of Political and Social Science*, 608, 1 (2006), p. 171.
[21] Tony Harcup and Deirdrie O'Neill, 'What is News? Galtung and Ruge Revisited', *Journalism Studies*, 2, 2 (2001), p. 261.
[22] Cited in F. Williams, *Dangerous Estate: The Anatomy of Newspapers* (London: Arrow, 1959), p. 15.

locally, C. P. Scott, the editor of the *Manchester Guardian* for 50 years, writing to commemorate the *Guardian*'s centenary in 1921, defined the press's function thus:

> The primary office is the gathering of news. At the peril of its soul it must see that the supply is not tainted. Comment is free, but facts are sacred ... The voice of opponents, no less than of friends, has a right to be heard. Comment also is justly subject to a self-imposed restraint. It is well to be frank; it is even better to be fair.[23]

Even during the war, Home Intelligence gave a contemporary definition of the function of the press as 'to gather, to make known, and to interpret news of public interest'.[24] But these definitions, while noble in intent, are not as simple as they might seem. What is the definition of a fact, for example, and who judges what is fair or what is of public interest? And who would originate opinion? Herman and Chomsky's top-down model of news would assert that the answer would be the government or other elites such as newspaper proprietors and editors. But there were other pressures as Knightley noted:

> From the very beginning, war correspondents faced a dilemma that remains unresolved to this day: whose side are they on? Correspondents have to choose because the aims of the military and the media are irreconcilable.[25]

Galtung and Ruge first brought an academic approach to the understanding of news values when they published a landmark paper 'The Structure of Foreign News' in 1965, but it is important for this book that Harcup and O'Neill felt the need to update these prerequisites when they revisited, and

---

[23] Ayerst, *The Manchester Guardian*, p. 435.
[24] Mass Observation, FR 126, *Report on the Press*, May 1940.
[25] Knightley, *The First Casualty*, p. xi.

applied domestic parameters nearly 40 years later.[26] This showed that news values alter with time and, certainly, Harcup and O'Neill's definitions would not have been wholly applicable in 1940 – witty headlines and celebrity gossip were either a rarity or largely publicity-driven, for example, by film studios. Importantly, however, the vast majority would stand. Andrew Marr, a former editor of *The Independent* and now a BBC journalist, stated: 'Most news values have not changed', noting *The Times*'s coverage of the Battle of Trafalgar was comparable to that of the war in Iraq in 2003.[27] He added: 'Over the centuries, newspapers change shape, order the news differently and target different groups of people. Some slant even hard news for political effect. But the hard news agenda itself seems an unalterable part of modern urban life.'[28]

Critical discourse analysis of newspapers also allows interpretations of the meanings of texts 'rather than just quantifying textual features and deriving meaning from this'.[29] An example was a report in the *Manchester Guardian* in December 1940 that stated 'several incendiaries fell in a square near to a war memorial'.[30] A grid of words would have noted 'incendiaries', 'memorial' and 'war' but would not have logged the mock outrage of the reporter or sub-editor. Anderson noted that 'no more arresting emblems of modern nationalism exist than cenotaphs and tombs of Unknown Soldiers' but no bomber several thousand feet in the air in the dark would have

---

[26] Johan Galtung and Mari Ruge, 'The Structure of Foreign News: The presentation of the Congo, Cuba and Cyprus crises in Four Norwegian Newspapers', *Journal of International Peace Research*, 1 (1965), pp. 64–91; Harcup and O'Neill, 'What is News?'
[27] Andrew Marr, *My Trade* (London: Macmillan, 2004) p. 113.
[28] Ibid.
[29] Richardson, *Analysing Newspapers*, p. 15.
[30] 'Night Raid on North-West', *Manchester Guardian*, 23 December 1940, p. 3.

aimed at such a militarily meaningless target and, in any case, the memorial was not hit.[31] This is a conventional propagandist technique as described by Nohrstedt et al. in which conflict is described in polarised terms: good and bad.[32]

Words can contain value judgements as well as the dictionary meanings. Billig noted that the crucial words of banal nationalism are often the smallest, 'we', 'this' and 'here', and Van Dijk's ideological square is characterised by positive self-representation and negative representation of others.[33] If this applied to newspaper reports, Van Dijk wrote:

> We may expect that Our good actions and Their bad ones will in general tend to be described at a lower, more specific level, with many (detailed) propositions. The opposite will be true for Our bad actions and Their good ones, which, if described at all, will both be described in rather general, abstract and hence 'distanced' terms, without giving much detail.

In war there are imperatives which make Van Dijk's theory the default position in newspapers, that tend to use words and language that 'deify a cause and satanize opponents', frequently linguistically assigning qualities to persons, animals, objects, events and social phenomena.[34] The copy was

---

[31] Anderson, *Imagined Communities*, p. 9.
[32] S. A. Nohrstedt, S. Kaitatzi-Witlock, R. Ottosen and K. Riegert 'From the Persian Gulf to Kosovo – War Journalism and Propaganda', *European Journal of Communication*, 15, 3 (2000), 383–404 (p. 384).
[33] Michael Billig, *Banal Nationalism* (London: Sage, 2008), p. 94; T. A. Van Dijk, 'Opinions and Ideologies in the Press' in Allan Bell and Peter Garrett, eds, *Approaches to Media Discourse* (Oxford: Blackwell, 2000), p. 35.
[34] Jowett and O'Donnell, *Propaganda*, p. 303; M. Reisigl and R. Wodak, *Discourse and Discrimination: Rhetorics of Racism and Anti-Semitism* (London: Routledge, 2001), p. 54.

Methodology

examined for references that represent the values and characteristics of the British and the Germans, a typical example appeared in the *Manchester Evening News* in December 1940. Under the headline 'A. F. S. men machine-gunned', a story alleging that, after dropping their bombs, 'Nazi planes swooped low and tried to machine-gun some of the firemen'.[35] Nobody is quoted to substantiate this story and German gunners, faced with a long flight home, would have been more likely to have wanted to conserve ammunition for possible encounters with British fighters. Nevertheless, the reporter has assigned their bad actions perpetrated against the good of the fire fighters.

Language is an indicator of subjectivity but where reports appear and what projection they receive is also a potentially important indicator of a lack of objectivity or symptoms of censorship. 'The design of a newspaper page, especially a news page, is its own menu', Hutt and James wrote, while Hodgson put it simply: 'The order which headlines appear on a page, and their size, signify the relative importance of the text in relation to the other items.'[36] The lead story on the main news page of relatively few words is more likely to receive attention and be read than a long report buried low down on the Foreign News page deep inside a newspaper. When the Manchester Blitz was not the lead story in a Manchester newspaper, this can be an indicator of censorship. Why this would happen is explored later in the book.

The column centimetres usually reflect the importance that the newspaper attaches to the article, although not always

---

[35] 'A. F. S. Men Machine-Gunned', *Manchester Evening News*, 24 December 1940, p. 1.
[36] Allen Hutt and Bob James, *Newspaper Design Today* (London: Lund Humphries, 1989), p. 12; F. W. Hodgson, *New Subediting* (Oxford: Butterworth-Heinemann, 1998), p. 35.

(as above), and in Chapter Nine there is a quantitative study of the amount of coverage of the war compared to other news stories, features and entertainment. This was done by analysing the number of stories, and the percentage of the newspaper they represent, allocating to seven categories: war news; non-war news; comment; entertainment and sport; business; cartoons and photographs; and advertisements. The findings were considered alongside the survey undertaken by the Royal Commission on the Press published in 1949 that analysed newspaper coverage in *The Times*, the *Daily Mail* and the *Daily Mirror* in 1927, 1937 and 1947.[37] This quantitative analysis was applied to the eight Tuesday editions of the three newspapers beginning 17 December 1940. Tuesday was chosen because Monday and Saturday editions are inclined to look backwards at, or forward to, the weekend, and consequently are frequently more entertainment focused, and Wednesday and Thursday papers would have had gaps in the analysis due to Christmas and New Year holidays. Friday was an alternative but was rejected because it would not have provided a proper perspective of a subsequent raid that finished in the early hours of Friday 10 January 1941. This study was conducted in the knowledge that entertainment would normally be given a greater priority by news desks during a holiday period but, while the newspaper of 17 December 1940 might have been affected by this seasonal aberration, this would have been more than compensated for by the gravity and importance of the local news in the aftermath of the Blitz in later editions. Entertainment news had strong competition for space in already ration-restricted newspapers so its inclusion was a strong indicator of the journalist's perception of the audience's desire to escape the war. Or even a propagandist's wish to cheer up people. As

---

[37] HMSO, *Royal Commission*, p. 249.

Methodology

Bingham stated, readers tend to select the paper that most closely fits their own preconceptions:

> Neither the editors nor the audience, nor indeed the advertisers, were likely to get exactly what they wanted, but there was a set of 'feedback loops' between each of them, in the form of sales figures and market research, which ensured that each party had some input into the newspaper.[38]

Those loops did not take into account the negative feelings of the people of Manchester in the immediate aftermath of Christmas 1940, and in any case they move at a slow pace rather than immediately, but as no newspaper was willing to confront these issues, there were no circulation or financial implications attached to this exclusion.

It is important to take into account the expectations placed on the *Manchester Guardian*, which had a national audience and the consequent journalistic obligations that implied, but Manchester's local newspapers also devoted considerable space in ration-reduced editions to the capital. Haley, editor of the *Manchester Evening News* during the war and a future editor of *The Times* and Director General of the BBC, stated: 'Only London mattered.' So, rather than self-restriction, was this kind of attitude simply the adoption of 'metropolitan values' by the Northern editorial/proprietorial elite?[39] Haley's comment, while not conclusive, suggests this was the case but a quantitative analysis was undertaken to chart the Manchester Blitz's fall down the news agenda. This was done by enumerating the references in the three newspapers to the bombing and Manchester from 24 December to the end of the study period. While local newspapers have a different audience and would be expected to linger longer on

---

[38] Bingham, *Gender, Modernity and the Popular Press,* p. 11.
[39] Woods Papers, 5 September 1963, cited in Koss, *The Rise and Fall,* p. 388.

Manchester stories, their coverage was compared to that of *The Times*, the *Daily Mirror* and, to give a hyper-local perspective, the *Salford City Reporter*.

4. The Audience

A fuller picture of how Manchester's press functioned in the face of the Blitz was drawn by comparing news reports to other, sometimes private, contemporary accounts. Consideration was given to conducting a series of semi-structured interviews with people who had been alive during Manchester's Blitz, but very few adults from the early 1940s survive and those aged 15 and below in 1940 may well have been sheltered from the grimmest news and darkest feelings by their parents. Instead, a variety of documentary sources, including contemporary written material, were examined, testing the accuracy of newspapers' representation of popular morale and the extent to which editors and journalists correctly judged the popular mood in the way they reported the Manchester Blitz. This process was completed partly through the study of archive material at the Mass Observation Project, based at the University of Sussex, which has contemporary reports from diarists in Manchester. These were relatively short engagements and virtually everything the diarists wrote pertinent to their collection of material and the city's reaction to the Blitz is included in this book.[40] There is also a small archive of Mancunian recollections at Stockport Library, Greater Manchester, which have been published online by the BBC as part of its *WW2 People's War* compilation.[41] Finally, there was a series of weekly reports compiled, via the resources of Home Intelligence, by the MOI

---

[40] Mass Observation Archive, University of Sussex.
[41] BBC, *People's War* <http://www.bbc.co.uk/ww2peopleswar> [accessed 25–31 May 2008].

Methodology

and distributed to the War Cabinet. These are also to be found at the University of Sussex and, importantly for this book, included a report on the morale of the Manchester public conducted in January 1941, just days after the Christmas Blitz.[42] This was used extensively as it is an official document that would have been read by the Cabinet or officials close to it and the team of government reporters would have had no obvious reason to be biased.

5. The Limits of the Research

This book focuses on the three newspapers that dominated the local market in Manchester. In 1940 and 1941 between them they sold more than 500,000 copies every day to a population of between double and treble that figure.[43] Even allowing for the geographical spread of the circulation that reached into outlying towns such as Bolton and Rochdale, this meant that the *Manchester Guardian*, *Manchester Evening News* and *Evening Chronicle*'s penetration into the local market was extensive. The research could have extended to other evening newspapers in the Greater Manchester area, for example the *Bolton Evening News* or *Oldham Chronicle*, but they did not have the influence and circulation (65,000 and 25,000 respectively in 1945) of the chosen sample.[44]

Thought was also given to making a direct comparison between Manchester and Liverpool's newspapers. Liverpool suffered more raids than any British city other than London and had a comparable population (856,000) and demography

---

[42] Mass Observation Archive, FR 538.
[43] *Census of Great Britain 1841–1931*, cited in Fielding, 'The Irish Catholics', p. 347.
[44] Audit Bureau of Circulations <http://www.abc.org.uk> [accessed 16 November 2012].

to Manchester.⁴⁵ It also had three daily newspapers, the morning *Liverpool Post*, and two evenings, the *Liverpool Echo* and *Liverpool Evening Express*, although it was not a national newspaper print centre like Manchester and had a far more local focus. But like Liverpool, other British cities and local newspapers in the Second World War are worthy of a separate study.

The three chosen newspapers represent a narrow spectrum of political opinion. The *Manchester Guardian* had supported the Liberal Party but, unlike the *News Chronicle*, had distanced itself when the party disintegrated after the First World War.⁴⁶ By 1939 it had no political allegiance, although A. P. Wadsworth, a future editor, articulated an editorial policy that pledged the paper to Churchill, who had 'the boldness, the imagination, the sense of social justice, the capacity to rouse the enthusiasm and devoted service that we need'.⁴⁷ The *Manchester Evening News* and *Evening Chronicle*, in common with most provincial and weekly newspapers, showed no obvious support to any political party, preferring 'journalism of consensus', although the former's link with the *Guardian* would make it liberal-leaning, while the latter's regular political commentator was the Conservative Party MP Beverley Baxter, who had an unofficial post with the Ministry of Aircraft Production where he was responsible for keeping up production of aero-engines.⁴⁸ The fact that his views were printed despite his lack of local connections – he was a

---

[45] Beaven and Thoms, 'The Blitz and Civilian Morale', p. 196; Demographia <http://www.demographia.com> [accessed 19 November 2012].
[46] Gannon, *The British Press*, p. 75.
[47] Ayerst, *The Manchester Guardian*, p. 535.
[48] Karin Wahl-Jorgensen, 'Op-ed Pages', in Bob Franklin, ed., *Pulling Newspapers Apart: Analysing Print Journalism* (London, Routledge, 2008), p. 72.

Methodology

Canadian and represented the constituency of Wood Green in north London – suggests his opinions did not differ significantly from the editorial policy. None of the papers in this study was among the most strident in terms of support for the main political parties and, although this is addressed in part by holding up the findings against *The Times* and the *Daily Mirror*, newspapers which tended to be Conservative and Labour by nature if not by proclamation, a more rigorous study of left-wing publications, for example, would include the *Daily Herald*, which supported the Labour Party, and the *Daily Worker*, which was set up in 1930 to support the Communist Party.[49]

Finally, the length of the study period could have been extended. Manchester and Salford suffered sporadic bombing throughout the Second World War, most notably in June 1941 when 14 nurses were killed after bombs landed on Salford Royal Hospital. The death rate and the damage were not comparable, however, and the strain on the local infrastructure was not as heavy. Nevertheless, there is scope for further study tracking the change of tone in Manchester's newspapers as the fear of invasion receded and the mood changed from *if* the war could be won to *when*?[50]

---

[49] HMSO, *Royal Commission*, p. 359.
[50] Hardy, Cooper and Hochland, *Manchester at War*, p. 44.

PART II

CHAPTER FOUR

THE NEWSPAPERS

1. Putting on the Battle Dress

Any study of British newspapers in the Second World War should acknowledge the exceptional circumstances in which they were published. Quite apart from the problems of printing and distribution caused by the Blitz, there were shortages of staff and other resources. By the end of 1943, substantially more than a third of the nation's 9,000 journalists had been called up by the armed forces, more were employed by the government and only around 25 per cent of staff photographers remained in Fleet Street.[1] The *Manchester Guardian*, for example, lost many of its reporters and editors, including its outstanding foreign correspondent Frederick Augustus Voigt, who was needed for what Ayerst described as 'political warfare', so former employees returned to bring out the newspaper.[2] Ayerst wrote that the war 'gave old men their chance … or a least their second wind' and among them was F. S. Attenborough, a former chief sub-editor who had turned 70 and returned to work under his previous deputy.[3] The three principal leader writers at the *Guardian* in 1939 had a combined age of 175 years, including Crozier who would die, still editor of the paper, on 16 April 1944, aged 64.[4] Haley wrote in tribute: 'Through 12 of the most difficult and troubled years in history, from the rise of Nazism in 1933 to 1944, the

---

[1] Calder, *The People's War*, p. 505.
[2] Ayerst, *The Manchester Guardian*, p. 531.
[3] Ibid., p. 529.
[4] Ibid., p. 530.

eve of its destruction, Crozier put the *Guardian* in the van of the fight.'[5]

Newsprint was rationed and restrictions were put on circulation, so that newspapers could increase sales only by reducing the number of their pages. The *Guardian*'s pagination came down to 40 per week compared to 120 for March 1938, allowing an increase in production to 58,000 in July 1941 and 60,000 by September of that year.[6] The *Manchester Evening News* and the *Evening Chronicle* were similarly reduced, the former's pagination going from 16 broadsheet pages to 10, then to eight, and, by July 1940, it had fallen to six. After the print allowance was cut by a further 17 per cent in March 1941, Haley took the decision to make the paper a five-column tabloid, circulating an office memo, 'we are putting on our battle dress', to pacify traditionalists on the paper.[7]

'Finance, shortages of raw material, and indeed every factor of production must have been a nightmare', Lord Burnham, who worked for *The Daily Telegraph* from 1955 to 1986, observed.[8] The Royal Commission on the Press 1947–1949 quantified the lack of newsprint, comparing the 1.25 million tons used before the war to the 350,000 tons in 1948 and, at the rock bottom of February 1943, only 4,320 tons were consumed weekly.[9] Newspapers were reduced by as much as 80 per cent and the Royal Commission noted:

---

[5] Sir William Haley, J. L. Hammond, H. D. Nichols and C. P. Scott, *C. P. Scott 1846–1932: The Making of The Manchester Guardian* (London: Muller, 1946), p. 14.
[6] Ayerst, *The Manchester Guardian*, p. 543.
[7] I. King, 'The Press at War: The *Manchester Evening News* 1939–1945' (unpublished undergraduate dissertation, University of Manchester, 1989), p. 17.
[8] Lord Burnham, *Peterborough Court: The Story of The Daily Telegraph* (London: Cassell, 1955), p. 181.
[9] HMSO, *Royal Commission*, p. 5.

The Newspapers

> The reduction to four or five pages of newspapers, which before the war averaged over 20, means that much important material cannot be published and that what is published must be highly compressed. Much news must be 'suppressed' for this reason alone and severe compression makes inaccuracy and distortion difficult to avoid. The likelihood that the Press will be subject of complaints is increased.[10]

Space was at a premium, so what was selected for publication became even more significant, not only because trivial reports were rejected but also because stories that were printed had greater impact in a regime of restricted news.

National newspapers voluntarily reduced the amount of advertising in 1940 because newsprint rationing reduced editions to a third of their pre-war size and, as a consequence, the reader became the most important source of cash, the London-based dailies deriving 69 per cent of their revenue in sales in 1943 compared to 30 per cent in 1938.[11] The Royal Commission on the Press in 1949 reported: 'The provincial newspapers in particular benefited from the greater demand for their advertising space and from the reduction of the competitive pressure of the London papers.'[12] In 1936 the *Daily Mail* carried 1,308 column inches (3,322 centimetres) of advertising, in 1947 it carried only 326 (828).[13] Instead of newspapers competing to sell advertising space, advertisers had to wait their turn for the limited space available for a number of years. The Royal Commission report added:

---

[10] Ibid., p. 6.
[11] The voluntary curtailment was formalised in 1942 when regulations restricted the proportion of space newspapers could devote to advertising (Curran and Seaton, *Power Without Responsibility*, p. 62); *Royal Commission*, p. 63.
[12] HMSO, *Royal Commission*, p. 5.
[13] Ibid.

'Nationwide advertising pushed out of the London papers were glad to find space in the provinces.'[14]

2. The Editors

Crozier, appointed editor of the *Manchester Guardian* in 1932, was indisputably the man in charge of editorial policy. John Scott, the son of C. P., was the managing director, but believed that a newspaper manager's duty was to 'make his paper as profitable as possible, and to refrain from taking part in editorial decisions'.[15] It was not that John Scott lacked interest in what appeared in the newspaper – *The Guardian* Archive has several examples of his non-judgemental comments – but he believed the editor 'must be as free editorially as if he were the proprietor'.[16] Crozier acted accordingly and memos showed his powers were matched by his attention to detail. He had a penchant for precise English, pronouncing: 'The best and most effective English for newspaper purposes ... simple, direct, lucid, concise, short.'[17] To the reporting staff he wrote in 1940:

> The verb 'to rock' or 'to be rocked' in such phrases as 'London Rocks' or 'Manchester Rocks' where there is a big explosion is forbidden. The verb 'to shock' or 'to be shocked' in phrases like 'Two wardens were shocked when this bomb fell' is also forbidden'.[18]

Production journalists were not spared either. A memo to Attenborough, when he was the chief sub-editor, read:

> I reckon that in the last four years I have sent to you personally not less than a hundred notes on 'both ... and' and 'either ... or' alone (say one per fortnight) and not less

---

[14] Ibid.
[15] Ayerst, *The Manchester Guardian*, p. 495.
[16] Ibid.
[17] John Rylands Library, *The Guardian* Archive, 3 January 1940.
[18] Ayerst, *The Manchester Guardian*, p. 497.

than fifty (I think far more) on the misuse of 'otherwise'. And, roughly speaking all wasted. Some people say these things are unimportant ... But, unfortunately I can't.[19]

With such scrutiny came conflict and Malcolm Muggeridge, a freelance reporter in the Soviet Union for the *Manchester Guardian* and later an author and broadcaster, wrote to Crozier in 1933 when his copy was toned down: 'From the way you cut my messages ... I realise that you don't want to know what is going on in Russia or to let your readers know.'[20]

Crozier was capable of a stinging retort too – in March 1936 he wrote to another reporter: 'Neither I nor my predecessors have been accustomed to be corrected by a member of the staff' – and Muggeridge's short-tempered exchange was not the only one.[21] Voigt, 'undoubtedly the greatest British political journalist of the 1930s', was relentless in exposing Germany's rearmament and was partly responsible for the *Guardian* being banned in Berlin.[22] The castigation of the Nazis was so consistent, however, that his writing was frequently toned down, usually by Crozier, causing rows. On one occasion in 1933 Voigt wrote to Crozier that his report about 'abductions, torture and secret executions' had been downgraded to rumours that 'may be "quite untrue".' He asked: 'What is the good of having a man in Berlin if he cannot establish the truth?'[23]

Crozier was a hard taskmaster but a human one, too, and there are several instances of personal feelings being expressed

---

[19] John Rylands Library, *The Guardian* Archive, Crozier to Attenborough, 25 January 1937.
[20] Ibid., Muggeridge to Crozier, 3 April 1933.
[21] Ayerst, *The Manchester Guardian*, p. 513.
[22] Gannon, *The British Press*, p. 80.
[23] John Rylands Library, *The Guardian* Archive, Voigt to Crozier, 15 March 1933.

by the editor and his staff. When Alexander Werth's reports from Berlin put him in physical danger, Crozier withdrew him to Paris writing: 'I have been uneasy about your safety all the time.'[24] During the war, when he had to intervene on the letters page because of the inexperience of a young journalist, Crozier insisted on calling on a trusted sub-editor, R. G. Garner, who would become night news editor later in 1941. In his diary he commented: 'Think for the future ... send all letters to R. G. – poor R. G.!'[25] Evelyn Montague, who was C. P. Scott's eldest grandson and the war correspondent for the *Guardian*, wrote on his posting to cover the BEF's deployment in France: 'I have never been as nervous since my wedding day as I am at this moment. ... But I'll do my best. It's a grand chance and I'm deeply grateful.'[26] The following year, Montague reported about the morale in the *Manchester Guardian*'s London office at the height of The Blitz:

> Shand and, to a much lesser extent, Ray are rattled. Scott and Miss Isitt are magnificently unmoved. Lambert is not so good; he is defeatist by nature, and was severely affected by the French collapse. I am not quite happy about Werth. Boardman shows no signs of nerves in his conversation, but is notably careful in looking after himself.[27]

He added: 'Our staff here are exhausted and rattled, and any effort which can be made to spare them will assist the production of a good paper.' Montague, himself, declared he was: 'not scared but exhilarated by the bombing' but fell ill not long afterwards.[28] An indication of the relationship between Crozier and his war correspondent, and the former's authority

---

[24] Ibid., Crozier to Werth, 20 March 1933.
[25] Ibid., Crozier, 11 February 1941.
[26] Ibid., Montague to Crozier, 7 October 1939.
[27] Ibid., 13 September 1940.
[28] Ibid.

over editorial matters even when up against relatives of the newspaper's former editor, was also revealed in Crozier's diary: 'E. A. M. [Montague] now writes a letter to me protesting against me spiking his pars. He finds it "mortifying and humiliating" that I should accept agency reports instead of his word.'[29] The following day, Crozier added: 'Letter of apology from E. A. M. for his outburst.'[30]

Despite the strains on the staff, circulations rose. Ayerst wrote: 'There was even a waiting list of about 3,000 would-be purchasers. As many *Guardian*s could be sold as could be printed. This was a common experience of all papers.'[31] The *Guardian* was still a relatively financially poor paper, however, as display advertising migrated to 'popular' papers, and in 1937 it could charge only £1 per column inch compared to *The Times*'s £3 and the *Daily Express*'s £6 10s.[32] Consequently most of its war coverage had to be done through others – the paper paid for the rights to use reports from *The Times*'s correspondents – and only when Montague landed in North Africa with the British First Army and then accompanied the Eighth Army in Sicily and Italy could the service be reciprocated.[33] This arrangement also testified to the lack of competition between the newspapers. The *Guardian* sold only around 3,000 copies in the London area while *The Times* barely penetrated Manchester and the North West.

The *Manchester Evening News* went into the Second World War under the editorship of Haley, who had joined the newspaper in 1922, became chief sub-editor three years later and was appointed a director of the *Manchester Guardian* and

---

[29] Ibid., Crozier, 10 December 1940.
[30] Ibid., 11 December 1940.
[31] Ayerst, *The Manchester Guardian*, p. 543.
[32] Ibid., p. 490.
[33] Ibid., pp. 547–48.

Manchester Evening News in 1930. A journalist who eschewed reporting because of shyness – 'that made him an embarrassing casual acquaintance' – but nevertheless a newspaperman of considerable repute, he would later become Director General of the BBC (1944) and the editor of *The Times* (1952).[34] Haley was a workaholic and an imposing man with a 'quiet but rasping voice, iron-grey wiry hair, a hard mouth and unsmiling eyes', while one person meeting him for the first time commented: 'I've met a chap with one glass eye before – but never a chap with two.'[35] Hamilton wrote that Haley came across as cold on first acquaintance: 'On the surface there was no warmth at all, but underneath, as I came to know, there was tremendous warmth, even passion.'[36] Appointed editor at the aged 29, Haley transformed the newspaper, made it more national in outlook and prepared the ground for the *Evening News*'s supremacy over the *Chronicle*.[37]

Haley became responsible for the day-to-day management of both the *Guardian* and the *Evening News* when war was declared but his grip on the editorial stance of his own newspaper remained. In his interview to be the editor he stated: 'One man must control news, distribution, advertising, the whole running of the paper.'[38] His appointment coincided with steady circulation growth from around 150,000 in 1930 to more than 200,000 when he left 13 years later and it was thanks to the *Evening News* that the *Manchester Guardian* survived.[39]

---

[34] 'Sir William Haley', *The Times*, 8 September 1987, p. 16.
[35] Oliver Woods and James Bishop, *The Story of The Times* (London: Michael Joseph, 1985), p. 331; Denis Hamilton, *Editor-in-Chief: Fleet Street Memoirs* (London: Hamish Hamilton, 1989), p. 133.
[36] Hamilton, *Editor-in-Chief*, p. 133.
[37] Ayerst, *The Manchester Guardian*, p. 491.
[38] Ibid., p. 490.
[39] Ibid., p. 491.

John Scott recognised this, paying Haley more than he did himself: 'After all, you make the money we spend.'[40]

Haley, whose judgement in being wary of Hitler's intentions had been vindicated in the build-up to the war, was less prescient when hostilities began. Writing in his diary on 3 September 1939, the day war was declared, he noted:

> For once it was inevitable. This is said untruly of most wars. It is true this time. So long as Hitler ruled Germany we could not escape ultimate conflict with him because he sought it. The only thing we could do was to see it was at our time rather than at his.
>
> The announcement of the Soviet-German pact spelt the beginning of the end. It may seem foolish to think it will be a short war; I feel it may be. Germany in 1914 was rich and strong after 40 years of peace. We were not one quarter so prepared as we are today.[41]

His short war never materialised and the *Evening News* was soon publishing with fewer reporters and less newsprint, a challenge Haley seemed to relish. When the number of his *Manchester Evening News* staff was reduced by three, he wrote in his diary in March 1940:

> This is a complete clear-out. And I feel exhilarated rather than depressed. We've done so well lately that we have got into a groove. This will give us all a chance to jump out of it and shake things up.[42]

The tone and news judgements at both the *Manchester Guardian* and the *Manchester Evening News* reflected the men in the editor's office, and reporters based in the city were tightly controlled, but much of the copy that appeared in the newspapers came from news agencies. Reuters and the Press

---

[40] Ibid.
[41] Churchill Archives, Sir William John Haley, 3 September 1939.
[42] Ibid., 25 March 1940.

Association, the principal providers, were based in one Fleet Street building, so the MOI could easily control the information flow and ensure that 'the journalism produced could communicate a sense of social unity in the war effort'.[43] Much of this copy came from official communiqués and within a fortnight of war being declared, Crozier was complaining: 'What makes me rather despair is the stuff that they are actually themselves putting out – wordy, woolly and thoroughly commonplace.'[44] The following chapters will include more examples of Crozier's dissatisfaction and he and Haley did not have far to go to complain. John Scott was made a government regional information officer (with the potential consequences for press freedom that suggested), while the chief regional information officer was George Mould, a former news editor of the *Manchester Evening News* who was given an office in the newspapers' Cross Street offices.[45] This was a convenient accommodation for *Evening News* journalists who could submit their items and have them returned very quickly. 'He had a real sense of a newspaper's urgent requirements', Bill Pepper, a journalist working on the paper, recalled.[46] The comment sums up the cosy nature of the relationship between Manchester's newspapers and the authorities during the war, a subject that will be explored in subsequent chapters.

If the editors shaped the editorial stances of the *Manchester Guardian* and *Manchester Evening News*, the line of control at the *Evening Chronicle* was more ambiguous. Lord Kemsley was the proprietor, and each of his newspapers carried the slogan 'a Kemsley newspaper' below the masthead, which prompted

---

[43] Conboy, *Journalism in Britain*, p. 63.
[44] John Rylands Library, *The Guardian* Archive, Crozier to Voigt, 11 September 1939.
[45] Ayerst, *The Manchester Guardian*, p. 288.
[46] King, 'The Press at War', p. 19.

Herbert Morrison, the Home Secretary for much of the war, to describe his publishing empire as 'the gramophone press'.[47] Yet he was 'largely preoccupied with the flagship of the group, the *Sunday Times*', and 'he relied on old-fashioned, able journalists to bring out the papers'.[48] In the case of the *Evening Chronicle* that was James Woodbridge, who had joined the paper in 1912 as a leader writer and who was editor from 1925 to 1943. The *Guardian* described him an editor who 'was able to inspire his staff, whose own views he always treated with courtesy'.[49]

Woodbridge needed his diplomatic skills because Kemsley, like Beaverbrook, generated strong opinions. One contemporary described him as a dim social climber with 'a genius for circulation and advertising', but Kemsley has been credited with creating the platform for the *Sunday Times*'s success in the 1960s, even if it was his brother Lord Camrose who, according to Greenslade, was 'the better journalist and the better man'.[50] Hamilton, who would edit the *Sunday Times* for Kemsley, was more scathing, describing him as 'a deeply conservative Conservative who had succeeded in life by clinging to his brother's coat-tails and was then saved from real competition ... by the war.'[51] Nevertheless, reporters on the *Evening Chronicle* would have been answerable to Kemsley

---

[47] Hamilton, *Editor-in-Chief*, p. 67.
[48] Ibid., pp. 55–57.
[49] 'Mr James Alfred Woodbridge', *The Guardian*, 9 January 1965, p. 4.
[50] Hamilton, *Editor-in-Chief*, p. 55; Roy Greenslade, *Press Gang: How Newspapers Make Profits from Propaganda* (London: Pan, 2004), p. 20.
[51] Hamilton, *Editor-in-Chief*, p. 71.

who 'reserved to himself final authority in all matters of policy'.[52]

This manifested itself in many ways but the National Union of Journalists, in its submission to the Royal Commission on the Press in 1949, claimed he kept a blacklist. The union described this as: 'lists of persons – and sometimes firms and organisations – mention of whom is completely banned in all circumstances in the columns of the papers concerned', and stated that the Kemsley organisation sent directives on the treatment of weekend speeches sent from London to the provinces during the war: 'Do not use Mr xxxx'.[53] Michael Foot, an MP, future leader of the Labour Party and a former journalist, reported to the Commission:

> I think for a period Lord Beaverbrook was on Lord Kemsley's black list; at any rate, it was an extraordinary fact that when Lord Beaverbrook was Minister for Aircraft Production there were no stories about the Ministry of Aircraft Production on Lord Kemsley's front page.[54]

The Royal Commission also heard from the Manchester editor of the *Daily Sketch*, who gave a further example of editorial interference from Kemsley after Hitler had delivered a speech before the Munich agreement. The editor received a call from Kemsley's headquarters in London saying the contents bill should include an 'agreeable' photograph of Hitler with one word: 'Peace'. He added:

> The comment of the chief sub-editor was: 'Well that's not my reading of Hitler's speech' and that was the general opinion. But we had to put out the bill just the same. It was another instance of journalistic knowledge, experience and sense of

---

[52] *Dictionary of National Biography*, cited in Greenslade, *Press Gang*, p. 19.
[53] HMSO, *Royal Commission*, p. 123.
[54] Ibid., p. 124.

responsibility to the public being overridden by the fiat of a Press Lord.[55]

That underlined the importance of Manchester in terms of the British newspaper industry, but it also showed that an editorial elite, conforming to Herman and Chomsky's top-down news model, heavily influenced the reports in the *Manchester Guardian*, *Manchester Evening News* and *Evening Chronicle*. In the case of the *Guardian* and the *Evening News* it was their editors, Crozier and Haley, albeit with the sanction of the owners, the Scott Trust, while the *Chronicle* had a less defined management structure. Woodbridge was editor, and his work led to his promotion to become editor of a national Sunday, the *Empire News,* in 1943, but it was the proprietor, Kemsley, who had the ultimate say on editorial policy.[56] The government set the parameters in terms of censorship, but it was Crozier, Haley and Kemsley who decided how far to test these limits.

3. 'Serious again in the morning'

Despite the *Manchester Guardian* being largely supportive of Germany in the 1920s and a consistent critic of the reparations imposed at Versailles, the Nazis banned it in 1933.[57] It opposed Hitler almost from his emergence in Germany, becoming exceptional in Britain in that it tried to print what it knew about what was happening in the Third Reich. Andrew Sharf wrote: 'During the first two years of Nazi rule ... the greatest amount of space given to the Jewish question was in the *Manchester Guardian*', while Gannon asserted that 'from the

---

[55] Ibid., Evidence and Papers, cited in Gannon, *The British Press*, pp. 53–54.
[56] 'Mr James Alfred Woodbridge', *The Guardian*, 9 January 1965, p. 4.
[57] Ayerst, *The Manchester Guardian*, p. 414.

very first there was no doubt but that the *Manchester Guardian* abhorred the Nazi regime, its racial theory and barbarous practices.'[58] A comment piece printed nine months before Hitler became German Chancellor was typically forthright: 'The following quotations from the speeches and writings of Hitler and his followers', it read, 'will explain why Jews have been mobbed in Germany, why the windows of Jewish shops have been smashed, why synagogues have been fouled and Jewish cemeteries desecrated.'[59] Crozier insisted it was important to keep the Jewish and other persecutions in the eye of a public, his determination in this regard springing from the conviction that the *Manchester Guardian* had been negligent in the years before the First World War in exposing the militarist ambitions of influential people in pre-1914 Germany. He wrote to one reporter: 'C. P. S. [C. P. Scott] had such a profound belief in the goodness of human nature … that he would just not believe that there was any important section of opinion in Germany who were a real danger to peace.'[60]

In the countdown to war the *Manchester Guardian* was less culpable than most other national newspapers in playing down the prospect of hostilities. Paradoxically in view of its regional roots, the newspaper provided comprehensive coverage of news directly related to British foreign policy, with Germany and Danzig in July and August 1939, averaging 305 centimetres of copy a day compared to *The Times*'s 208

---

[58] Andrew Sharf, *The British Press and Jews under Nazi Rule* (London: Oxford University Press, 1964), p. 11; Gannon, *The British Press*, p. 76.
[59] 'Campaign of abuse against Jews', *Manchester Guardian*, 9 April 1932, p. 11.
[60] John Rylands Library, *The Guardian* Archive, Crozier to Voigt, 25 January 1934.

centimetres, the *Daily Express*'s 157 and the *Daily Mail*'s 132.[61] This was partly due to the newspaper's letters pages that, in contrast to the other publications, dealt extensively with Germany and, in particular, the Munich agreement. The tone of the newspaper's coverage was critical of the Nazi regime and there was a negligible amount of the false optimism of the *Daily Express*. A leader printed on 24 July 1939 calling for the inclusion of Churchill and Anthony Eden in the Cabinet was indicative of the sense of foreboding, while a report from Germany read: 'It is possible Herr Hitler will decide in favour of war this year', but said the feeling in Berlin was that he preferred the following spring.[62] It was not a matter of if the war would start, but when.

Even so, the *Manchester Guardian*'s own voice, via its leader articles, was more hopeful, although it described Goebbels as an 'arch illusionist' and his propaganda as 'shriller, wilder and, to put it bluntly, more panic-stricken'.[63] Contrarily, Hitler was described as 'the great man' in another leader on 16 August and even when the Soviet-German pact was announced the newspaper almost mirrored Beaverbrook's optimism when it claimed the crisis was 'extremely threatening, but not beyond remedy'.[64] Reality dawned the following day when the *Guardian* bemoaned the lack of a Franco-British agreement with Stalin: 'The front which was

---

[61] Guy Hodgson, 'Sir Nevile Henderson, Appeasement and the Press' (unpublished Master's dissertation, Open University, 2005), p. 64.

[62] 'Herr Hitler's Desire for an "Eastern Munich"', *Manchester Guardian*, 24 July 1939, p. 12.

[63] 'The Gentle Art of Making Enemies', *Manchester Guardian*, 28 July 1939, p. 10.

[64] 'A Time of Waiting', *Manchester Guardian*, 16 August 1939, p. 8; 'Cabinet and Country', *Manchester Guardian*, 22 August 1939, p. 8.

not merely to win a war, but to prevent a war will be much weaker than it might have been, both in a military and moral sense'.[65] The *Manchester Guardian*, like other newspapers, had its reason swayed by the evacuation from Dunkirk. Its reporter 'watched with incredulous joy the happening of a miracle', as he saw a destroyer dock with rescued soldiers: 'They at any rate did not regard themselves as the central figures of tragic drama ... Their eyes were red with weariness above bags of tired skin, but they were still soldiers and still in good heart.'[66]

While the *Manchester Guardian* was undoubtedly earnest in the 1930s, the *Evening Chronicle*, James Agate argued, had a lighter touch:

> The effect of the *Guardian* was to make one feel that the previous day had been one of grave moral questioning and serious responsibility at home and abroad. The *Chronicle* gave one the impression that the day one had just lived through had been full of exciting and, on the whole, jolly happenings. One would be serious again in the morning.[67]

Agate, the *Sunday Times* theatre critic and, therefore, an employee of Kemsley Newspapers, had a vested interest in preferring the *Evening Chronicle*, but its tone was generally lighter and less reverent. Like the *Manchester Evening News*, the *Evening Chronicle* sold at three halfpence (just over 0.5 of a modern penny) a copy and both newspapers printed first editions at 11 am. These were followed by the 'home', 'last', 'last edition extra' and the 'late night final' editions that

---

[65] 'The Russo-German Pact', *Manchester Guardian*, 23 August 1939, p. 8.
[66] 'The Miracle of the BEF's Return', *Manchester Guardian*, 1 June 1940, p. 7.
[67] James Agate, 'As It Was ...', in Henry J. Bradley, *Fifty Great Years: Through The Eyes of the Evening Chronicle, 1897–1947* (Manchester: Kemsley, 1997), p. 10.

reached vendors just before 5 pm. The edition was denoted at the top of the title page. Local news came from the paper's reporters and freelance journalists, while Manchester's satellite towns were covered by the Press Association and Extel, the national news agencies, and other national and international news was provided by the British United Press and Reuters. Not that there was much space for these reports because newsprint restrictions meant that by the summer of 1940 the *Evening Chronicle* was down to six pages.

The *Chronicle*'s response to the talks at Munich in 1938 was to describe Chamberlain as 'a spectacular figure' whose virtues shone through a crisis and the paper's regular political commentator, Baxter, praised the Prime Minister for treating Hitler like a 'gentleman'.[68] On 30 September, the day the agreement was announced, the newspaper stated: 'All the world today is hailing Mr Chamberlain as a peacemaker.'[69] The following day it reported: 'The thoughts of British people have turned inevitably to rejoicing and thanksgiving.'[70]

Six months later, after the Germans occupied the whole of Czechoslovakia, Baxter's tone had changed. 'The present occupation of Prague is the greatest offence Herr Hitler has committed against international decency', his column read, before condemning the invasion of a country 'which has no more relation to Germany than the moon'.[71] As war loomed, the *Chronicle* assumed a perceptiveness that its previous work

---

[68] Beverley Baxter, 'And Now … We Can Look Ahead', *Evening Chronicle,* 29 September 1938, p. 8.
[69] 'Manchester May Offer Premier its freedom', *Evening Chronicle,* 30 September 1938, p. 1.
[70] 'Millions to Give Peace Thanks Tomorrow', *Evening Chronicle,* 1 October 1938, p. 5.
[71] Beverley Baxter, 'Hitler Again', *Evening Chronicle,* 16 March 1939, p. 8.

could not justify. 'In the end the world always has a day of reckoning with men like Hitler', its leading article read on 1 September 1939. 'Our hands are clean. We have pursued conciliation to the utmost, but in the last resort we stand ready and united.'[72] On 4 September, the first edition after war was officially declared, an indicator appeared of what was to come in terms of propaganda that demonised the enemy. The lead headline read: 'Liner was torpedoed without warning: 311 Americans aboard', while the subhead was: 'Treaty has been callously broken'.[73] There was also an attempt to lift morale with an article on making the most of the blackout. 'Even though the windows might be darkened at night so that not even a pencil of light shows through on the outside, there is no reason why the inside of a room should be dark and depressing.'[74]

Given the censorship of news of the evacuation of Dunkirk, the *Evening Chronicle* probably did not appreciate the irony in its sub-headline on 27 May 1940 that read 'Our offensive not yet started'.[75] On 14 June, with the beaten British Army back in England, 'our Special Correspondent' reported from the South Coast: 'To a gay eightsome reel, which a man from Motherwell solemnly assured me is called "Hitler's lament" at home, thousands of British troops left a Southern port for France.'[76] Three days later, with the true position

---

[72] 'The Attack on Poland', *Evening Chronicle*, 1 September 1939, p. 6.
[73] 'Liner was Torpedoed Without Warning: 311 Americans Aboard', *Evening Chronicle*, 4 September 1939, p. 1.
[74] Black-out Without Gloom' *Evening Chronicle*, 4 September 1939, p. 2.
[75] Allies Move Back from Region of Valenciennes', *Evening Chronicle*, 27 May 1940, p. 1.
[76] 'New BEF Dance and Sing as They Leave', *Evening Chronicle*, 14 June 1940, p. 1.

dawning, there was a rush to apportion blame: 'France has given up the battle'.[77] By the height of the Battle of Britain, the *Evening Chronicle* had abandoned all pretence at objectivity. 'The RAF is hitting Germany hard – infinitely harder than Goering's Luftwaffe has been hitting', it reported, neglecting the obvious flaw in its argument that the battle was being fought over British territory. It added:

> The only thing Hitler can do in the air is to continue on a larger scale the type of bombing we have been getting in recent weeks. The enemy's air force has scarcely hit a military target in Britain but it has managed to do a certain amount of damage to civilian life and property and has also wantonly machine-gunned the streets of open towns.[78]

The alleged futility of the enemy's attacks, along with the attribution of negative characteristics, was emphasised, the words 'wantonly' and 'open' stressing the unashamed attacks on undefended areas. Nine days later the *Chronicle* followed that up with a report of raids at 'three places in North-West England', adding 'one person is said to be slightly injured and the damage was only trivial'.[79]

The *Manchester Evening News* became increasingly concerned with politics and foreign affairs under the editorship of Haley, questioning Chamberlain's policies in early 1938. On 16 February its editorial accused the Prime Minister of failing to recognise the singular threat posed by Germany.[80] 'The time has come for the ordinary man to stop avoiding the

---

[77] 'French Army Ceases Hostilities', *Evening Chronicle,* 17 June 1940, p. 1.
[78] 'RAF Drive Hitler to Wild Threats', *Evening Chronicle,* 20 July 1940, p. 4.
[79] 'Big Air Battle: "20 Raiders Down"', *Evening Chronicle,* 29 July 1940, p. 1.
[80] 'After Austria', *Manchester Evening News,* 16 February 1938, p. 8.

truth ... he knows in reality ... where the only danger to the peace in Europe lies.' On 15 March 1938 it called for the inclusion of Churchill in the Cabinet.[81]

While the *Evening News* had stood apart in early 1938, it joined the consensus in the build-up to Munich, praising Chamberlain for his 'courage', although it did warn a fortnight later: 'Today the world rejoices. It should not do so without care for the morrow.'[82] The leader added prophetically: 'Hitler's troops will still march ... The settlement terms the world is so gratefully applauding today are terrible proof how far aggression has managed to travel along its "peaceful" road.' When the Germans moved on Prague in March 1939 the paper adopted an 'I told you so' stance, stating that the time to act had been six months earlier. It asked if the rest of the world regarded Britain as a nation of clever lawyers who could wriggle out of any agreement and would not stand up to Hitler as long as 'they didn't touch Britain'?[83] A day later it stated: 'The free people of the world await a lead.'[84]

A study of the *Evening News* in the four weeks leading up to the war marks a journey towards unhappy resignation that the conflict was inevitable. On 21 August 1939 the paper commented: 'During the next fortnight the fate of European civilisation may be decided', while the signing of the Nazi-Soviet non-aggression pact on 23 August led to the question: 'Can any life be worth living in which force and not justice

---

[81] 'The Free Peoples', *Manchester Evening News*, 15 March 1938, p. 8.
[82] 'The Wonderful Visit', *Manchester Evening News*, 15 September 1938, p. 6; 'The End of a Nation', *Manchester Evening News*, 30 September 1938, p. 8.
[83] 'The Ides of March', *Manchester Evening News*, 15 March 1939, p. 6.
[84] 'Without Blinkers', *Manchester Evening News*, 16 March 1939, p. 6.

The Newspapers

governs the affairs of nations and men?'[85] The same editorial asked: 'Is a man to be conceived as a free, if still imperfect individual ... or a mere robot ... having no freedom ... or rights within himself?' The 1 September edition, two days before war was declared, carried the grim headline 'Warsaw bombed' under which was a report of Germany's invasion of Poland.[86]

The *Evening News*, unlike its rival the *Evening Chronicle*, had a realistic vision of what was going on in France in May 1940, notwithstanding its sub-headlined claim that 'Germans had five casualties to every British'. Its leader noted: 'The BEF are getting out. Despite fearful odds, relentlessly beset and harried by a determined and ruthless aggressor, our men are slowly being extricated from a position made desperate by no fault of their own.'[87] During the Battle of Britain the *Evening News* printed tables giving 'scores' referring to the number of German planes shot down that week. When Churchill made his 'finest hour' speech the newspaper reacted with an editorial: 'Compare that speech with Hitler's last effort. In that comparison you will find the inner reasons why this is a war Britain will win.'[88]

---

[85] 'The Moving Finger', *Manchester Evening News,* 21 August 1939, p. 6; 'The Choice', *Manchester Evening News,* 25 August 1939, p. 8.

[86] 'Warsaw Bombed', *Manchester Evening News,* 1 September 1939, p. 1.

[87] 'BEF Heroes Pouring Home' *Manchester Evening News,* 31 May 1940, p. 1; 'Who is for Liberty?' *Manchester Evening News,* 31 May 1940, p. 4.

[88] *Hansard,* HC Debate, 18 June 1940; 'Britain Speaks', *Manchester Evening News,* 21 August 1940, p. 2.

CHAPTER FIVE

CENSORSHIP

1. A Barrage of D-Notices

In terms of censorship, newspapers were made aware of potential government coercion well before the Second World War began. The Emergency Powers (Defence) Act passed on 28 August 1938, Knightley observed, authorised the government to do virtually what it liked to prosecute war without reference to Parliament:

> Every press, commercial or private message leaving Britain, whether by mail, cable, wireless or telephone was censored. Everyone, including newspaper editors, was prohibited from 'obtaining, recording communicating to any other person or publishing information, which might be useful to the enemy'.[1]

The signing of the Nazi-Soviet Pact on 23 August 1939 increased the government's readiness to control the press and the following day Crozier, the editor in chief of the *Manchester Guardian*, wrote to the London editor Bone about a meeting with officials concerning reporting restrictions. It will be voluntary, he reported, 'in the sense that all editors were expected to do as much of the censorship as they could themselves'.[2]

The MOI was formed the day after the outbreak of war and expanded from a staff of 12 to a reputed numerically resonant 999 within a matter of weeks (in reality it grew

---

[1] Knightley, *The First Casualty*, p. 238.
[2] John Rylands Library, *The Guardian* Archive, Crozier to Bone, 24 August 1939.

steadily to be 1,385 by 31 July 1940 and 3,000 by 1945).[3] Taylor wrote:

> Britain went to war with a wealth of peacetime experience in censorship and with the basis of a censorship machinery that, once its wheels began to turn when the correct lubrication was added by 1941, was to run remarkably smoothly.[4]

Since Britain was fighting for democracy, it was decided that censorship should be conducted on what outwardly appeared to be a liberal basis with editors invited to submit copy they thought might infringe regulations.[5] The censors would then have the right to cut or withhold this material, thus absolving newspapers of any legal responsibility should it later transpire publication aided the enemy. Even if the press ignored the censors' cuts, the government still needed to prove that the offending publication had actually aided the enemy before prosecution could take place. It seemed a benign regime; in reality, the censors exercised comprehensive control over what appeared in newspapers. Editors, the chief censor George Thomson noted, were issued with such a barrage of D-notices that the restrictions 'covered nearly every conceivable human activity'.[6]

This was acknowledged even in Parliament where MP Sydney Silverman, speaking against the restrictions, said they would put the government 'in a position by no means inferior,

---

[3] *Hansard*, HC Debate, 11 October 1939, 352, cols 376–484; *Hansard*, HL Debate, 8 August 1940, 117, cols 158–60; Williams, *Get Me a Murder!*, p. 125.
[4] Philip M. Taylor, *British Propaganda in the Twentieth Century* (Edinburgh: Edinburgh University Press, 1999), p. 136.
[5] George P. Thomson, *The Blue Pencil Admiral: The Inside Story of Press Censorship* (London: Sampson Low, Marston, 1947), p. 6.
[6] Ibid.

as regards the scope of its powers over newspapers, to that occupied by the distinguished Dr Goebbels in Germany'.[7] This system was constructed by Chamberlain and reinforced from May 1940 by Churchill, who forsook his previous occupation as a journalist to bear down on his former Fleet Street employers. Margach noted:

> Fleet Street was the foundation of his fortunes and, during his long years in the political wilderness, it sustained him as a national figure. Yet when he became Prime Minister he became authoritarian and repressive, incapable of tolerating any form of criticism in the press. Criticism he viewed as treasonable.[8]

According to Margach, Churchill used the 'majesty of his office to steamroller Fleet Street' so that coverage of the war became a series of good news stories or columns listing examples of Nazi inhumanity.[9] Its success was down to the expedient of censoring at source – the principal national and international news agencies – so as to avoid the French system whereby information that might be useful to the enemy was blanked out in the newspapers. That French method allowed the public to see the extent of the censorship, whereas British readers could not quantify the work of the MOI.[10] That work ensured that attempts at objectivity became replaced by the reporting of more subjective and 'biased' comments via official press releases, government communiqués and, when journalists went out into bombed-out areas, simple propaganda.

---

[7] *Hansard*, HC Debate, 31 July 1940, 363, cols 1307–49.
[8] James Margach, *The Abuse of Power: The War Between Downing Street and the Media* (London: Allen, 1978), p. 64.
[9] Ibid.
[10] Jacquie L'Etang, *Public Relations in Britain: A History of Professional Practice in the Twentieth Century* (Mahwah, NJ: Lawrence Erlbaum Associates, 2004), p. 39.

Censorship

In short, the press stopped reporting the news. Cyril Dunn, a *Yorkshire Post* journalist, was sent to Manchester on Boxing Day 1940 to report on the bombing, making a telling comment in his notebook under the heading 'Bombing is a Messy Business':

> There were big fires everywhere, the air stank of smoke and the streets were full of black ash as if there'd been a volcanic eruption ... I went around nervously collecting the same old stories. 'All I want to do,' said one publican who'd been blasted out of his cellar 'is to get out of here and stop out. I've had enough.' And a woman, 'If only I could feel it was worth it, was helping to win the war. But this [the ruins of her pub] is everything we've worked for ...' I wrote the usual story about the cheerful courage and determined endurance of the Manchester folk.[11]

2. 'Any use to us?'

Taylor wrote that propaganda and censorship are 'really different sides of the same medal: the manipulation of opinion', but despite Britain's alleged expertise in the former, which will be explored in the next chapter, the war began in terms of censorship with a series of misunderstandings that reduced the credibility and threatened the existence of the MOI.[12] Partly this was down to a decision, unknown to editors, by the Allied chiefs of staff to make the war 'newsless'.[13] Initially British military action was limited mainly to the Royal Navy, who refused to relay information to the press even though the First Lord of the Admiralty was a former journalist,

---

[11] Cyril Dunn. 'Bombing is a Messy Business', *Notebook XIV, November 1940 to April 1941*, 26 December 1940, cited in Gardiner, *The Blitz*, p. 215.

[12] Taylor, *British Propaganda*, p. 153; Williams, *Get Me a Murder!*, p. 126.

[13] Knightley, *The First Casualty*, p. 238.

Churchill, and when American newspapers began to be filled with information coming from Berlin, there was an outcry in Britain.[14] This mood was not improved when a Commons statement revealed that only 43 of the nearly 1,000 MOI staff had been journalists.[15] Knightley wrote:

> The *Daily Express* said that soon Britain would need leaflet raids on itself to tell its own people how the war was going. *Manchester Guardian* said that the official communiqués could not help the enemy but 'are they any use to us'?[16]

The situation reached farcical proportions in September 1939 when an embargo of news of the British Expeditionary Force being sent to France was lifted and re-imposed in a matter of hours so that the police guarded printing presses and newspapers were confiscated from commuters.[17] The blackout was lifted again shortly afterwards. When the British Army's attempt at a second front in Norway in 1940 ended ignominiously, but with barely a report in British newspapers, Ed Murrow, of the Columbia Broadcasting System, was scathing.[18] He told his American listeners from London on 22 April 1940: 'The handling by the press and radio in this country of the news from Norway in the past 10 days has undermined the confidence of a considerable section of the

---

[14] Ibid., p. 241.
[15] *Hansard*, HC Debate, 27 September 1939, 351, cols 1330–34.
[16] Knightley, *The First Casualty*, p. 242.
[17] Philip M. Taylor, *Munitions of the Mind. A History of Propaganda from the Ancient World to the Present Era*, 2nd edn (Manchester: Manchester University Press, 1995), p. 212.
[18] The *Manchester Guardian* reported that the military position was 'extremely favourable' the same day Allied forces in Norway were evacuated ('Allied Progress in Narvik', *Manchester Guardian*, 10 June 1940, p. 8).

Censorship

British public in the integrity and accuracy of its news sources.'[19]

What Murrow did not acknowledge, and, as an American broadcast journalist, may not have fully appreciated, was the threat hanging over Fleet Street of a *British Gazette*-style newspaper that could be produced by the government as competition. The *British Gazette* had been published by the government during the General Strike 14 years earlier and the fact that Churchill had been the editor of a paper that rose from 200,000 sales to two million in eight editions emphasised the threat.[20] In June 1940 Duff Cooper, back in government as the Minister for Information, met the Editorial Committee, a combination of senior journalists representing Fleet Street, and was asked if there was foundation in the rumour that a government newspaper would take the place of existing newspapers? 'Mr Duff Cooper did not give an emphatic denial to the rumour', a report of the meeting read. 'He said he had heard the matter discussed, but it had not been considered by the Cabinet. He smiled at the suggestion that there might be another "*British Gazette*".'[21] Six weeks later, with newspapers generally compliant, the government withdrew from its aggressive position when Duff Cooper organised a dinner meeting with journalists (including future Labour leader Michael Foot and future *Daily Mirror* editor Hugh Cudlipp), arranged 'so that they could talk to him in an atmosphere less formal and less bitter than usually exists'.[22] Montague re-

---

[19] Knightley, *The First Casualty*, pp. 248-49.
[20] Price, *Where Power Lies*, p. 115.
[21] John Rylands Library, *The Guardian* Archive, 223/19/1-18, *Wartime Arrangements on the Manchester Guardian*, 1939-42, 21 June 1940.
[22] John Rylands Library, *The Guardian* Archive, Montague to Crozier, 6 August 1940.

ported to Crozier that 'Cooper had mentioned the *British Gazette*, so he says, as a joke, quoting it as an example of which nobody wanted.'[23] Nevertheless, a warning had been delivered.

Relations between Fleet Street and the government improved with the appointment of Thomson, first as deputy and then, from 1940, chief censor for the duration of the war.[24] The Rear Admiral felt the press had genuine grievances and adopted the policy to 'prevent the enemy from gaining military information of value, but also to ensure that the Press and the BBC should have complete freedom to inform the British people and the world at large of every thing that was happening'.[25] The freedom was never as encompassing as Thomson suggested, but the press, after initial scepticism, eventually came to a working relationship with the MOI.

Thomson acknowledged that air raids presented a problem for those responsible for information and security on both sides. There was the basic question of whether the effects of bombing should be played up or down. If one opted for the former, the chief advantage would be that it would provoke anger and stiffen resistance, but that had to be balanced against the risk of encouraging the enemy and spreading alarm and despondency. Playing down raids, however, would risk belittling the credibility of official communiqués, encourage the spread of rumours and antagonise victims in bombed areas. In May 1941, for example, raids on Glasgow and Liverpool were described as light when casualty figures published a few days later showed this to be false. Thomson reported that this provoked considerable anger:

---

[23] Ibid.
[24] Williams, *Get Me a Murder!*, p. 131.
[25] Thomson, *The Blue Pencil Admiral*, p. 2.

Censorship

> We had to try and satisfy the natural desire of the inhabitants of a town which had been raided so that their menfolk at the front and their relatives and friends in other parts of the country should know what they were having to endure. They had seen with their own eyes ancient, familiar and homely things turned into heaps of ash and rubble. They knew with what resolution and courage they and the ordinary folk around them had stood up to it and they wanted the whole world to know.[26]

One way out of the difficulty was to allow local newspapers more extensive reports than national newspapers, thus satisfying the victims of raids while restricting the spread of knowledge that might aid the Germans.[27]

A frequent problem was whether to reveal places that had been hit. The Air Ministry allowed national newspapers to name bombed cities only after it was certain the Germans knew where they had raided, normally meaning a delay of two days, and it was forbidden to identify localities and damage to buildings for 28 days. But, as Thomson pointed out, Goebbels did not wait until aircrew reports had been checked before he put out news of a bombing raid, German radio often proclaiming that London, Liverpool or Manchester had been devastated even before the bombers had returned home:

> On the other hand it was most important that the British Press and radio should not give the enemy information of which he was in need. The first essential was to conceal the name of the town raided until the Air Ministry were quite satisfied that the enemy knew it.[28]

The Germans did not always know which cities they were hitting because large conurbations in England were often close together, leading to potential confusion, and the wireless

---

[26] Ibid., p. 77.
[27] Ibid., p. 78.
[28] Ibid., pp. 77–78.

beams used to guide the bombers were jammed by the British. As a consequence, national newspapers frequently were forced to be vague, using large areas: North, North East, North West, East, South East, etc. Thus a raid on Bristol would be described as an attack on a town in South West England.[29] Casualties also presented a problem. If the casualty was a doctor, solicitor or shopkeeper, whose name and address appeared in a telephone directory, both the name and the occupation were not permitted in order to prevent the Germans knowing precisely where a bomb had landed.[30] It was a sign of the relative scarcity of telephones, and Thomson's preconceptions, that he wrote: 'In the case of a miner, steelworker or manual worker this difficulty did not of course arise.'[31]

Even though there were improved relations brought about by the appointment of Thomson, there were serious clashes between Fleet Street and Downing Street, particularly after Parliament passed new defence regulations in the wake of Dunkirk in which section 2D allowed for the suppression of newspapers and 18B provided for imprisonment without trial. In July 1940 the *Daily Worker* was warned that its pacifist line contravened these regulations and in the following January the Home Secretary, Morrison, stopped the presses of the newspaper and they were allowed to resume only in August 1942 after Germany invaded Russia.[32] More significant in terms of size was the relationship between the government and the *Daily Mirror*, whose circulation rose from 1.33 million in 1937 to 3.7 million in 1947.[33] Churchill, who had used the

---

[29] Ibid., p. 78.
[30] Ibid., p. 81–2.
[31] Ibid., p. 82.
[32] Curran and Seaton, *Power Without Responsibility*, p. 56.
[33] HMSO, *Royal Commission*, p. 190.

paper as his platform as a backbencher in 1939, made representations to the *Mirror* to moderate its 'guilty men' attack on Chamberlain in early 1940 and, after he had become Prime Minister, was so angered by the paper in January 1941 that he accused it of:

> Creating a spirit of hatred and malice against the government ... which surpasses anything I have ever seen in English journalism. One might have thought that in these hard times some hatred might be kept for the enemy.[34]

Relations soured further in March 1942 when the *Mirror* published a cartoon by Philip Zec that depicted a half-drowned merchant seaman clinging to some wreckage.[35] The caption read: 'The price of petrol has been increased by one penny – Official', and the intention had been to attack any needless waste of petrol. Home Intelligence stated that was how it was understood by most people, but the government, or rather Churchill, saw it as an attack and part of a campaign that had begun with an editorial in the *Mirror* the month before.[36] That had read:

> The assumption that whatever blunders are committed and whatever faults are plainly visible in organisation, we must still go on applauding men who muddle our lives away, is a travesty of history and a rhetorical defiance of all the bitter lessons of past wars.[37]

The implication of Zec's cartoon, in the minds of Churchill and his Cabinet colleagues, was that sailors were risking their lives for the benefit of higher profits for private enterprise at the

---

[34] Hugh Cudlipp, *Publish and be Damned* (London: Dakers, 1953), p. 11; Maurice Edelman, *The Mirror: A Political History* (London: Hamish Hamilton, 1966), pp. 104–05.
[35] *Daily Mirror*, 5 March 1942, p. 3.
[36] Curran and Seaton, *Power Without Responsibility*, p. 60.
[37] 'After Singapore', *Daily Mirror*, 16 February 1942, p. 3.

government's connivance and caused fury in Downing Street. Churchill wanted to close the *Mirror*, was reined back by Beaverbrook and Morrison, but nevertheless a Parliamentary debate followed on 19 March in which the latter's attack on the paper could hardly have been more damning:

> The cartoon in question is only one example, but a particularly evil example, of the policy and methods of a newspaper which, intent on exploiting an appetite for sensation and with a reckless indifference to the national interest and to the prejudicial effect on the war effort, has repeatedly published scurrilous misrepresentations, distorted and exaggerated statements and irresponsible generalisations.[38]

In private, Churchill was equally scathing. Crozier revealing a conversation with the Prime Minister on 20 March:

> He turned to the *Daily Mirror* question and was very hot and strong about it. He said it was dangerous to have a constant stream of stuff calculated to undermine the morale of the soldier; very serious issues were involved.[39]

And in another conversation with Crozier, Churchill commented: 'The paper that I can't stand, the worst of all, is the *Daily Mirror* ... It makes me spit.'[40]

Despite Churchill's anger, newspaper proprietors sided with the *Mirror* and it soon became clear that suppressing it would lead to a 'major confrontation with a powerful section of the press'.[41] This flexing of Fleet Street's muscles was underlined when another campaign led to the lifting of the ban on the *Daily Worker* in August 1942, but also poses a question: if the press had resisted the pressure of the government, would

---

[38] *Hansard*, HC Debate, 19 March 1942, 378, cols 1665–9.
[39] Crozier, *Off The Record*, p. 312.
[40] Ibid., pp. 349–50.
[41] Curran and Seaton, *Power Without Responsibility*, p. 61.

the censor's grip have been so tight? This is an important indicator that the relationship between Downing Street and the press was more complex than the straightforward pushing of propaganda with proprietors intent on ingratiating themselves with the government. Fleet Street rallied behind the *Mirror* on the grounds of freedom of speech, but later it was apparent that the warning had been grave enough to place all newspapers on their guard for the rest of the war. According to Harrison the threat of 2D hovered over all editors and 'unofficial proposals were mooted for the closing down of all newspapers except *The Times,* the *Daily Herald* and the *Daily Express'*.[42] The *Daily Mirror,* which 'minded its ways without quite mending them', continued to attack examples of inefficiency but not on the scale of March 1942, although it did play a significant role in the defeat of Churchill and the Conservative Party in the General Election of 1945.[43] The effect has divided observers. Williams noted that the government never again attempted to use Regulation 2D to suppress publication and Taylor wrote: 'Opinion had not actually been censored or punished, only threatened with it.'[44] Margach was less sanguine:

> The crises between the Churchill government and Fleet Street continued over most of the war years, covering many papers ... It was a miracle, particularly since newsprint rationing kept papers down to four or six pages, that journalism survived the experience.[45]

---

[42] Stanley Harrison, *Poor Men's Guardians: A Survey of the Struggle for a Democratic Newspaper Press 1763–1973* (Southampton: Camelot, 1974), p. 210.
[43] Koss, *Rise and Fall*, p. 607.
[44] Williams, *Get Me a Murder!*, p. 136; Taylor, *British Propaganda*, p. 164.
[45] Margach, *The Abuse of Power*, p. 84.

3. Guidance to Editors

Price noted that Churchill 'read more newspapers with greater attention than almost any other Prime Minister' so, although the threat of the *British Gazette* was averted, the scrutiny of Fleet Street was constant.[46] The archive of the *Manchester Guardian* memos and correspondence has several examples of the generic pressure being applied by the government and, at a more specific level, the censor. In June 1940 a telegram from the MOI was received under the title 'Guidance to Editors (Not for Publication)', and it laid out the government's policy concerning the reporting of war news with a particular reference to air raids:

> Germany exercises rigid censorship over news of air raids. Very little information is released for publication and the meagre particulars which appear in the German press are always misleading when compared to authentic reports.
>
> In this country, whilst no one would suggest that the enemy should be given useful information as to the result of his air attacks, it would be contrary to the traditions and spirit of our country that we should adopt such extreme methods as those employed by Germany in keeping facts from its people. We pride ourselves on the fact that 'we can take it'.[47]

The memo went on to say that the Luftwaffe was bound to get through, particularly at night and that 'many casualties and severe damage are inevitable'. Then, contradicting the spirit it had initially espoused, the memo issued orders to the press, stating there should be: delays to the full description of air raids; delays to lists and numbers of casualties; and restrictions on the mention of bombed areas 'even of large towns'.

---

[46] Price, *Where Power Lies*, p. 115.
[47] John Rylands Library, *The Guardian* Archive, 223/19/1–18, *Wartime Arrangements*, June 1940.

Censorship

In the same month Duff Cooper was also quoted as saying as saying that the voluntary system of censorship had not been satisfactory, and 'it must now give place to a compulsory system'.[48] The Minister for Information asked the committee to consider three 'possible solutions'. Namely:

1. Complete compulsory censorship using French system (delay of two to three days in publishing news).
2. Compulsory source of news so that newspapers could publish from official sources only.
3. Board of Censors, consisting of two members from the MOI, Admiralty, War Office, Air Ministry, Ministry of Home Security and the Press. Would meet twice a day and would decide what should be said on certain matters.

These reforms were successfully resisted by Fleet Street, but individual editors continued to feel the overt presence of the censor. In June 1940 Crozier warned the *Guardian*'s London editor Bone that complaints had been made 'from certain quarters (the P.M.) about attacks in the *Manchester Guardian*' and five months later Cyril Ray, a war correspondent, reported that three newspapers, the *Melbourne Argus*, *Toronto Star* and *Winnipeg Free Press*, had withdrawn their London correspondents because of the heavy-handed censorship. 'Representations to the Ministry of Information', he wrote, 'have generally been answered in an offhand way and have resulted in no improvement.'[49]

In December 1940, at a lunch hosted by the Minister for Information, Duff Cooper, and the Home Secretary, Morrison, journalists were told: 'The censorship as it affects air raids is to

---

[48] Ibid, 21 June 1940.
[49] John Rylands Library, *The Guardian* Archive, Ray to Crozier, 13 November 1940.

be tightened up ... We are telling Germany too much about air raids.'⁵⁰ Morrison listed the new restrictions:

1. No mention of water shortages (for fear the enemy would return to finish the job in the knowledge there would be little water to put our fires).
2. No criticism of the railway, post office or telephone breakdowns.
3. No mention of people moving out of towns and cities.
4. No mention of fires not being extinguished.
5. Unwise to mention the efficiency in putting out fires.
6. No mention of emergency services moving to help other towns.
7. Don't mention land mines (had a fault and would not explode unless it hit the ground in a certain way).

Morrison finished this lecture by saying: 'If the press is willing to go slow on all this, it is better to do it wholeheartedly. Tell your readers what you are going to do to cheat the enemy and make a patriotic virtue out of necessity.' Within a matter of days, Manchester's newspapers were given ample opportunity to practise their 'patriotic virtue' in the aftermath of the Christmas Blitz.

At a more mundane level there was the constant irritant of having to adhere to, and be under the scrutiny of, the censor. Even in 1943, with the war swinging the Allies' way, Crozier was still being upbraided by a 'very courteous gentleman from the MOI who reads leaders from all over the world each night'. The reprimand read:

> The nightly extract from Manchester tends to criticise the government or to tell people not to be too optimistic, or, in short, all is not supremely well in the best of all possible worlds. They have difficulty, they say, in sending extracts abroad and ask for something not so critical.⁵¹

---

⁵⁰ Ibid., 223/19/1–18, *Wartime Arrangements*, December 1940.
⁵¹ Ibid., 2 February 1943.

Censorship

By then, the dialogue between the MOI and the *Guardian*'s offices was well established. In November 1941 Crozier had written to the Ministry complaining of its 'technical ignorance' of the cotton industry:

> All references – and there have been many – to labour shortages in the cotton mills have spoken of the shortage in the cardroom, because that is the only department in a mule spinning mill in which women happen to be employed. The deletion of the word 'cardroom' safeguards nothing from the enemy but merely destroys the point of the sentence.[52]

Three months later he had to defend himself against the censor after the *Guardian* reported there was a shortage of ARP wardens in Salford. Emergency committees, he argued, had to use the press to draw attention to their needs. If the publicity was denied 'the need will not be met and the deficiencies will not be remedied'.[53] In June 1942 Crozier was forced to apologise after the *Manchester Guardian* carried a small story under the headline 'The Two Uncles'. It read: 'In a recent letter received here from a prisoners' camp in Germany this passage had been uncensored: "I hear that Uncle Sam and Uncle Joe are doing well".'[54] The response from the censor was: 'It is thought that any suggestion in our press of laxity on the part of German censorship may result in steps being taken to make it stricter.'[55] The fact that it took the MOI nearly three weeks to respond to the above was indicative of the delays brought by censorial involvement. On 8 December 1942 Crozier complained: 'Montague's message tonight, dated December 5, is

---

[52] John Rylands Library, *The Guardian* Archive, Crozier to the MOI, 18 November 1941.
[53] Ibid., 18 February 1942.
[54] 'The Two Uncles', *Manchester Guardian*, 21 May 1942, p. 4.
[55] John Rylands Library, *The Guardian* Archive, MOI to the *Manchester Guardian*, 10 June 1942.

useless, being covered by this morning's news, so it goes on the spike ... Our service is being almost completely ruined.'[56]

The system for war time photographs was also complex and slow. To get a permit from the MOI, a photographer had to have accreditation, usually from a newspaper or news agency.[57] Their work had to be given to the censor before it could be distributed, often to a pool for general use, although, to save time, the photographers would self-censor beforehand. Inevitably, given the pressures of deadlines, there was friction. On 26 December 1940, two days after the Manchester Blitz, Crozier complained of the problems of getting photographs into the approved pool for publication: 'I want to get them there as soon as possible lest by chance the Censor should release other people's before he releases ours. In which case we shall be undone.'[58] A month later Crozier, normally succinct to the point of brusqueness in his diary, was so irritated with the censorial dithering about photographs that he noted:

> Censor stopped Duke of Kent in Manchester at 8 pm. Pictures now in page. Said he did not know what the MOI in Manchester had promised. (2 of them had said the stuff was all right for Thursday's paper). *D Herald* protested because its stuff had gone in early editions. Censor rescinded his prohibition and the stuff went in – we took emergency pictures off machine and restored normal page.[59]

For Crozier's diary this number of words amounted to an essay and was perhaps indicative of his frustration at having to deal with such overt control.

---

[56] Ibid, Crozier to Bone, 8 December 1942.
[57] Amy Helen Bell, *London Was Ours: Diaries and Memoirs of the London Blitz*, (London: Tauris, 2011), p. 29.
[58] John Rylands Library, *The Guardian* Archive, Crozier to Haley, 26 December 1940.
[59] Crozier, 15 January 1941, cited in Ayerst, *The Manchester Guardian*, p. 542.

Censorship

Crozier rarely let his exasperation spill out into the newspaper, but the fall of Tobruk, Libya, in June 1942 was a rare example of the *Manchester Guardian* openly criticising the running of the war.[60] Even then, the criticism was buried below an introduction to the editorial that read: 'The edge has gone off the political threat to the Government in the Commons. The "no confidence" men have shown themselves to be a small muster', but below was forthright condemnation:

> We have had our share of disillusionment and disappointment ... But Libya, as the ordinary man sees it, is another matter. Here at least we were prepared to be strong ... The government will have to put itself in the place of the workers who find that after they have worked so hard and so long their production is thrown away in the field, battered by superior weight, or left as booty to the enemy.

This was exceptional, and perhaps the *Guardian* was emboldened because Churchill was being criticised in Parliament, but six days and five editions later it had reverted to type. Its editorial on 3 July read: 'The government has beaten off the vote of "no confidence" by 475 to 25 votes. We must be all un-feignedly glad at the result.'[61]

4. Fit to Print: Censorship and the Manchester Blitz

Crozier's occasional outbursts revealed the frustrations felt by editors, whose job, after all, was to bring news to the public as quickly as possible. The MOI monitored every report about air raids and the only items of news newspapers could report without submission to the censor were: anti-aircraft guns and British fighters had been in action; bombs had been dropped; enemy aircraft had been brought down; and eye-witness

---

[60] 'The Discontents', *Manchester Guardian*, 27 June 1942, p. 6.
[61] 'The Premier's Defence', *Manchester Guardian*, 3 July 1942, p. 4.

accounts of fights in the air.[62] A typical headline appeared on the *Evening Chronicle's* front page in December 1940: 'Nazis try "sneak raids" on N-West'.[63] The choice of words here is significant. The Germans 'try' rather than succeed in their bombing mission, and they were described pejoratively as 'sneak raids' when a similar mission by the RAF would have provoked adjectives such as 'daring' or 'secret'. Propaganda will be examined more thoroughly in the next chapter, but the work of the censor is apparent too. The N-West was used when the place under fire was Manchester, and the placing and prominence of the report was also indicative. Typically, it would require a very strong news story to supplant a bombing as the lead story, but the raid on the city was a single column under the shoulder of the second lead article in columns six and seven of an eight-column page. The apparent downplaying of this story by a Manchester paper was deliberate in that to have led the front page with it would have been an indication that the main destruction was in the city. The report, too, contained typical phrases that diminished the effect of the raid and disguised the geography, beginning: 'A short but concentrated attack was made on a district of an inland town ... Damage was not heavy, although there were a number of casualties, some fatal.'[64] Normal news-writing conventions would dictate that the deaths would have been in the first sentence.

This was typical of the censorship throughout the study period and showed that newspapers' willingness to suppress reports of casualties and bomb damage was as keen in the immediate build-up to Manchester's Blitz as it was in the

---

[62] Thomson, *The Blue Pencil Admiral*, p. 77.
[63] 'Nazis Try "Sneak Raids" on N-West', *Evening Chronicle*, 17 December 1940, p. 1.
[64] Ibid.

Censorship

weeks afterwards. If there was an exception it was in the immediate aftermath of 22 and 23 December 1940 when Manchester's local newspapers were allowed to refer to the city as the Luftwaffe's target. As Mancunians could see the bombed-out buildings in the city centre, Salford and Old Trafford with their own eyes, and German radio was announcing that Manchester had been blitzed, the need for secrecy became redundant. Only the timing of the details were influenced and it was 3 January 1941, 10 days after the first heavy raid, that the *Manchester Guardian* announced that the Free Trade Hall, the Royal Exchange, Chetham's Hospital and Manchester Cathedral had suffered substantial damage.[65] These details had appeared a day earlier in the *Manchester Evening News* and *Evening Chronicle*, which may have been a nod to the freer licence given to local newspapers, and the *Evening News* acknowledged the censor's role with the headline: 'First proper report on damage to Manchester', which neither explained why it had taken 10 days, nor how the previous reports had been less than proper.[66] Under a sub-headline 'Free Trade Hall in ruins: Royal 'change [*sic*] roofless', the report read:

> Manchester today revealed to the world how the Germans attack 'military objectives'. Historic buildings dating back more than 500 years and known the world over now bear the scar of the Hun, wantonly damaged in recent pitiless raids. They have been named for the first time.

The expression 'the scar of the Hun' was deeply subjective, and attributed negative characteristics on the enemy, but just in case the reader was left in doubt about the crimes against

---

[65] 'Raid Damage in Manchester', *Manchester Guardian*, 3 January 1941, p. 6.
[66] 'First Proper Report on Damage to Manchester', *Manchester Evening News*, 2 January 1941, p. 1.

the city's heritage, the *Evening News* emphasised the cultural loss to the city. The Royal Exchange was described as 'one of the largest of its kind in the world'; the Free Trade Hall as the 'home of many great Hallé concerts'; and Chetham's Hospital and Manchester Cathedral were listed as 'two architectural gems'. The censor ensured no mention was made of the considerable damage to the city's industrial infrastructure.

The government's restrictions on casualty figures meant that no Manchester newspaper issued the true numbers of the dead, although they did acknowledge the numbers were high. Gardiner wrote:

> The War Cabinet had taken the decision that it would be ill-advised to make casualty figures public, but once the Blitz started it became clear that rumours often exaggerated the number of deaths and serious injuries, so stark notices were posted outside town halls giving the number of those killed and injured, but without identifying the location of the 'incidents' and insisting that the information 'must not be published in the press', lest it prove helpful to the Germans by informing them how successful their raids had been.[67]

The *Manchester Evening News* printed a report a week after the Christmas Blitz in which it was stated:

> Although no official figure can be obtained of the total number of deaths caused during recent air raids in the Manchester area, it is estimated that nearly 500 men, women and children were killed. In addition, there were many injured.[68]

The *Manchester Guardian* followed that up the next day, although the censor's hand can clearly be detected:

---

[67] Gardiner, *The Blitz*, p. 37.
[68] '500 Killed in Manchester Blitz', *Manchester Evening News*, 30 December 1940, p. 1.

Censorship

> In view of the rumours which have circulated both within and outside the city, it is important to point out a *'Manchester Guardian'* representative was informed by a member of the City Council yesterday, that the position on December 27 was that the fatality list was substantially less than 500.[69]

The newspaper was careful to attribute the figure to the council official but its dissembling was to no avail because, as the previous and following chapters show, the public, distrusting what they read in their newspapers, believed that the figures were being kept deliberately low. They had grounds because the figures for the dead and wounded were later estimated at 972 and nearly 4,000 respectively.[70]

The Births, Marriages and Deaths section did not bring clarity. Eight of the death notices in the *Manchester Guardian* on 27 December did not give a date, but stated typically: 'In December, by enemy action', thus still apparently trying to keep German intelligence wondering whether the Luftwaffe's radio beams led its bombers to the right destination. The work of the censor is apparent because the lack of detail in terms of dates is in contrast to other material that was printed: the home addresses were Whalley Range, Heaton Norris, Stretford, Knutsford and Hulme; the Hulme victim was a Catholic priest; two victims were a married couple.[71]

The mass funerals for the dead at the city's Southern Cemetery were covered, although the number of victims was kept deliberately vague. Surprisingly, the report was not the lead story in the *Evening Chronicle* on 28 December 1940 – that was reserved for an attack by RAF torpedo planes – which was

---

[69] 'Manchester Air-Raid Deaths', *Manchester Guardian*, 31 December 1940, p. 5.
[70] IWM North, *Manchester Blitz*.
[71] 'Births, Marriages, and Deaths', *The Manchester Guardian*, 27 December 1940, p. 8.

an idiosyncratic choice for a Manchester local newspaper, and, instead of specifics, the *Chronicle* concentrated on the mood.[72] The introduction read: 'They died together; they are buried together. Rich man, poor man, the aged and the children, the victims of the Manchester Blitz were buried today. And over them the Last Post was sounded.'[73] The language, harking back to the trenches, emphasised the egalitarianism of the dead, but, like the casualties of the First World War, there was a lack of detail in terms of numbers. The report, too, did not linger over the deceased and, instead, there was an urgency to emphasise a community on the road to recovery. A sub-head lower down the report announced: 'City returning to normal', while the sentence that followed was: 'Throughout the raided areas of Manchester there were sure signs today of the great works that have been accomplished in bringing a return to smooth running.' A later chapter will show this was not the case even a week later.[74] The *Manchester Guardian*, of 30 December, was more forthcoming in stating that 'seventy-two people were buried in the civic service' but by then, with funeral services occurring on a daily basis, the numbers had become so confused as to be meaningless.[75] The details were more illuminating when it came to the fire service and on 1 January 1941 the *Guardian* reported that 17 fire fighters had died 'in the raid'.[76]

---

[72] 'RAF Torpedo Planes in North Sea Raid', *Evening Chronicle*, 28 December 1940, p. 1.
[73] 'Last Post Sounds Over Manchester Dead', *Evening Chronicle*, 28 December 1940, p. 1.
[74] Mass Observation Archive, FR 538.
[75] 'Raid Victims: Manchester Funeral Services', *Manchester Guardian*, 30 December 1940, p. 6.
[76] 'Manchester's Fire-Fighters', *Manchester Guardian*, 1 January 1941, p. 5.

Censorship

Manchester was bombed again on the night of 9/10 January 1941 and there was a sense of growing confidence in the evening papers' dealings with the censor, conforming to the guidelines but using German reports to identify the city. The *Manchester Evening News* did not reveal the target was Manchester in its second lead on page one, reporting: 'Scattered attacks with high-explosive and incendiary bombs were made on a North-West inland town last night, but although many incendiaries were dropped, only a few fires were started.'[77] Immediately below it, however, was a short report: 'Manchester bore the weight of last night's German air attack, and was heavily hit, the Berlin radio said today.'[78] On the same day the *Evening Chronicle* was even bolder, proclaiming: 'The fire bomb fighters – men and women organized among themselves to protect their homes against fire in air attack – went into action during the night and thwarted an attempted Blitz on a wide scale by the Nazi raiders.'[79] The report went on to list damage to houses, shops and a cinema, all civilian targets, but while there was not even a reference to a North-West town, the 'you' in the headline made it obvious where the incendiaries had fallen. A cut out – an insert used as a layout device to break up blocks of type – within the report stated: 'Strong formations of the German air force directed their attacks last night against important military objectives in Manchester', says the official German News Agency.[80]

---

[77] 'Nazis scatter explosives and incendiaries in NW', *Manchester Evening News,* 10 January 1941, p. 1.
[78] 'Would You Believe It?', *Manchester Evening News,* 10 January 1941, p. 1.
[79] 'You beat the fire-raisers', *Evening Chronicle,* 10 January 1941, p. 1.
[80] 'Manchester Say Nazis', *Evening Chronicle,* 10 January 1941, p. 1.

The Home Intelligence report in January highlighted several shortcomings in Manchester's preparation for its Blitz and its reaction afterwards, yet obvious stories for a local newspaper were virtually ignored. On Saturday 4 January, an *Evening Chronicle* headline read 'Criticisms answered by city transport chief', but, while this was the first hint of public dismay at the city's response, the report was unquestioning.[81] Instead it merely reported the official's response to a letter to a newspaper that claimed there were insufficient buses, traffic chaos, and inflexibility over routes so that buses stuck to old routes even though they were bombed out and impassable. An uncensored report would have led on the alleged deficiencies.

Four days later two headlines on one report also suggested that the city had made mistakes. 'Lessons of the Manchester Blitz' the main headline announced, with the subhead reading: 'Grim, heroic page in city history'.[82] Instead of listing the lessons, however, the story quoted Manchester's Lord Mayor saying: 'Never in their history have the citizens shown greater courage or determination.' The only whiff of criticism was a mention of the need for more firewatchers and more rest centres within reasonable reach of the congested areas 'where heavy casualties were likely to occur'. Both were couched in terms of praise for the people who had been on duty. The words 'pride', 'thankfulness' and 'gratitude' were used liberally.

The *Manchester Guardian* was equally circumspect in its criticism, its reports often failing to deliver what was promised in the headline. So a report with the subsidiary headline 'Neglect of Precautions in Manchester' ignored several

---

[81] 'Criticisms answered by city transport chief', *Evening Chronicle*, 4 January 1941, p. 4.
[82] 'Lessons of the Manchester Blitz', *Evening Chronicle*, 8 January 1941, p. 1.

obvious news stories. Its second paragraph listed recommendations in a report, reading:

> These included firewatchers thoroughly trained in fire fighting on duty during raids ... It was also suggested that employees should be given elementary instruction in the use of fire appliances, that water tanks should be installed to supplement mains supplies, that special risks should be notified to the local fire authorities, that hydrant points should be clearly shown, and the advisability of having a direct telephone line to the nearest fire station should be considered. [83]

There were several elements of news in that list that would have merited a better introduction than the one it got: 'The *Manchester Guardian* understands that a full report on all fires caused in Manchester during last week's raid is being prepared for the Emergency Committee.' This was bland stuff that hardly encouraged the reader to go on, and the criticism was instead lower in the report and attributed to another newspaper. *The Observer* was quoted by the *Guardian:* 'It is admitted that much of the damage caused by fire in the raid on Manchester would have been averted by proper precautions.'

Another censorial restriction was the reporting of the weather. There were fears that trains and other vital transport would become easy targets for the bombers if they were halted in drifts so the weather was a banned topic, which posed many problems for editors, particularly as in the first winter of the war was the coldest for 45 years.[84] A front page headline in the *Manchester Evening News* on 29 January 1940 read: 'Road and

---

[83] 'Fire-Watchers', *Manchester Guardian*, 30 December 1940, p. 6.
[84] Freethy, *Lancashire 1939–45*, p. 21; Weatherworld <http://www.ukweatherworld.co.uk/forum/index.php?/topic/49321-the-severe-winter-of-1939-40-a-special-report/> [accessed 1 April 2013].

Rail chaos in Britain's severest hold-up', above an article which reported that certain Manchester satellite towns had been cut off without post or papers, and how people had been stranded and unable to report for work, without any mention of snow and ice.[85] The only quoted reference in the report referred to concerns for children, who were suffering in the cold, although the newspaper did carry the headline 'Cheshire is stagnant' on the back page.[86] The following day the *Evening News* found the means of overcoming the ban by printing a photograph of children playing in the snow in Piccadilly with the caption 'taken during the cold spell, which began last month'.[87]

5. Self-Censorship at the *Manchester Guardian*

Fleet Street operated from 1939 to 1945 with the censor watching keenly, but editors and reporters, while aware of this disapproving eye, also seemed willing to go beyond even the strictures set by the MOI. The restrictions imposed on newspaper reporters, whether through official pressure or through editorial and personal conviction, were articulated by Montague in a memo to his editor Crozier on 13 September 1940, a year into the war and at the height of the London Blitz. The memo gave an insight into the self-censoring mindset of the reporter in that it was entitled: 'Picture of what is happening here in London and cannot be published'. He wrote:

> The fundamental fact here is that the East End is scared out of its wits, and is eager to accept any kind of settlement

---

[85] 'Road and Rail Chaos in Britain's Severest Hold-up', *Manchester Evening News*, 29 January 1940, p. 1.
[86] 'Cheshire is Stagnant', *Manchester Evening News*, 29 January 1940, p. 6.
[87] *Manchester Evening News*, 30 January 1940, p. 1.

which would put a stop to the bombing. Doctors who have been working in rest centres say that the East Enders recover in an incredibly short space of time when once evacuated. I can confirm from my own experience. My wife lost her nerve a few days ago when a bomb burst 20 yards from our house; when I told her to clear out, she recovered her nerve entirely a quarter of an hour later, merely through the knowledge that she was going to be out of it before long.[88]

The suggestion that Londoners had been bombed to the point where they would have been keen to talk peace terms with Hitler fundamentally contradicts the myth of the Blitz. No-one reported it then, and it is at odds with today's popular conception of fortitude under fire that was summed up by Marr who stated: 'The Blitz was a devastating attack from the air that everyone had dreaded, yet it didn't break the spirit of the people or dim their humour.'[89] Montague suggested that the real picture was that humour was difficult to locate in a large part of the capital 'scared out of its wits'.

Montague's memo urged Crozier to use the *Manchester Guardian* to campaign for the evacuation of the East End 'within the limits allowed by the censorship', describing the bombing as worse than anything he had endured with the British Expeditionary in France.[90] He added:

For the East End it is particularly hard to bear. Those living near the big fires are in the position of soldiers lying out in no man's land with flares all around them; their position is known and they can only lie there and wait to be bombed.

---

[88] John Rylands Library, *The Guardian* Archive, Montague to Crozier, 13 September 1940.
[89] *Andrew Marr's The Making of Modern Britain*, episode 6, dir. by Roger Parsons (BBC2, broadcast on 4 December 2009).
[90] John Rylands Library, *The Guardian* Archive, Montague to Crozier, 13 September 1940.

This First World War imagery emphasised Montague's fear that the war effort 'may be torpedoed' unless the East End was quickly evacuated. Giving an insight into the prevailing inclination towards self-censorship in Fleet Street, he added:

> Pictorial descriptions of the raids and their results are more or less limited nowadays by the censorship to word-pictures of bombs falling and buildings in ruins, and I propose, again with your approval, to ease on these, which are monotonous and depressing.

This was a *Guardian* reporter exercising self-censorship although there is evidence in the *Guardian* Archive that Crozier, too, was wary of printing newsworthy items for fear of the reaction of the authorities. In a memo to Bone, the editor gave his reasons why he refused to print a report in June 1940 of plans to unite Britain and France into one country in an attempt to prevent the surrender of French forces.[91] By any standard, that was a hugely significant news story, historically, socially and militarily, yet Crozier, along with every other Fleet Street editor, chose to ignore or downplay it.[92] 'I should not use the story … about Sunday's proceedings. I think it would sound too irresponsible for so tremendous an act of State', he wrote.[93]

Nearly a year later, when Rudolf Hess, Hitler's deputy, inexplicably parachuted into Scotland in an attempt to meet the Duke of Hamilton and negotiate a peace with Britain, Churchill insisted: 'We must not make a hero of him'.[94] Hess

---

[91] Ibid., Crozier to Bone, 18 June 1940.
[92] *The Times* of 18 June 1940 put the report halfway down page 6, albeit its main news page, but it amounted to a single-column story 20 centimetres long.
[93] John Rylands Library, *The Guardian* Archive, Crozier to Bone, 18 June 1940.
[94] Cited in Gardiner, *The Blitz*, p. 354.

was placed in the Tower of London, Churchill insisted he should be 'strictly isolated' and editors were urged to:

1. Emphasise his [Hess's] importance and popularity in Germany.
2. Write up his past.
3. Speculate on correspondents' own authority as to the reasons for the flight.
4. Write up the achievements of the flight, which may in itself be regarded as evidence of his complete sanity.[95]

The instructions were also explicit about what could not be reported, including any conversations or messages which Hess may have and any mention of the Duke of Hamilton. In response, Charles Lambert, the *Guardian*'s diplomatic correspondent who had been based in Berlin before the war, wrote to Crozier: 'From what I hear about Hess I should think he is insane, or at least that his mind is unbalanced.'[96] No indication of Lambert's opinion, nor any questioning of Hess's mission – something that had the potential to fracture the Soviet-German Pact – appeared in the *Manchester Guardian.*

If these were glaring omissions, there was a greater one in June 1941 when Crozier took the decision to ignore reports of what was a pivotal moment of the Second World War, Germany's invasion of the Soviet Union in Operation Barbarossa. In a 'confidential report' that was unattributed, it was stated:

> Germany sees she has got to nullify the ultimate Russian menace now because the war is going to be a long one. No confirmation of any clash yet but present tension cannot go

---

[95] Winston S. Churchill, *The Second World War*, III, *The Grand Alliance* (London: Cassell, 1952), p. 55; *The Guardian* Archive, 13 May 1941.
[96] John Rylands Library, *The Guardian* Archive, Lambert to Crozier, 14 May 1941.

on … His object therefore is to kill the Russian bogey now and thus improve his war position against us.[97]

The report, which continued 'Germany's main bombing strength believed to be held in readiness for Russia', was dated 19 June 1941 and, as Germany and the Soviet Union were allied at the time, there is no obvious reason why Crozier chose not to run a story that under any circumstances meets the criteria as newsworthy. Operation Barbarossa began on 22 June.

This reluctance to tackle larger news events is extraordinary in terms of normal news values in a newspaper, and emphasises that the *Manchester Guardian* was subject to self-censorship, although this was not unique in the 1930s and 1940s. Indeed, it mirrored the British press's attitude to another landmark event, the Abdication Crisis in 1936, when Fleet Street chose to ignore Edward VIII's relationship with Wallis Simpson even though newspapers throughout the world were reporting it. As a consequence, it came as a greater shock when the British public were finally informed, it inflamed the constitutional crisis, and undermined public trust in the press (Mass Observation was formed partly because the newspaper coverage of the public's reaction was considered inadequate).[98] Crozier made reference to this in a letter in August 1940, to a reader, J. W. Dulanty, who had asked whether newspaper accounts that the UK was considering invading Éire to pre-empt similar plans by Germany had been 'inspired' and encouraged by the government. The question itself indicated a mood of scepticism and Crozier's reply, while defending the reputation of Fleet Street, did nothing to dispel the notion that the British press lacked boldness:

---

[97] John Rylands Library, *The Guardian* Archive, 19 June 1941.
[98] Charles Madge and Tom Harrisson, *Britain by Mass-Observation* (London: Penguin, 1939), p. 23.

Censorship

> You will remember that for some time before the Abdication Crisis the newspapers maintained complete silence although they knew what was afoot. It was afterwards suggested by many people in this country, and it was widely believed in the United States, that the newspapers had agreed among themselves to keep silent and that they had been 'inspired' to do this by the government. This was, in fact, a complete misconception, for we acted independently, each of us hoping it would be unnecessary to wash the dirty linen in public and each, I may add, wondering whether some rival contemporary might not one fine day, decide to 'blow the gaff'. But there was no agreement and no 'inspiration'.[99]

While the Abdication Crisis fell before the war, Crozier's response, written in August 1940, betrayed an attitude of self-imposed compliance that was relevant in respect of the reporting of the Blitz. It did not meet the self-proclaimed fiction of neutral news values, and nor did it follow the assertion of one of Crozier's predecessors as editor of the *Manchester Guardian*, C. P. Scott, who had asserted that the journalist's primary function was the gathering of news.

Bingham wrote: 'While texts usually contain a "preferred" meaning, this meaning can always be negotiated, resisted, or ignored by the reader', and Manchester's public had reason to be sceptical.[100] If their newspapers were to be believed, the Luftwaffe damaged hospitals, schools, shops and houses while the city's industrial infrastructure remained untouched. Yet the RAF's bombsights were so honed that their precision bombing wiped out arms factories, transport links and power utilities at no loss to civilian life. The Manchester public could see that factories were in ruins, that they could not get public transport to work even if their workplace was undamaged, that hundreds of their fellow citizens were homeless and

---

[99] John Rylands Library, *The Guardian* Archive, 2 August 1940.
[100] Bingham, *Gender, Modernity and the Popular Press*, p. 11.

housed in under-resourced and overcrowded shelters and, as the next chapter will show, that they could not even drink water without boiling it first.[101] The consequence was widespread cynicism. Hylton wrote:

> Along with direct censorship, journalistic euphemisms for war-time reverses became commonplace. A rout became a 'retrograde movement', a 'disengagement' or simply 'straightening the line'. Insanity caused by exposure to the fighting became 'battle fatigue' or 'exhaustion'.[102]

He noted that other examples included the initial blaming of damage caused by V2 rockets on gas explosions, leading to their being christened 'flying gas mains'.[103] Even the armed forces became euphemistic and bomber crews participating in raids that spectacularly failed to find their targets spoke of major assaults 'on German agriculture'.[104] The MOI, which could have made reporting any news a near-impossible process for journalists, did not approach the extent of its potential draconian powers and became known, according to Koss, as 'Minnie', 'a fusspot dreaded not so much for what she did as what she might do.'[105] Price stated:

> The press, by promising to be on its best behaviour, had seen off the danger of direct government control ... The mainstream media had fought an effective rearguard action to protect their liberties. It was a campaign based more on self-interest than high principle and didn't extend to protecting those people who wished to use the right to free expression to propound more extreme views.[106]

---

[101] *Manchester Guardian*, 24 December 1940, p. 1.
[102] Stuart Hylton, *Their Darkest Hour: The Hidden History of the Home Front 1939–1945* (Stroud: Sutton, 2001), p. 137.
[103] Ibid.
[104] Ibid.
[105] Koss, *The Rise and Fall*, p. 604.
[106] Price, *Where Power Lies*, pp. 117–18.

CHAPTER SIX
PROPAGANDA AND THE MANAGEMENT OF OPINION

1. The First World War Model

The Second World War, according to Taylor, witnessed the biggest propaganda battle in the history of warfare and by 1939 Britain, in terms of conflict by word, was prepared.[1] Twelve years earlier Lasswell had written: 'There is no question but that government management of opinion is an inescapable corollary of large-scale modern war' and in 1936 the Committee of Imperial Defence formed a sub-committee to prepare plans for a Ministry of Information on the outbreak of war.[2] The template came from the First World War, which was, according to Carruthers, the first 'in which propaganda was a vital, and thoroughly organised instrument' and, to Ferguson, 'the first media war'.[3] The author John Buchan commented in 1917: 'So far as Britain is concerned, the war could not have been fought for one month without its newspapers.'[4]

The British combined manipulation with suppression between 1914 and 1918, demonising the enemy – the German soldier was depicted as a murderer who committed 'all sorts of atrocities' – while embarking on campaign of censorship

---

[1] Taylor, *Munitions*, p. 208.
[2] Harold D. Lasswell, *Propaganda Technique in the World War* (London: Kegan, 1927), p. 15.
[3] Carruthers, *The Media at War*, p. 29; Niall Ferguson, *The Pity of War* (London: Penguin, 1998), p. 212.
[4] Cited in Ferguson, *The Pity of War*, p. 213.

and news management.⁵ Goldfarb Marquis wrote that the latter was achieved by the close control of news from the trenches by the military authorities combined with news management provided by a 'tight-knit group of "press lords" who (over lunch or dinner with Lloyd George) decided what was "good for the country to know"'.⁶ As a consequence, newspapers frequently failed to mention losses or battles, including the sinking of the battleship *Audacious* in 1914, and the Battle of Jutland occurred in a news vacuum because, as Lord Balfour told the managing director of the *News of the World* George Riddell, 'it would have occasioned un-necessary anxiety'.⁷ Why were journalists so willing to suppress important news? Goldfarb Marquis wrote:

> The obvious answer is that they all belonged to the same club, whose membership also included the most powerful politicians. Publishing a casualty list … would have meant expulsion from the club; social ostracism apparently meant more to the newsmen than their professional duty to inform the public.⁸

It was a successful model and not only Britain re-created it. Goebbels used it in Germany and Hitler wrote admiringly in *Mein Kampf* of press baron Lord Northcliffe's work as director of external propaganda, describing it as 'an inspired work of genius'. He added: 'I myself learned enormously from this

---

5   Eberhard Demm, 'Propaganda and Caricature in the First World War', *Journal of Contemporary History*, 28, 1 (1993), 163–92 (p. 181).
6   Alice Goldfarb Marquis, 'War as Weapons: Propaganda in Britain and Germany during the First World War', *Journal of Contemporary History*, 13, 3 (1978), p. 476.
7   Ibid., pp. 477–78.
8   Ibid., p. 478.

enemy propaganda.'⁹ This became part of the myth propagated by the Nazis that the German army had not been defeated but had been betrayed by Jews, financiers and the management of opinion. Eugen Hadamovsky, a Nazi propagandist, wrote in *Propaganda and National Power* in 1933: 'The German people were not beaten on the battlefield, but were defeated in the war of words.' ¹⁰ Erich Ludendorff, commander of the German army in 1918, wrote: 'Words today are battles. The right words, battles won; the wrong words, battles lost.'¹¹

Britain's propaganda in the first two years of the Second World War had external and internal targets. The former was aimed at enemy countries and the United States, whom Churchill hoped to persuade into the conflict, but there were imperatives at home too.¹² There was pessimism in government circles about Britain's willingness to fight borne by a cynicism in working class circles caused by the slaughter in the First World War and the 'false promises' made to returning soldiers about 'homes fit for heroes'.¹³ The 1930s had also seen the rise of the pacifism movement and the widening of social divisions brought on by unemployment. These discordant

---

[9] A. Hitler, *Mein Kampf*, p. 213, cited in Ferguson, *The Pity of War*, p. 161.
[10] Cited in Ferguson, *The Pity of War*, p. 213.
[11] Goldfarb Marquis, 'Words as Weapons', p. 468.
[12] In terms of the United States, the results were mixed. There was a major congressional investigation begun in 1940 into the levels of pro-British propaganda being published through Hollywood until Pearl Harbor brought it to an end. Cited in Nicholas Pronay and Jeremy Croft, 'British Film Censorship and Propaganda Policy in the Second World War', in James Curran and Vincent Porter, eds, *British Cinema History* (London: Weidenfeld and Nicolson, 1983), p. 155.
[13] Williams, *Get Me a Murder!*, p. 125.

voices will be covered in a later chapter, but Williams wrote: 'On the outbreak of war in 1939, those in authority believed that the experience of the 1930s had made the British worker so militant that he wouldn't fight and that class divisions would weaken morale.'[14]

The MOI's earliest attempts at propaganda were based on building resolve and were rooted in traditional themes, national feelings, of King, country and 'our past'.[15] Williams described the campaign as 'inept', and 'lacking knowledge of public opinion' but overlooked the ministry's more persuasive work with the press because newspapers delivered government-derived propaganda to people's homes from September 1939.[16] Curran and Seaton wrote: 'The press, including critical and independent-minded papers such as the *Daily Mirror*, consciously sought to bolster public morale at the expense of objective reporting. Coercive censorship was made, to some extent, unnecessary by self-censorship.'[17] Lord Reith, Minister for Information from January to May 1940, said famously 'News is the shock troops of propaganda' and this chapter will look at how the words used by the 'other Fleet Street' were mobilised before and after the Manchester Blitz.[18] The first section will analyse the preceding week to set the coverage of the Blitz in context; the second will look at the editions of 23 and 24 December in detail; and the third will examine post-

---

[14] Ibid.
[15] Simon Cottle, *Mediatized Conflict* (Maidenhead: Open University Press, 2006), p. 77; Williams, *Get Me a Murder!*, p. 125.
[16] Williams, *Get Me a Murder!*, p. 126.
[17] Curran and Seaton, *Power Without Responsibility*, p. 63.
[18] N. Pronay, 'The News Media at War', in N. Pronay and D. W. Spring, eds, *Propaganda, Politics and Film, 1918–45* (London: Macmillan, 1982), p. 178.

Blitz newspapers when Manchester's press had time to reflect and to investigate any shortcomings exposed by the bombing.

2. Before the Manchester Blitz

2.1 *Manchester Guardian*

Bernays described propaganda as an 'unseen mechanism', and part of the mastery of manipulation of opinions is to deny or minimise propaganda's existence.[19] The *Manchester Guardian* carried a report on 16 December 1940 on a radio broadcast to the United States by the novelist and playwright J. B. Priestley, in which he stated that Britain's government did not take propaganda seriously. 'Instead of doing too much propaganda we did not do half enough', he was paraphrased as saying.[20] This was the *Guardian's* interpretation of Priestley's broadcast because, when he was quoted directly lower in the report, the tone was different:

> He complained that the people of Britain were left too much in the dark, 'not so much because somebody wants to deceive it [sic] and hide the truth as that there are too many censors who are afraid of making a mistake and at the same time have no particular enthusiasm for keeping the public informed'.

A study of the *Manchester Guardian* in the week before the city was attacked suggests that the newspaper's enthusiasm for keeping its readers informed was tempered by other considerations. The night after reports of Priestley's broadcast appeared, Manchester suffered a bombing raid and the *Guardian's* news story complied with the polarised propaganda technique framed by Nohrstedt et al. and identified

---

[19] E. L. Bernays, *Propaganda*, (New York: Liveright, 1928), republished (New York: Ig Publishing, 2005), p. 37.
[20] 'Mr. Priestley on Our Censorship', *Manchester Guardian*, 16 December 1940, p. 2.

earlier. It was not the lead story on its main news page, which was an unusual display of news judgement even allowing for the obligations placed on a newspaper that purported to be national. Instead, the bombing of the city was confined to a single-column story in column three and its introduction read: 'High-explosive and incendiary bombs were dropped in a North-West inland area last night during a raid which lasted for about an hour. Heavy bursts of AA fire were directed against the bombers.'[21] Although Manchester was not named, the level of detail in the ensuing paragraphs, in the circumstances of a raid taking place as page deadlines were coming and going, suggested the Manchester-based paper had its own reporters very close to the scene. This would have told any serious analyst that the city had been hit. In keeping with accepted news values, the second sentence of the above ought to have focused on the extent of the damage, so the prominence given to the work of the ack-ack gunners seemed an intentional attempt to boost morale. The damage and loss of life (vaguely worded) came immediately after the tribute to the ack-ack. 'One district of a North-West inland town suffered considerable damage and there were a number of casualties, some of which were fatal.'

The report was keen to underline German bad points and Allied good. To emphasise the German 'crimes', the list of damage mentioned civilian targets – houses, business premises, a chemist's shop, buses, a public house, two churches, the rectory of one of them, some lock-up shops, a cinema, two pubs, a girls' hostel, a savings bank, and a children's playing field. The only 'military' target mentioned was an Air Raid Patrol (ARP) post, but, from a propaganda point of view, the public at the time would have seen it in the

---

[21] 'Night Raid on the North-West', *Manchester Guardian*, 17 December 1940, p. 5.

same category as the others – it was the local centre to which one's civilian husband or father went after putting on his dark navy uniform and steel helmet with the 'W' for warden.[22] The minor nature of some of the damage to the more emotive targets did not deter the reporter from using it. 'Slight damage was done to a stained-glass window of a church' and splinters struck the outside of another church. By contrast, a report under the byline of the Air Ministry News Service listed targets of RAF raids on Naples and various towns in Germany. These were warships, an aerodrome, railway stations, junctions and goods yards, factories, merchant vessels, munitions factories, power stations, grain elevators and oil plants.[23]

2.2 *Manchester Evening News*

Propaganda has a role to play in shaping the attitudes of the British and a report on shelter etiquette in the *Manchester Evening News* on 17 December 1940 attempted to 'direct behaviour'.[24] The report read: 'The practice of leaving children unattended in shelters must stop.'[25] The article probably stemmed from an official source (although that was not acknowledged) and, while it is debatable how much power and social influence the newspaper would have on the missing mothers, it could have strengthened the resolve of its readers to enforce good practice. That was on page three, while the bombing raid on Manchester the previous night was on the front page, although, like the *Guardian* and the *Evening Chronicle*, it was

---

[22] Peter Stansky, *The First Day of the Blitz* (London: Yale University Press, 2007), p. 78.
[23] 'Direct hits among cruisers at Naples', *Manchester Guardian*, 17 December 1940, p. 5.
[24] Jowett and O'Donnell, *Propaganda*, p. 289.
[25] 'Shelters Not for Lazy Mothers', *Manchester Evening News*, 17 December 1940, p. 3.

not the lead but the third most prominent story. Surprisingly given that it was its readers that came under attack, the newspaper attempted to shape behaviour again: 'Hundreds of sightseers ignored all appeals to keep roads and pavements clear, risked death and impeded the work of wardens and ambulance men after a working class district of a North-Western town had been raided last night.'[26] On the back page, there was a portentous piece of reporting given that five days later Manchester was about to be attacked. On 17 December Mancunians could read:

> Rest centre accommodation for Manchester people, who might be bombed out of their homes, has been speeded up in the last few days so that there are now in the city 21 permanent fully-equipped centres to house 8,000 people. And, within the next few days the *Manchester Evening News* learned today, there will be many more.[27]

The intention of the propaganda was to reassure, but, as Manchester would discover within a week, the city was not prepared. The reassurance was hollow.

This was not the only instance of the *Evening News* tempting providence. After Coventry was bombed in November 1940, the newspaper's London editor Malcolm Gunn wrote a comment piece in his column 'In Fleet Street today', asking why some towns like Coventry were named but others, like Manchester and Birmingham, were not. His conclusion was that it was down to the Air Ministry – a strange assertion when he knew full well it was down to the MOI – and civic pride:

> 'Brum' has less of a grievance than that mysterious 'North West town' which up to now has suffered complete

---

[26] 'Foolish Crowds Risk Bomb Death', *Manchester Evening News*, 17 December 1940, p. 1.
[27] '8,000 Homeless can be Housed in Manchester', *Manchester Evening News*, 17 December 1940, p. 6.

anonymity and can't get any publicity at all. One's heart bleeds for this brave little known and essentially modest people, who up to now, have not even been officially credited with a Molotov breadbasket.[28]

It was a light-hearted, facile, comment that created an 'us' and 'them' confrontation even if the 'them' on this occasion were fellow-Britons in bombed cities. The intention, presumably, was to demand attention for Mancunians who had survived attacks by the Luftwaffe and it backfired three weeks later when the city received publicity by being bombed to an extent that morale plummeted.

2.3 *Evening Chronicle*

It was not difficult to locate the *Evening Chronicle*'s attempt to polarise opinion. On the top of every edition, just below the paper's main title, was the message 'Hitler's War – xxth Day', the number rising every 24 hours. In addition, 'Nazi' appeared three times on the front page of 17 December 1940, a use that had a value in typographical terms in that the word was short and would fit in headlines, but it also had connotations that 'Germans' did not carry. The semiotics of the most prominent, 'Nazis try "sneak raids" on N-West', were referred to earlier but the report also provided a contrast to a story on the same page about the RAF's attacks on the Italian port of Bari and the German city of Mannheim.[29] The story told of how 'many important targets were left in flames', contrasting with the churches attacked by the Luftwaffe. The report of the raid on Manchester had two cross-heads – lay-out devices to break up type but used to emphasise aspects of a story that the sub-editor

---

[28] 'N-West Town', *Manchester Evening News*, 29 November 1940, p. 2.
[29] 'Mannheim and Bari Bombed', *Evening Chronicle*, 17 December 1940, p. 1.

considers important – that set an upbeat tone: 'Fires soon out' and 'Warden hero'.[30] The report read: 'Incendiaries were dropped on a number of other North-West inland districts, but where fires were started they were quickly put out by the ARP services.' The warden story began: 'Hero of the attack on one North-West town was a 34-year-old warden, John Molloy, father of two children, who gave his life while sticking to his post.' There was a description of how Molloy, who was in charge of a public shelter, remained in the doorway while bombs were 'whistling down', and tried to persuade people still outside to take cover. One of the bombs injured him, and he died in hospital. The image of the hero is carefully drawn and the futility of the enemy's work was underlined by the report of the damage that focused on a block of property already scheduled for demolition. A more artful use of propaganda was the reference to the 'heavy anti-aircraft barrage' that was going on at the time.

The target audience would have had every right to question some of the reports and the comment in their newspapers that were anxiously looking for optimistic news to print. On 19 December 1940 a report from Istanbul quoted a Turk who was not named and who, allegedly, had returned from a visit to Britain. It read: 'Morale has not been in any way affected … What the German bombs will never be able to destroy is such a nation's underlying morale and resistance and determination to fight on.'[31] In the same newspaper Baxter wrote of 'Hitler's setbacks', adding: 'He can truly say that his victories have outpaced those of Napoleon himself and no conqueror has ever accomplished so much in so short a time.'

---

[30] 'Nazis try "Sneak Raids" on N-West', *Evening Chronicle*, 17 December 1940.
[31] 'A Turk Tells of British Morale', *Evening Chronicle*, 19 December 1940, p. 6.

Propaganda and Opinion

Two sentences further on he added without irony: 'Diplomatically Hitler has suffered a heavy defeat'.[32]

3. The Blitz editions

3.1 *Manchester Guardian*

The raid of 16 December 1940 proved to be a trial run for both the Luftwaffe and Manchester's newspapers because the propaganda techniques (and the headline) were repeated six days later on the first night of the Christmas Blitz. The final edition of the *Manchester Guardian* on Monday 23 December comprised four pages, 86 per cent of the editorial (non-advertising) space of which was devoted to war related items. The bombing of Manchester was not the lead, but a single-column running down the middle of page three, the main news page. This may have indicated the pressures on deadlines – the Blitz began at 7.45 the previous evening and printing was disrupted by 11 incendiary bombs falling on the *Guardian* roof in that night – but more probably there was a concern that leading with it would tell the Luftwaffe that its pilots had successfully targeted the city.[33] The four decks of the headline were:

NIGHT RAID ON NORTH-WEST

Heavy Attack on Inland Town

MANY FIRE-BOMBS

People Trapped in Shelter Rescued

while the introduction read:

> The German Air Force, continuing its campaign of heavy night bombing, concentrated its attack last night on an inland town in North-West England. Hundreds of incendiary bombs and many high-explosives were dropped

---

[32] Beverley Baxter, 'Hitler's New Year Plans', *Evening Chronicle*, 19 December 1940, p. 2.

[33] Ayerst, *The Manchester Guardian*, p. 541.

and some fires were started in different parts of the town, but the entire staffs of the fire brigades were quickly called out and fought the outbreaks. The firemen worked through the barrage and amid falling bombs.[34]

Manchester was not mentioned by name, although the *Guardian*'s sister paper the *Manchester Evening News*, published later the same day, felt free to identify the city. In terms of propaganda, four points were made: the town concerned did not take the bombing passively; the highest possible number of firemen fought the outbreaks; there was no delay in calling them out; and they worked courageously under enemy attack. In reality, there was a shortage of civilian defence staff, who had been moved to Liverpool the night before; contemporary accounts wrote of fires raging out of hand and buildings being dynamited to stop the flames spreading; and 700 fire fighters were rushed from London and its outskirts to help put out the blazes.[35] The effect of the bombing was also minimised with a good news element on the bottom deck of the headlines; civilians had been trapped but had been rescued.

Subsequent paragraphs continued to stress the plus points in line with the propaganda theory that if a message is 'consistent and repetitious' people are unlikely to challenge it.[36] Thus, the enemy aircraft 'were met by sharp bursts of fire from ground defences'; in a number of cases civilians used sandbags to extinguish the incendiary bomb fires; nurses helped to put out fires when a hospital was hit; and when people were trapped in the wreckage of a public house, rescue

---

[34] 'Night Raid on North-West', *Manchester Guardian*, 23 December 1940, p. 3.
[35] Hylton, *A History*, p. 253; Cliff Hayes, ed., *Our Blitz: Red Skies over Manchester* (Bolton: Aurora, 1995), p. 18; M. J. Gaskin, *Blitz: The Story of 29th December 1940* (London: Faber and Faber, 2005), p. 38.
[36] Jowett and O'Donnell, *Propaganda*, p. 302.

squads 'worked strenuously to rescue them'. The *Guardian* staff themselves played their part, but, although reference was made to bombs landing on a newspaper office, censorship as well as modesty forced them to withhold which was involved: 'A newspaper office was hit by incendiaries, but the office fire-fighters put out the flames before any damage was done.' Nowhere were there pictures or reports of the damage done or the casualties inflicted, an absence that could be explained by the extraordinary circumstances in which the newspaper was printed, but the publications that followed on 24 and 27 December proved there would have been no desire to print them even if the journalists and the production team had the time and information.

That was propaganda by omission, a study of the language elsewhere on page three exposes propaganda by inclusion. A cross-head proclaimed: 'Three hospitals hit', while the Luftwaffe's targets were identified as houses, schools, shops, business premises, public buildings and hospitals, all non-combatant constructions. Unity was stressed in a report about the homeless who found shelter with friends or at public rest centres staffed by the Women's Voluntary Service. The desired effect on the target audience would have been to cause outrage, and attribute bad actions to 'them', that sick and innocent patients had been targeted, while comfort that care was being provided for those who had suffered in the bombing ('us').

The *Manchester Guardian* of 24 December was also produced while the city was under attack but also had the benefit of a day in which to report what had happened on the night of 22/23 December. Yet the most revealing information did not come in the news reports, but in the advertisements, nearly all small, that filled the front page. Two prominent display adverts said more about the true state of the city, the first, signed by the Town Clerk, reading: 'All water for drinking purposes should, until further notice, be boiled before use.'[37] There was also a display advertisement of the same size opposite consisting of a Christmas message from the Minister of Transport, urging people not to travel over Christmas. The message was of a city's basic functions close to collapse, but no news reports tackled this. Page two was nearly all commercial and financial news, sports results and radio listings, but there was still an element of censorship. A brief statement that daily services at Manchester Cathedral had been suspended for the present failed to give the reason: the cathedral had been bombed.[38]

The facing page was extraordinary in that, with a city still smouldering, its transport infrastructure creaking and Mancunians needing to boil water to drink, more than half was devoted to photographs stressing defiance: Whitley bombers under construction at a northern factory; a Whitley in flight; anti-aircraft ammunition production for the Fleet; Australian troops in the Western Desert; and a Cecil Beaton photograph of Churchill looking ready for a fight. To emphasise German 'crimes', a bombed House of Commons completed the set. The lower half of the page was almost entirely on subjects other than the war, although there was an underlying theme of how to behave. 'Lucio', in the 'Miscellany Column', recalled being in the British Museum, close to a '100-per-cent-safe air-raid shelter', when an attendant informed the researchers that aircraft were overhead. 'Not one of 'em budged or indeed took the slightest notice', he reported with obvious approval. The use of the abbreviation for 'them' has a (perhaps ironical) *Boy's Own Paper* ring.[39]

---

[37] *Manchester Guardian,* 24 December 1940, p. 1.
[38] 'Manchester Cathedral', *Manchester Guardian,* 24 December 1940, p. 2.
[39] 'Miscellany', *Manchester Guardian,* 24 December 1940, p. 3.

Propaganda and Opinion

The main news page focused on the previous night's (23/24 December) attacks. The lead headline read:

NIGHT RAIDERS AGAIN IN THE NORTH-WEST

Heavy Attack on an Inland Town

HOSPITALS, PUBLIC BUILDING, AND A CINEMA HIT [40]

The city was disguised in the introduction as 'a North-West town', although the sub-editor responsible for the headline had decided it was safe to go beyond the text and call it an 'inland town'. This was perhaps done to make it clear that it was not another attack on Liverpool, which was still burning from the raid by 294 bombers on the Saturday night. The propaganda was most obvious in the third deck of the headline that emphasised the civilian status of the damage, while the report read: 'High explosive bombs caused damage to house property, public buildings, and hospitals and a cinema were hit in one district.' It added: 'The raiders had to run the gauntlet of fire from the ground defences.' This 'running the gauntlet' metaphor exaggerated the effectiveness of the gun batteries as Erich Sommer, a German airman, stated: 'We laughed off the enemy defences … The flak didn't worry us as it was mostly badly directed.'[41] Shrapnel from British anti-aircraft shells killed more people on the ground than it killed German aircrew, but the noise of the guns was, nevertheless, good for civilian morale.[42] One enemy bomber shot down was therefore a good-news story, and the flak may have scored at least one hit: a sentence was included,

---

[40] 'Night Raiders Again in the North-West', *Manchester Guardian*, 24 December 1940, p. 5.
[41] J. Richard Smith and Eddie J. Creek, *Kampfflieger*, II, (Hersham: Ian Allan Publishing, 2004), p. 102.
[42] Gaskin, *Blitz*, pp. 186-87.

attributed to the Press Association, stating that a raider was reported as shot down at Old Trafford, Manchester.

The raid on the first night of the Blitz was demonised as part of a 'Nazi attack on the civilians of Britain', as if this were its sole purpose. 'Wave upon wave of bombers, drawn like iron filings to a magnet, swept over the burning buildings' and dropped high explosives among the fire fighters. Many families were 'made homeless', and 'innumerable decent homes' were 'broken and laid down by the enemy'.[43] The language was designed to underline it was 'us' under attack – 'families', 'decent', and 'homes', while 'laid down' was resonant of a deceased relative – and the indictments were emphasised by a cross-head: 'Schools suffer'. As in previous pages, there was an attempt to minimise the Germans' success. The report stated that many hours of intense bombing produced 'a surprisingly small number of casualties'. The information was attributed to the town clerk, but a truer picture emerged in the first paper after Christmas, on 27 December, when it reported that 'a mass funeral of the victims of the raid in Manchester will take place at Southern Cemetery tomorrow'.[44]

The propaganda message of 'we can take it', reinforcing 'the cultural myths and stereotypes', ensured the mood of the 24 December paper was resolutely upbeat. The public transport vehicles were said to be undamaged, apart from a few broken windows; two schools had been taken over to supplement the rest centres; and 'One group of firemen could talk of nothing but the courage of three girls who stayed in town all night making cups of tea and carrying them round to

---

[43] 'Sunday Night's Bombardment of Manchester', *Manchester Guardian,* 24 December 1940, p. 5.
[44] 'A Mass Funeral', *Manchester Guardian,* 27 December 1940, p. 5.

the bomb teams.'⁴⁵ But a reporter stated plainly: 'It was a bad night.' He asserted, however, that although civilian damage was great, the people were 'still, in Mr Churchill's phrase, "grim and gay"'. As a subsequent chapter will show, Home Intelligence reported to the government that some people in Manchester were close to despair.

3.2 Manchester Evening News

There was no attempt by the four-page, three-halfpence, *Manchester Evening News* of 23 December 1940 to disguise where the bombs had fallen the previous night. Page one, which was the main news page, led with a report on the raid, its introduction stating: 'Manchester had its longest and most severe aerial bombardment last night'.[46] The propaganda impact lay in the second deck of the lead headline that referred to 'Two raiders believed down in North-West'. To put that into context, it represented a success rate of little more than 0.7 per cent given that 270 aircraft took part, but it was not an isolated piece of morale boosting. Under the left-hand 'shoulder' of the main head there was a bold headline across three columns asserting: 'Chins up in the North-West', while under the right-hand shoulder was the headline: 'Mannheim again left in flames' – another 'hitting back' piece.[47] Elsewhere on the page

---

[45] 'Sunday Night's Bombardment of Manchester', *Manchester Guardian*, 24 December 1940, p. 5.
[46] 'Manchester Blitz: Many Buildings Fired', *Manchester Evening News*, 23 December 1940, p. 1.
[47] 'Chins Up in the North-West' and 'Mannheim Again Left in Flames', *Manchester Evening News*, 23 December 1940, p. 1; Had the facts about Mannheim been known at the time, they would not have helped much in the propaganda war. The first big attack on Mannheim on 16 December was a trial run for area bombing, but aerial photographs obtained on 21 December had shown the operation 'failed in its primary object' (John Terraine, *The Right of*

there were examples of attempts to shape values, attitudes and behaviour. Role models were provided in the shape of nurses who stayed at their posts despite a hospital being bombed, while the anti-model was provided by a report headlined 'Soldiers accused of looting'.[48]

The 23 December *Evening News* had openly identified Manchester as the targeted city, but there was more reticence in the last extra edition the following day. Page one's lead headline read: 'Buildings dynamited in Lancashire town'.[49] This did not refer to the second night of bombing but to the deliberate dynamiting of buildings to stop fires spreading. This seems at odds with normal news values, which would have reported the raid of 23/24 December, but it served to show that the authorities were doing something positive. The story admitted that by morning 'a number of buildings' had been either destroyed or badly damaged, and that 'some firemen' were killed. The introduction to the story began by emphasising the non-military status of the targets:

> Hospitals, two shelters, and a number of shops, houses and commercial buildings in a Lancashire town were damaged or destroyed in another heavy raid on the North-West last night.

The report's cross-heads included 'Church burnt out' and 'Four halls hit', civilian targets.

The reporting generally was a case of minimising bad things happening in Britain, maximising the bad things happening to Germany, maximising the good things

---

the Line: The Royal Air Force in the European War 1939–1945 (Ware: Wordsworth, 1997), p. 269).
[48] 'Soldiers Accused of Looting', *Manchester Evening News*, 23 December 1940, p. 1.
[49] 'Buildings Dynamited in Lancashire Town', *Manchester Evening News*, 24 December 1940, p. 1.

happening to 'us', minimising the good things happening to 'them', an example of the Van Dijk's ideological square. This edition also contained the familiar theme of hitting back at the Germans. Another deck of the page-lead headlines claimed: 'Bomber brought down at Old Trafford'. There was no source for this story, which was slightly less strong than the headline: the bomber was only 'reported to have been brought down'. A scrupulous sub-editor would want quotation marks round 'brought down at Old Trafford', to indicate some uncertainty. 'Transport keeps on' was another cross-head, emphasising a claim that 'transport is functioning almost normally'. There was no mention of the fact that railway stations and the main bus depot had been hit the previous night. The picture of traffic functioning 'almost normally' was put into question by the back-page' lead on the previous night's paper (23 December) which had appealed to motorists to give lifts to stranded pedestrians.[50]

The 24 December paper reinforced that message when it reported that drivers had entered into the spirit of 'free lifts' that morning:

> It was a common sight to see people being driven into town, smartly dressed typists crowded in with workers in their rough clothing. But all were smiling, and it is almost impossible to speak too highly of the way Lancashire folk have faced up to the intensive raiding with real courage.[51]

The needs of propaganda included showing that the different classes worked cheerfully together for the common cause, a picture exposed as idealised when Home Intelligence and Mass Observation reporters described a different landscape.

---

[50] 'Manchester SOS to Motorists is 'Give Lifts', *Manchester Evening News*, 23 December 1940, p. 6.
[51] 'Buildings Dynamited in Lancashire Town', *Manchester Evening News*, 24 December 1940, p. 1.

Manchester people put out of work by the previous night's bombing were provided with a role-model in a story tied with the lead: 'Work gone, they helped hungry tired A. R. P. men'.[52] Citizens were assured that their forces were retaliating on land, at sea and in the air: there were headlines on 'Navy planes sink two ships' and 'Our night fighters are scoring'.[53] This last headline reflected wishful thinking: Britain had no specially designed night fighters at that time.[54]

In the same edition, another propaganda message came in the form of civic pride at the foot of the front page. A message to citizens, stated to be from 'the Lord Mayor of Manchester, Alderman R. G. Edwards', blew away the censorial smokescreen of 'a Lancashire town'. The Mayor, having made an extensive tour of the city, was 'profoundly impressed' by the way citizens had faced the ordeals they had suffered. He paid tribute to the 'untiring' work done and still being done by all branches of the civil defence.[55] This showed the newspaper performing its war-time role as a line of communication between authorities and public. It could also have shown any enemy agents, by the Mayor's references to 'an extensive tour', and 'untiring' work, that the Luftwaffe had identified and attacked its intended target, causing widespread damage.

3.3 *Evening Chronicle*

The *Evening Chronicle* of 23 December 1940 had to search hard for the positive, as the three decks of headlines testified:

---

[52] 'Work Gone, They Helped Hungry Tired A. R. P. Men', *Manchester Evening News*, 24 December 1940, p. 1.
[53] 'Navy Planes Sink Two Ships' and 'Our Night Fighters are Scoring', *Manchester Evening News*, 24 December 1940, p. 1.
[54] Ramsey, *The Blitz Then and Now*, p. 35.
[55] 'True Citizens', *Manchester Evening News*, 24 December 1940, p. 1.

Propaganda and Opinion

SAVAGE GERMAN AIR ATTACK MADE ON MANCHESTER
MANY FIRES IN CITY 12-HOUR BLITZ
TWO GERMANS DOWN, ONE IN SEA OFF BLACKPOOL[56]

The introduction read: 'Manchester had its longest and most severe aerial bombardment last night, and after a 12 hours' Blitz a pall of smoke hung over the city today. A church and other historic buildings were damaged.' The description of the bombers' approach to the city – how they 'spread fanwise over a wide area, and adopted the familiar tactics of flare-dropping, followed by incendiaries and high explosives' – had almost exactly the same wording as the report in the *Manchester Evening News*, and must have come from the same source, probably an official one. There was no attempt to play down the raid, which was described as 'savage' and lasting 12 hours, although there was a clear emphasis on attributing negative characteristics on the Germans. The placing of the damage to 'a church and other historic buildings' in the introduction showed the Luftwaffe in a bad light and lower down in the report there were references to hotels, commercial premises, business houses, shops, stores, cinemas and schools being 'victims of indiscriminate bombing'. High-explosives and incendiaries 'dealt death to people and destruction to property'.

The degradation of 'them' continued in the leader on page two which began: 'The Blitz has come again to the north, following the usual Nazi pattern of concentrating not on military objects but on ancient and historic buildings, business premises and residential areas.'[57] Note that it was normative

---

[56] 'Savage German Air Attack Made on Manchester', *Evening Chronicle*, 23 December 1940, p. 1.
[57] 'Foiling the Raiders', *Evening Chronicle*, 23 December 1940, p. 2.

behaviour, and that the Germans were not damaging local landmarks by accident, thus offering an interesting contrast with the story alongside about an RAF attack on Mannheim. Here the bombed areas were ports, aerodromes, docks, barges, railway yards, goods yards, munitions works, oil stores and factories. Yet, Robert Kee, a British airman, articulated in his diary for 1941 the contradictions between his experience and what was appearing:

> I've now been on many raids where owing to total cloud it's been impossible to do anything but fling the bombs out somewhere near the flak and the searchlights, and yet I have invariably read the next morning of 'attacks on rail communications or industrial premises'.[58]

The leader went on to claim that the aim of the Germans, 'as Manchester is now able to judge', was to terrorise and cause dislocation.[59] This was propaganda, a reiteration of the crimes of the Nazis, but it could also be read as an admission that the bombing had this effect, or was threatening to have this effect, in Manchester.

No Second World War British newspaper could continue in the vein for very long, however, and local pride was evoked almost immediately, another element of the discourse between the newspaper and its readers. Keeble wrote that local pride is used by newspapers as a marketing strategy and the *Chronicle* gave an example: thanks to the precautions taken in Manchester, the 'full blast of the Nazis' enmity' had been foiled.[60] The leader continued: 'Manchester, a city proud of its

---

[58] 'Mercury on a Fork', *Listener*, 18 February 1971, p. 208, cited in Fussell, *Wartime*, p. 16.
[59] 'Foiling the Raiders', *Evening Chronicle*, 23 December 1940, p. 2.
[60] Richard Keeble, *The Newspapers Handbook*, 3rd edn (London: Routledge, 2005), p. 8; 'Foiling the Raiders', *Evening Chronicle*, 23 December 1940, p. 2.

record and of its preparations to meet attack, has maintained and more than maintained this standard of efficiency and heroism.' This, as this book shows, was wishful thinking but it required scrupulous reading between the lines to detect deviations from the predominant message. 'Those who have work should go to it', the leader added, suggesting there had been some absenteeism, while the unemployed were urged stay at home and not go sightseeing. It could be inferred that there had been some form of bombsite tourism.

The demonisation of the enemy is a common propaganda technique and the lead headline, across three columns, in the *Evening Chronicle* of 24 December conformed:

FIVE HOSPITALS HIT IN A NEW LANCASHIRE BLITZ

Churches, houses and business places suffer[61]

The message was reinforced by the copy. 'Five hospitals in two towns were among the places damaged by bombs', the introduction read, and the second paragraph added to the list of civilian targets: churches, houses, shops, business houses and public houses. At one point, the report stated, civil defence workers, particularly firemen – local figures with no means to fight back – were machine-gunned by individual raiders, although no casualties were reported. The report also mentioned an 'oil bomb' falling into 'one of the town's thoroughfares', which contained business premises and shops.[62] The choice of 'thoroughfare', rather than 'road' or 'street', evoked an image of a fire-bomb in a busy area full of people.

---

[61] 'Five Hospitals Hit in a New Lancashire Blitz', *Evening Chronicle*, 24 December 1940, p. 1.

[62] This would have been one of the German bombs that were filled with liquid mixtures, which could include petrol and crude oil (Wolfgang Fleischer, *German Air-Dropped Weapons to 1945* (Hinckley: Midland), p. 69.

Conventional news writing techniques would have concentrated on the deaths and the damage and it was an example of propaganda that the third paragraph of the story concentrated on retribution. One enemy plane was reported to have been brought down close to Old Trafford, Manchester, 'near to the cricket ground' – a detail that contrasted the Nazi war machine with the peaceful and most English of national games. Armstrong and Barth have stated that symbols are crucial to the survival of ethnic identification because they act as 'border guards' distinguishing 'us' from 'them' and there is an implicit evocation of a pre-war idyll of willow and leather and the vision of what the nation was fighting for.[63] The report also provided details of some of the victims. For example, in a 'rural district' Miss Harriet Lomas was killed by a bomb, while Mr and Mrs Harold Worth died sitting beside the fire in their farmhouse. The semiotics of phraseology were designed to paint a bucolic picture, to the target audience the victims were people 'like us'.

Like its local rivals, the *Evening Chronicle* provided role models, conforming to Jowett and O'Donnell's propaganda criteria in which messages seem to be more resonant when 'they seem to be coming from within the audience'.[64] The civil defence services 'went quickly into action', and firefighters worked 'heroically', as did nurses at one of the hospitals, who were 'heedless of the danger'.[65] There was special praise for

---

[63] John Armstrong, *Nations before Nationalism* (Chapel Hill: University of North Carolina Press, 1982) and Fredrik Barth, *Ethnic Groups and Boundaries* (Boston, MA: Little, Brown, 1969), cited in Anthony D. Smith, *Nationalism and Modernism* (Abingdon: Routledge, 2000), p. 182.
[64] Jowett and O'Donnell, *Propaganda*, p. 299.
[65] 'Lancashire Patients Praise Nurses who Removed Them', *Evening Chronicle*, 24 December 1940, p. 1.

the calmness of the nurses as they worked to transfer patients to safety after hospital walls were brought down by a bomb blast and hundreds of windows shattered. There were quotations from a soldier in hospital with bomb splinter injuries to his face and arms; from a man temporarily blinded by an incendiary bomb; and from another man suffering from burns sustained in rescuing three children. One patient was quoted as saying: 'If only Hitler could see how these nurses behaved he would soon realise that all his bombs cannot weaken the spirit of the British people.' This quotation read like it was made up by the journalist, or, at the very least, prompted.

4. The Post-Blitz Editions
4.1 *Manchester Guardian*

There were no newspapers published on 25 and 26 December 1940, Christmas Eve and Christmas Day being traditional journalism holidays until the 1980s, and the German bombing offensive on Britain also came to a halt until the night of 27/28 December.[66] The hiatus allowed Manchester's newspapers an opportunity to reflect on the bombing of the city and the *Guardian* of 27 December was critical of preparations, noting the failures in fire-watching on the night of 22/23 December.[67] Its main criticism was aimed at industry rather than the authorities, however, recalling that the MOI had stated that the people responsible for certain buildings apparently neglected their legal obligation to provide an efficient service of fire watchers. It suggested that the Fire Watchers Order did not go far enough.

---

[66] Roy Greenslade, 'The Sun Publishes on Christmas Day' (*The Guardian*, 2010) <http://www.guardian.co.uk/media/greenslade/2010/dec/23/sun-christmas> [accessed 21 January 2013]; Ramsey, *The Blitz Then and Now*, pp. 355–56.

[67] "Manning Roofs', *Manchester Guardian*, 27 December 1940, p. 4.

On page five a survey, dated 26 December, expressed in its introduction the propaganda values of carrying on, working together, and thus hitting back. It began: 'Manchester men and women have used the Christmas holiday to put right, so far as possible, what has been torn down and burnt out by the German bombs.' The 'carrying on' theme appeared again in the report insisting that the Christmas festivals at home have gone ahead 'somewhat normally'. [68] The reporter stated that it was not possible to name the places the bombs hit, implicitly telling the readers that his report was censored, but he was able to report that they included churches, chapels, eight infirmaries and hospitals, schools, various institutions and many commercial buildings, offices and homes. It is worth noting that, apart from 'homes', the list seemed to be given, consciously or unconsciously, in order of propaganda value. The placing of the emotionally charged word 'homes' in the final position may even have been done for climactic value. A communiqué from the Air Ministry and Ministry of Home Security admitted that 'considerable damage was done' in the Monday night raid (on a Lancashire town). But preliminary reports, it was claimed, indicated that casualties were not heavy'.[69]

Examples of distorted news values were revealed by separate, small items. In one Captain David Drummond, chief officer of Manchester Fire Brigade, reported: 'I hope that the authorities will see that fire-watching parties will speedily be brought up to the strength which we had expected, and that

---

[68] 'A Manchester Survey After the Attack', *Manchester Guardian*, 27 December 1940, p. 5.
[69] 'Monday Night's Air Attack', *Manchester Guardian*, 27 December 1940, p. 5.

they will be kept at their posts night and day.'[70] There is a lot of implied criticism in that statement and in normal circumstances it would be the basis of a big story. Here it was just four centimetres, including the headlines. In another report, the sinking of a Royal Navy ship was dealt with as a very small paragraph at the foot of the page: 'The Board of Admiralty regrets to announce that HM Destroyer *Acheron* (Lieut J. R. Wilson RN) has been sunk. The next of kin of casualties have been informed.'[71] The 'voice' of this piece was clearly that of the Admiralty press release, not that of a journalist.

No Manchester newspaper reported what Home Intelligence was telling the MOI in January 1941, which will be examined in a later chapter, but there was evidence of Britain's 'Other Fleet Street' making attempts to improve the mood in the city. On 30 January the *Manchester Guardian* headlines on page six read:

BUILDING THE NEW MANCHESTER

An Unexampled Opportunity to Tidy Up the City[72]

Under it the president of the Royal Institute of Builders and Architects, Mr W. H. Ansell, was paraphrased as saying: 'The dictators would be entirely dis-satisfied if they knew that the result of their destructiveness had been to create a high resolve to build better cities and better lives.'[73]

The *Manchester Guardian*'s autopsy of the aftermath of the Blitz was equally upbeat. A reporter visited a centre housing nearly 1,000 people made homeless by the bombing, and

---

[70] 'Fire-Watching Parties', *Manchester Guardian*, 27 December 1940, p. 6.
[71] 'Destroyer Lost', *Manchester Guardian*, 27 December 1940, p. 6.
[72] 'Building the New Manchester', *Manchester Guardian*, 30 January 1941, p. 6.
[73] Ibid.

quoted a 69-year-old widow saying she had been 'sleeping warm and comfortable'.[74] The piece went on: 'At all centres visited the catering arrangements seem to be admirable. In every shelter in the city turkey was served for Christmas Day dinner.'[75] The Home Intelligence inspectors, who visited the city, were scathing: 'This, like many other press versions, is alas untrue.'[76]

4.2 *Manchester Evening News*

The *Manchester Evening News* of 27 December 1940 had less than 15 per cent of the editorial copy devoted to the city's Blitz. There were no reports on the aftermath of the bombing on the front page, which, by most editorial standards, is a surprising example of news values. The other main reports on the page were overt examples of propaganda.[77] Signs of the hand of the censors, who insisted on minimising reports of suffering, were manifest, but a Manchester newspaper could have found news stories amid the bombed-out buildings and chose not to. It is as if the *Manchester Evening News* wished to find a new focus as quickly as possible.

The city's plight was reserved to page three and a report headed 'All Manchester homeless will be re-housed again in few days time', although those who could detect good news in that headline would also have to contemplate the counterpoint

---

[74] 'Manchester's Rest Centres', *Manchester Guardian*, 2 January 1941, p. 6.
[75] Ibid.
[76] Mass Observation Archive, FR 538.
[77] 'RAF bomb Bordeaux' and 'Officer on defeatist talk charge', *Manchester Evening News*, 27 December 1940, p. 1.

Propaganda and Opinion

of the report next to it: 'Last chance for child evacuation'.[78] This would have been a sobering thought for the parents of the 80,000 Mancunian children who had to choose between sending their children to strangers or to keep them in a city that might be targeted by the Luftwaffe at any time. The *Evening News* was determined to find the silver lining, however, and the potential boom for one of the city's main thoroughfares, Oxford Road, provided it. It read:

> Manchester's Blitz is likely to bring an unexpected prosperity to the Oxford Road area. It is estimated that about 100 houses and shops are empty in that area and already firms are making inquiries with the object of taking over these vacant properties.[79]

A more accurate comment came in the private diary of the *Evening News*'s editor three days later. 'The city still has not resumed its normal life', Haley wrote, strongly contrasting what his newspaper was reporting.[80] Mancunians could read these headlines while witnessing the chaos of their own city that was only hinted at in their newspapers – 'From today it is no longer necessary to boil water for drinking purposes' – and make comparisons with reports of the alleged damage being done to German cities and towns. [81] For example, the principal headline on 28 December had read:

---

[78] 'All Manchester Homeless will be Re-Housed Again in Few Days Time' and 'Last Chance for Child Evacuation', *Manchester Evening News*, 27 December 1940, p. 3.
[79] 'Oxford Road May Boom Again', *Manchester Evening News*, 27 December 1940, p. 3.
[80] Churchill Archives, Sir William John Haley, 30 December 1940.
[81] 'Water Need Not Be Boiled Now', *Manchester Evening News*, 10 January 1941, p. 6.

MORE NEWS OF HAVOC IN BERLIN AND PORTS
Accuracy of the RAF Bombing[82]

Three days later the *Evening News* was making more mountains from rubble in its leader: 'Hitler has promised complete victory, Churchill promised nothing. Therein lies one of the weaknesses of his position. The Dictatorships must have triumphs or their hold weakens. Spectacles must take the place of bread. Without conquests they die.'[83] Later it read: 'We, too, have been assaulted and we have not cracked.' The attempt to restore morale included official visits. Wendell Willkie, who had stood against Franklin D. Roosevelt in the 1940 United States election and who became an international ambassador for the American president, toured Manchester in February. 'I'll tell the States they're not downhearted here', he was reported as saying.[84]

4.3 *Evening Chronicle*

Just as the *Evening News* appeared to abandon normal journalistic practices by switching its news focus from Manchester prematurely, the *Evening Chronicle* also moved on in its 27 December edition. There were just six reports on the city's Blitz, which accounted, in terms of column centimetres, for around one page of a six-page newspaper, approximately 16 per cent. There were no photographs. Unlike the *Evening News*, the lead story in the *Evening Chronicle* did focus on the city.

The headline 'Manchester Gets Down to Work Behind Boards' extended over three columns, while the introduction read: 'Manchester is rapidly assuming its normal workday

---

[82] 'More News of Havoc in Berlin and Ports', *Manchester Evening News*, 28 December 1940, p. 1.
[83] '1941', *Manchester Evening News*, 1 January 1941, p. 2
[84] 'Willkie to Manchester: Your Spirit is Grand', *Manchester Evening News*, 3 February 1941, p. 1

aspect after the Blitz. Its countenance may be scarred and in some parts battered, but the people, after the Christmas respite, returned to work with determination.'[85]

The message chimed with the 'Manchester can take it' discourse and might have stirred admiration in parts of the city that had escaped relatively unscathed, but for the grieving and the homeless this must have come across as blatant untruths, and possibly offensive.

The propaganda techniques of the *Chronicle* were to ignore the worst aspects of the bombing and to 'other' the enemy. On page three the main headline read 'Christmas post beats the Blitz', stressing a return to normality, while a sports report on the following page recorded a new challenge for Manchester United, because they were now playing their home games at Stockport County's Edgeley Park.[86] There was no mention that United's ground was unusable because of bombing.[87] Ten days later there was evidence of an inclination to ascribe animal-like language to the enemy. 'Defenders creep out of cave', one headline read, describing surrendering Italians, with the underhand and sinister connotations contained in the word 'creep'. 'Cave', too, has a primitive or sub-human undertone to it. In comparison, the same report highlighted the overt bravery of the Allies, the subsidiary headline reading: 'Australians went into battle singing'.[88]

---

[85] 'Manchester Gets Down to Work Behind Boards', *Evening Chronicle,* 27 December 1940, p. 1.
[86] 'Christmas Post Beats the Blitz', *Evening Chronicle,* 27 December 1940, p. 3
[87] 'Big Task Ahead of United', *Evening Chronicle,* 27 December 1940, p. 4.
[88] 'Defenders Creep out of Cave', *Evening Chronicle,* 6 January 1941, p. 1.

5. 'No one dare report the tears'

A Home Intelligence report in February 1941 quoted a remark '(private of course) by a famous columnist'.[89] It read: 'Journalists report the cheers. No one dare report the tears', and this was borne out by Manchester's newspapers from December 1940 to February 1941. The number of casualties was worse than reported; the destruction to factories and the city's infrastructure was minimised; efforts were made to increase the success of air defences; shortcomings in firefighting were virtually ignored; heroes were plentiful and promoted; the Luftwaffe's successes were dismissed as rare; and it was civilian rather than industrial targets that were hit. All were distortions designed to maintain morale and demonise the enemy.

The censor was sitting in the offices of the *Manchester Evening News* to monitor the copy coming out in the city's newspapers, but there is little in the editions to suggest journalists were pushing at the boundaries of what would have been considered acceptable. Indeed senior journalists congratulated themselves on the service they provided. On 27 December 1940 Crozier wrote to Haley:

> You were saying the other night that the appearance of newspapers after a heavy raid was a powerful agent in steadying people's nerves. I have two interesting pieces of evidence.
>
> 1 An air-raid warden, who at a Christmas gathering said that he and his friends were overjoyed when they got the four-page MG *[Manchester Guardian]*, because they thought that if the MG came out 'with all its features' after such a night, Manchester must still be standing firm.

---

[89] Mass Observation Archive, FR 568, *Report on Morale in 1941*, February 1941.

2 At the aircraft place where my daughter works, various directors and bosses came up to her, knowing of her connection with me, and expressed high delight at having received the paper. Some of them had not received it until pretty late, but they felt retrospectively that it had been a great comfort after they had been fearing the worst sort of news.[90]

This self-congratulation came at a cost.[91] Billig wrote that the metonymic image of banal nationalism 'is not a flag which is being consciously waved with fervent passion; it is the flag hanging un-noticed on the public building' and, by following Fleet Street's lead, Manchester's newspapers pushed propaganda to the point that it became so institutionalised in the rhetoric of politicians, the editorials in the comment pages and the favoured narratives within the reporting of news that it became the norm.[92] Home Intelligence reports showed the consequence was that trust in the press was eroded.

---

[90] John Rylands Library, *The Guardian* Archive, Crozier to Haley, 27 December 1940.
[91] Brian McNair, *News and Journalism in the UK*, 4th edn (London: Routledge, 2003), p. 68; Boyd-Barrett, 'Understanding the Second Casualty', p. 29.
[92] Billig, *Banal Nationalism*, p. 8.

Plate 1: Oxford Road at war: A bomb appears to have destroyed buildings close to the University of Manchester (courtesy of the Greater Manchester Police Museum & Archives).

Plates

Plate 2: Inspecting the wreckage: The Lord Mayor of Manchester, Robert Edwards amid the ruins of the Free Trade Hall. The bombing left much of the interior destroyed and a new building was constructed behind the original façade. The hall reopened in 1951 with a concert featuring the English contralto Kathleen Ferrier (courtesy of the Greater Manchester Police Museum & Archives).

Plate 3. Manchester in the Blitz: The Piccadilly bus station ablaze at the height of the Manchester Blitz (courtesy of the Greater Manchester Police Museum & Archives).

Plates

Plate 4: Manchester Christmas Blitz 1940: Firefighters face the blaze on the corner of Silver Street (courtesy of the Greater Manchester Police Museum & Archives).

Plate 5: Surveying the damage: Officials tour Piccadilly Gardens in the wake of the Manchester Blitz. Note that only the humble soldier (second from left) is without a gas mask (courtesy of the Greater Manchester Police Museum & Archives).

Plates

Plate 6: Rising from the destruction on Miller Street and Shude Hill. Miller Street is now the site of the CIS Tower, which was Britain's tallest building when it was completed in 1962 (courtesy of the Greater Manchester Police Museum & Archives).

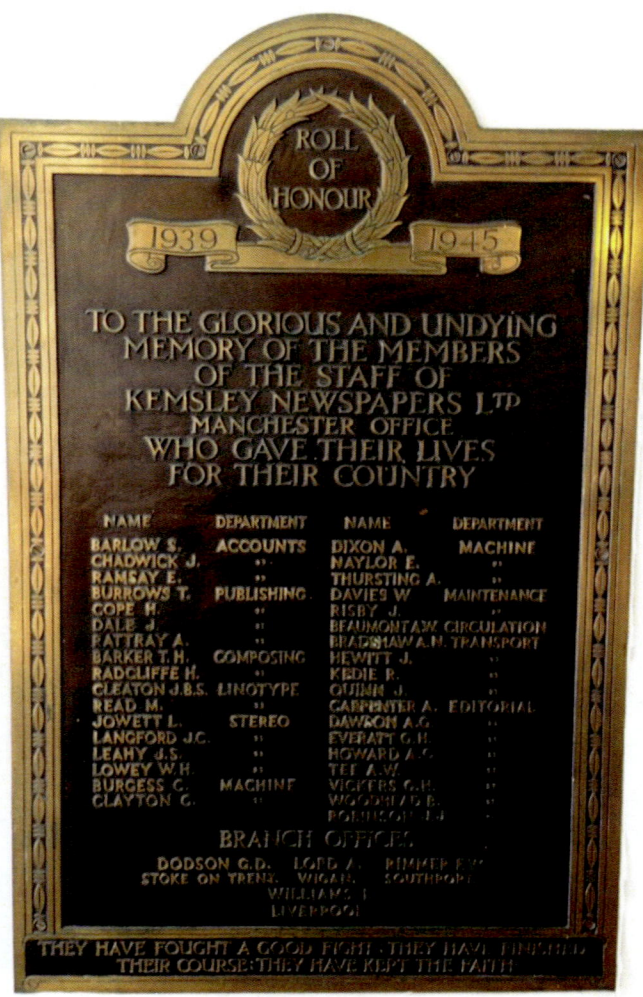

Plate 7: Echoes of the past: The Roll of Honour 1939–45 at the entrance to Manchester's Printworks entertainment venue. The site is in the former Kemsley Newspapers headquarters at Withy Grove.

Plates

Plate 8: The Fire Window in Manchester Cathedral: The stained-glass commemoration to the Blitz in Manchester Cathedral's Regimental Chapel. It was designed by Margaret Traherne, who also supervised its reconstruction after it was damaged by the IRA bomb attack in 1996.

CHAPTER SEVEN

ALL IN THIS TOGETHER?

1. The Social Divide

The expression 'we're all in this together' is a legacy of the Second World War that derived from the message that social barriers had been broken down by the conflict.[1] It was a proclamation that has since been interrogated by historians, who have discovered less equality.[2] Ponting wrote:

> One of the central myths of 1940, cultivated at the time and embellished since, was that Britain was galvanised by crisis to change old ways of working, and became united as never before, with a strong bond of equality of sacrifice ... The reality was very different.[3]

Britain entered the war with significant social difficulties that were a hangover from the Great Depression. In January 1940, with the country straining to build as many tanks, ships and planes as possible, 1.47 million people were out of work and that figure did not fall below 200,000 until June 1941.[4] The surplus of labour did not soothe industrial relations, more than 1.5 million days being lost to strikes in 1942, a figure that

---

[1] The expression 'we're all in this together' came originally from the US, where it became a common war cry in the Second World War before spreading to Britain (National WW2 Museum <http://www.nationalww2museum.org/history/pearlharbor.html> [accessed 11 March 2013]).
[2] Calder, *The Myth of the Blitz*; Gardiner, *The Blitz*; Ponting, *1940*.
[3] Ponting, *1940*, p. 138.
[4] Butler and Sloman, *British Political Facts*, p. 341; Ponting, *1940*, p. 138.

rose to 3.7 million in 1944.[5] Inflation also took a toll on household incomes with a knock-on effect of severe deprivation in some of the poorer areas.[6] MP Russell Thomson reported in 1942 that 25 per cent of children in Merseyside were living below the poverty line, while a doctor in West Sussex had found that 72 per cent of the elementary school children were living below the line of nutrition laid down by the Children's Minimum Council.[7]

Other evidence countered the myth of equality. Hastings stated that: 'Privileged Britons remained privileged indeed. "The extraordinary thing about the war was that people who really didn't want to be involved in it were not," the novelist Anthony Powell wrote afterwards.'[8] Rich parents sent 17,000 children abroad in the last six months of 1940 and former public schoolboys were 14 times more likely to be officers in the army.[9] Knightley wrote that the Blitz was not the great social leveller: 'The protection a Londoner got from German bombs depended on how much money he had.'[10] In 1940 an American journalist Ralph Ingersoll found just six overflowing buckets acting as toilets for 8,000 people when he visited a

---

[5] Butler and Sloman, *British Political Facts*, p. 341.
[6] In 1940 average prices rose 19 per cent compared to an 11 per cent rise in salaries (Ponting, *1940*, p. 138).
[7] *Hansard*, HC Debate, 30 June 1942, 381, cols 38–182. In the same debate it was revealed that pupils at Christ's Hospital, a public school in Sussex, were 2.4 inches (6.1 centimetres) taller at the age of 13 than comparable boys at elementary schools. At 17 the difference was 3.8 inches (9.7 centimetres).
[8] Max Hastings, *All Hell Let Loose: The World at War 1939–45*. (London: Harper, 2011), p. 342; Anthony Powell, *A Writer's Handbook* (London: Heinemann, 2001), p. 94, cited in Hastings, *All Hell Let Loose*, pp. 342–43.
[9] Ponting, *1940*, pp. 148–49; Hylton, *Their Darkest Hour*, p. 58
[10] Knightley, *The First Casualty*, p. 261.

shelter in the Isle of Dogs. 'The whole experience shocked so that it numbed', he wrote, before driving to the Dorchester in the West End where guests slept in individual beds in a subterranean area that had been the hotel's Turkish baths. There was a note pinned to one berth reading 'Reserved for Lord Halifax', the Foreign Secretary.[11]

While the war was largely supported by the public – a poll conducted by the British Institute of Public Opinion in October 1939 found that 89 per cent favoured fighting 'until Hitlerism goes' – the reaction was not unanimous.[12] Home Intelligence reported there was little national unity at the start of the war and, initially, many had misgivings about the conflict.[13] In December 1939 a Manchester student reported to Mass Observation that the war was a 'taboo' subject in his family, adding: 'I still don't support it, but my family ... seem to forget all the dirty tricks (in my opinion) which they [the government] played before.'[14] Three months later a railway draughtsman reporting from Wilmslow, 14 miles south of Manchester, wrote: 'I suppose I must agree that the WAR AIMS [his capitals] of the orthodox propagandists are reasonable, but somehow I feel no enthusiasm ... I am mostly floundering around, undecided and sad.'[15] These were voices in the North-West, nationally, the sceptics included members of the far left and right, Irish republicans and even miners,

---

[11] N. Longmate, ed., *The Home Front: An Anthology 1938–1945* (London: Chatto and Windus, 1981), p. 78.
[12] War Morale, 6 October 1939, cited in Sheila Elizabeth Rosemary Watson, 'The Ministry of Information and the Home Front in Britain 1939–42' (unpublished doctoral thesis, University of London, 1980), p. 189.
[13] University of Sussex, Mass Observation Archive, FR 568.
[14] Ibid., D5104, Male Student, 16 December, 1939.
[15] Ibid., D5199, G. W. Shipway, 31 March 1940.

who harboured grievances against Churchill dating back to the General Strike.[16]

There was also the peace movement. Nearly 130,000 Britons had joined the Peace Pledge Union by the outbreak of war and the above Wilmslow Mass Observation correspondent, surveying Manchester's bomb damage, felt aggrieved enough about the government's efforts to preserve peace to write in January 1941: 'I must say that all this destruction of cities is no more than England deserves for its wanton destruction of the League of Nations.'[17] The government put pressure on the BBC and Fleet Street to make sure pacifist voices remained virtually unheard, Bingham noting that Vera Brittain, a leading advocate for peace throughout the hostilities, found it difficult to find space in newspapers to promote her views, as she was 'perceived to be challenging the "national interest"'.[18] A reader's letter in the *Manchester Guardian* voiced the mood of intolerance towards those who shared Brittain's views. It read:

> By its action in protecting the public from the pernicious singing of the Orpheus Choir under the direction of the pacifist Sir Hugh Robertson the BBC has earned the plaudits of all prudent patriots. It therefore came as a great shock to read in the *Radio Times* that a lifelong pacifist Sir Arthur Eddington was actually being allowed to disseminate his insidious astronomical theories in a talk with the significant title 'Other Worlds'. Should not the person responsible for

---

[16] Calder, *The Myth of the Blitz*, pp. 65–89.
[17] David C. Lukowitz, 'British Pacifists and Appeasement: The Peace Pledge Union', *Journal of Contemporary History*, 9, 1 (1974), p. 117; University of Sussex, Mass Observation Archive, D5199, Shipway, 17 January 1941.
[18] Williams, *Get Me a Murder!*, p. 125; Bingham, *Gender, Modernity and the Popular Press*, p. 208.

subjecting the nation to so grave a risk be immediately removed from office?[19]

There is scant indication there of latitude or forgiveness, and little was shown to Germans, some of them Jews who had fled their native country to escape Hitler's persecution, and Italians, whose shops, including those in Manchester, were ransacked. Many were imprisoned in the Isle of Man or in a makeshift prison camp in Warth Mills, a vermin-invested cotton mill in Bury, nine miles north of Manchester.[20] In July 1940 more than a thousand of these prisoners set sail from Liverpool for Canadian internment on the *Arandora Star* and 600 perished when they were torpedoed by a U-Boat. The dead included a well-known German socialist opponent of Hitler and the secretary of the Italian League of the Rights of Man.[21] The *Manchester Guardian* reported that there had been panic among the internees, adding: 'There was great hostility between the Germans and Italians, and even on board the rescue ship they had to be guarded by British troops to prevent them from coming to blows.'[22] According to the *Daily Express*:

> Soldiers and sailors … told of panic among the aliens when they realised the ship was sinking. All condemned the cowardice of the Germans, who fought madly to get into the boats. 'The Germans, fighting with Italians to escape, were great hulking brutes,' said one soldier. 'They punched and kicked their way past the Italians. We had to restrain them forcibly … But the Italians were just as bad. The whole mob

---

[19] 'Pacifists and Broadcasting', *Manchester Guardian*, 2 January 1941, p. 8.
[20] Calder, *The Myth of the Blitz*, p. 113.
[21] Ibid.
[22] 'Shipload of Internees Torpedoed', *Manchester Guardian*, 4 July 1940, p. 5.

thought of their own skins first. The scramble for the boats was sickening.'[23]

A subsequent investigation proved this account to be false and this helped change the national mood, the proportion of the public in favour of internment falling from 55 per cent in July 1940 to 30 per cent in August.[24]

While the public's antagonism to British-based Germans and Italians moderated, anti-Semitism was more ingrained. Mass Observation found evidence of anti-Jewish sentiments among more than 55 per cent of respondents in one survey and a Home Intelligence report in 1943 stated there was 'much latent anti-Semitism':

> The Manchester *Daily Dispatch*, for instance, published a letter in which it was suggested Jewish names predominated in black market prosecutions, army dodging trials, clothing coupon rackets, petrol ramps and the like, the writer suggesting that the Jews should be put in their place. [25]

The investigator reported this letter was widely discussed, overhearing several comments, including: 'there's no doubt they (the Jews) have too much power'; 'stinking lot of cowards they are, the Jews'; and 'Jews [sic] shops are always stocked up'. An accompanying survey of Mass Observation's national panel of observers – credited as: 'a section of the population more intelligent and better informed' – revealed that only 25 per cent of them felt 'favourable' towards Jews'.[26]

---

[23] 'Germans Torpedo Germans', *Daily Express*, 4 July 1940, p. 1.
[24] Hylton, *Their Darkest Hour*, p. 18.
[25] Ibid., p. 21; University of Sussex, Mass Observation Archive, FR 1648, *Recent Trends in Anti-Semitism*, March 1943.
[26] University of Sussex, Mass Observation Archive, FR 1648, *Recent Trends in Anti-Semitism*, March 1943. As late as January 1944 another Mass Observation survey revealed that 24 per cent of the population wanted stricter controls on the activities of British

Ironically, the bombing of London initially focused on the East End, which before the war had provided a geographical foundation for the anti-Semitic British Union of Fascists.[27] 'Everybody is worried about the feeling in the East End', Nicolson wrote in his diary on 17 September, 'where there is much bitterness. It is said that even the King and Queen were booed the other day when they visited the destroyed areas.'[28] Bernard Kops, a boy in the East End, recalled desperate nights on London Tube platforms:

> Some people feel a certain nostalgia for those days, recall a poetic dream about the Blitz. They talk about those days as if they were time of true communal spirit. Not to me. It was the beginning of an era of utter terror, of fear and horror.[29]

Calder stated that versions of the Blitz often suggested 'it was a mean and pusillanimous Londoner indeed who did not emerge from the debris with a wisecrack on his lips'.[30] He noted, however, that the witty remarks often masked hysteria and often the authors of this humour were found sobbing a few hours later. For example, Sansom cited an anecdote where an elderly woman refused to leave the cooking pot she was stirring in the remains of her bombed-out home. To humour her, a man agreed to taste her food only to find the pan contained plaster and bricks.[31]

Fascists but only two per cent saw the need for curbs on anti-Semitism (Hylton, *Their Darkest Hour*, p. 21).

[27] Stephen Dorril, *Black Shirt: Sir Oswald Mosley and British Fascism* (London: Penguin, 2007), p. 394.

[28] H. Nicolson, *Diaries and Letters 1939–1945* (London: Fontana, 1970), p. 112.

[29] Longmate, *The Home Front*, p. 66.

[30] Calder, *The People's War*, p. 187.

[31] William Sansom, *The Blitz: Westminster at War*, 3rd edn (London: Faber and Faber, 1947), p. 63.

All in This Together?

When Coventry was blitzed in November 1940, the *Daily Express* reported the city was wounded 'but keeps its courage and sanity'.[32] Three Home Intelligence inspectors disagreed:

> There were more open signs of hysteria, terror, neurosis, observed in one evening than during the whole of the past two months together in all areas. Women were seen to cry, to scream, to tremble all over, to faint in the street, to attack a fireman, and so on. The overwhelmingly dominant feeling on Friday was the feeling of utter helplessness ... There were several signs of suppressed panic as darkness approached. In two cases people were seen to be fighting to get on to cars, which they thought would take them out into the country, though in fact, the drivers insisted, the cars were just going up the road to the garage.[33]

Knightley wrote that the reaction of the local population was ignored because it did not fit the myth.[34] Newspapers were complicit in this, often without urging from the authorities yet, curiously, obliquely acknowledged the destruction of Coventry, and the German use of *Coventration* or *Coventried*, later in the war:

> British newspapers, adept as always at turning the serious into the trivial, made many cute usages in aid of morale. One was the term *Coventried* to describe any place as bomb-ruined as Coventry. This led ultimately to such a headline as 'Hamburg has been Hamburgered'.[35]

One psychiatrist estimated that children who stayed in Bristol were eight times more likely to be psychologically disturbed than those who were evacuated and there are other

---

[32] "A Very Gallant City', *Daily Express*, 16 November 1940, p. 1.
[33] University of Sussex, Mass Observation Archive, FR 495, *Coventry*, November 1940.
[34] Knightley, *The First Casualty*, p. 262.
[35] Fussell, *Wartime*, p. 148.

statistics testifying to the mental strain.[36] The number of teenage girls arrested doubled in the three years after 1939, more infants than usual choked or were suffocated in their cots, there were fewer cars but more children were killed on the roads and more children drowned. In contrast, the suicide rate fell.[37]

2. Crime and Newspaper Coverage of the Courts

Reported crimes rose from 303,711 in England and Wales in 1939 to 478,394 in 1945 and the number of people convicted went up 54 per cent.[38] Police numbers in England and Wales fell from 82,232 to 59,574, making catching criminals more difficult, so the high number of convictions indicates a significant increase in crime.[39] Hylton wrote: 'There were new classes of offence for people to commit in a heavily regulated wartime society, and the opportunity to commit them was enhanced by the cover of the blackout and the substantial reduction in police numbers.'[40] Duncan Campbell, a former crime correspondent for the *Guardian*, noted that the war was a criminal watershed: 'Hundreds of emergency regulations protected the nation but many were seen as petty, even ludicrous, and led to a loss of respect for the law.'[41] The imposition of rationing and wartime shortages led to a rise in thefts from work, threefold in Birkenhead docks during 1940, and in the same year 500 policemen had to be sent to France to stop mass pilfering of supplies and equipment from the British

---

[36] Calder, *The People's War*, p. 225.
[37] Ibid.
[38] Hylton, *Their Darkest Hour*, p. 154
[39] Ibid.
[40] Ibid.
[41] *Bandits of the Blitz*, prod. by Liz Carney (BBC Radio 4, Broadcast 8 September 2010).

All in This Together?

Expeditionary Force.[42] The railways lost goods valued at £1 million in 1941 alone; looters regularly raided bombed out houses despite the imposition of the death penalty for the offence (it was never carried out); and on 8 March 1941 a notorious incident occurred when two bombs hit the underground *Café de Paris*, in the West End, when it was packed with Canadian nurses and young officers on leave, killing 34.[43] Delays by the emergency services led to an inquiry and several unsavoury incidents, including rings and jewellery being stripped from dead bodies by thieves.[44]

Although Lord Northcliffe was not the first to realise the importance of crime reporting to newspapers – the historian Dr Andrew Cook has put forward the theory that Jack the Ripper was a forgery invented by journalists who linked a series of unrelated murders in 1888 to boost circulations – the founder of the *Daily Mail*, did articulate the attraction of courts and justice to editors.[45] Williams wrote: 'He placed great emphasis on crime stories as a staple feature of the paper. Crime featured prominently with interviews with murderers as well as the police. Northcliffe's motto was "get me a murder a day".'[46] Court reporting is a staple item in every newspaper because it is easily, and cheaply, acquired copy and because 'courts are a marvellous source of human interest and crime stories'.[47] Throughout the study period, the *Manchester Guardian*, *Manchester Evening News* and the *Evening Chronicle* gave significant space to reports from the courts, devoting

---

[42] Ponting, *1940*, p. 142.
[43] Hylton, *Their Darkest Hour*, p. 156; Gardiner, *The Blitz*, p. 323.
[44] Gardiner, *The Blitz*, p. 324.
[45] Andrew Cook, *Jack The Ripper: Case Closed* (Stroud: Amberley, 2009).
[46] Williams, *Get Me a Murder!*, p. 56.
[47] Keeble, *The Newspapers Handbook*, p. 173.

approximately a page in each of the evening newspapers and around half a page in the *Guardian*. In a time when much of the news was subject to official approval, and travel and communication were complicated by air raids and bomb damage, the attraction of guaranteed stories that rarely required the attention of the censor, was obvious.

All three newspapers reported court cases at length, but none made the link between the special circumstances of war and the degree of lawlessness they provoked. On 1 January 1941 the *Guardian* reported the comments of Noel B. Goldie, the Recorder at Manchester Quarter Sessions, who noted the 56 youths before him and said 'something had to be done'. He added:

> I have no doubt that in the first instance it was due to a lack of parental control, but I have a strong suspicion that receivers in this great city are using youths for the purpose of committing these most serious offences ... We are, in Manchester at the moment breeding a race of young criminals.[48]

On 9 January the *Manchester Evening News* added to this debate under the headline 'Looting becoming serious in Manchester, court told'.[49] On the same page it was noted that Manchester had suffered a three-fold increase in crime in a three-month period, Recorder Goldie blaming a lack of parental control: 'It is not merely an increase in petty pilfering. We are now getting serious crimes such as breaking and entering. And the boys who are responsible show complete hardness when they are

---

[48] 'Manchester Breeding Young Criminals', *Manchester Guardian*, 1 January 1941, p. 2.
[49] 'Looting Becoming Serious in Manchester, Court Told', *Manchester Evening News*, 9 January 1941, p. 6.

caught.'[50] Below were other headlines: '50-mile joy ride in van', 'Roaming town like wild things', 'Gas meters robbed in bombed houses' and 'Father suspected own son'.[51] The accused in each case was aged between nine and 14. Later that month the *Evening News* columnist Eileen Elias wrote:

> The gangsters are here. No, this is not something from an American film. Police, parents and magistrates wish it were. It is just a plain statement of fact about the country today in the midst of war.
>
> For juvenile crime is on the increase. In Manchester alone during the past three months it has trebled. Never before have we been faced with so serious a problem in the life of young Britain.[52]

No link was made to the effect of raids on young attitudes, but Roy Lee, a teenager in 1940, articulated a sense of futility once his best friend Matthew was killed in the Manchester Blitz:

> When he went my clock stopped ticking. I remember saying to myself: 'That's it. No matter what happens now it could be me tomorrow.' I made up my mind there and then to live for me and my mum and to hell with everyone else.[53]

Lee would wait for the all clear and then loot bombed-out buildings. He added:

---

[50] 'Young Crime Trebles Since September', *Manchester Evening News*, 9 January 1941, p. 6.
[51] '50-Mile Joy Ride in Van', 'Roaming Town Like Wild Things', 'Gas Meters Robbed in Bombed Houses' and 'Father Suspected Own Son', *Manchester Evening News*, 9 January 1941, p. 6.
[52] Eileen Elias, 'The Gangsters are Here', *Manchester Evening News*, 20 January 1941, p. 2.
[53] *Secrets of the Blitz*, dir. by Steve Humphries (Channel 5, Broadcast 20 January 2011).

Obviously money was the first thing you looked for, and then, of course, there was always food, packets of tea and this, that and the other, anything that had been blown up in people's kitchens. You never handed it back. Anything that was worthwhile we just stuck in our pockets and away we'd go.[54]

Lee lived in Manchester but theft was not unique to him or his city. Gardiner said that looting was the 'largely unspoken, unacknowledged underside of the "blitz spirit", the fissure that crazed the pulling together to face a common enemy – and it was widespread'.[55]

Had journalists examined this underside they would have noticed it was not just youths who were breaking the law but people who normally would be regarded as pillars of the society. So it was a war reserve policeman (aged 34) and a customs office watcher (46) who were convicted of stealing 12 bottles of whisky, a 30-year-old soldier who was given a three-month prison sentence for looting and a 39-year-old shopkeeper charged with stealing £4 10s. in cash and a £20 cash register from a bombed-out inn.[56] An Air Raid Patrol officer was gaoled for 'neglecting duty', beginning his one-month sentence to the words of the Manchester Stipendiary Magistrate, who said: 'If you had lived under a different regime you might have been shot.'[57] Violence did not end with bombs and

---

[54] Ibid.
[55] Gardiner, *The Blitz*, p. 324.
[56] 'Whisky Stolen from Docks', *Manchester Guardian*, 30 December 1940, p. 2; 'Looting After Air Raid', *Manchester Guardian*, 31 December 1940, p. 10; 'Looting Charges', *Manchester Guardian*, 2 January 1941, p. 3.
[57] 'ARP Rescue Man Gaoled for Neglecting Duty', *Manchester Evening News*, 29 January 1941, p. 6.

anti-aircraft shells, and in December 1940 the *Evening Chronicle* reported the execution of a soldier for a domestic murder.[58]

3. Letters to the Editor

The feedback loops that ensure there is a two-way communication between newspapers and their audience were referred to earlier, but the most overt come in the readers' letters column. These form an important part of a newspaper in that they 'enable both the press and the readership to keep an ear to the ground and listen in to some of the leading themes of local conversation'.[59] All readers' letters are subject to the gate-keeping of journalists, however, and Wahl-Jorgensen listed four criteria by which letters are selected for publication. These are the letter's entertainment value, its brevity, the writer's authority and command of English and, finally, its relevance or news-worthiness.[60] All four criteria are open to the kind of journalistic judgements, but the last is particularly so as readers' attempts to introduce their own items to the news agenda will 'almost invariably fail'.[61] With newspapers promoting the notion of unity, not many letters contradicting this theme would have been allowed in the newspaper.

Nevertheless, the *Manchester Guardian* allowed its readers to criticise both itself and the government over the suppression

---

[58] 'Soldier's Execution Date', *Evening Chronicle*, 20 December 1940, p. 4.
[59] I. Jackson, *The Provincial Press and the Community* (Manchester: University of Manchester Press, 1971), p. 174, cited in John Richardson, 'Readers' Letters' in Bob Franklin, ed., *Pulling Newspapers Apart*, p. 56.
[60] Karin Wahl-Jorgensen, 'Understanding the Conditions for Public Discourse: Four Rules for Selecting Letters to the Editor', *Journalism Studies*, 3, 1 (2002), pp. 73–78.
[61] Ibid., p. 73.

of the *Daily Worker*, a decision that prompted a series of letters. The *Guardian*'s editorial on the subject concluded: 'The *Daily Worker* did not believe in the war or in democracy; its only aim was to confuse and weaken. We can well spare it.'[62] This was a surprising position given the *Guardian*'s stance on pre-war freedoms in Nazi Germany and a majority of the letters printed on the subject condemned it. The comments included: 'It is a step which the executive of a democratic country should never take'; 'We have taken a perilous step towards the totalitarian concept of journalism'; 'Criticism has been driven underground', and 'Why use a Coalition steam-hammer to crack a Communist nut?'[63] Crozier was forced to defend the *Guardian*'s position, stating: 'We would hold strongly that freedom to criticise the executive is as vital in time of war as it is in peace', before adding the critical qualification 'subject to the inevitable abridgements that a virtual state of siege may impose'. This is a key point because Crozier was accepting, and transmitting to his readers, the 'necessary' role of the press in time of war. Later in his response he wrote that the suppression of the *Daily Worker* was a 'choice of evils'.[64]

This book has shown the *Manchester Guardian*'s eagerness to criticise was overstated by Crozier, but the readers were less inhibited (or the censors were more willing to allow them to be). In December 1940 a letter complained that a shortage of workers in munitions and aeroplane factories had not

---

[62] 'The Daily Worker', *Manchester Guardian*, 22 January 1941, p. 4.
[63] 'The Right of Criticism', *Manchester Guardian*, 27 January 1941, p. 8; 'A Blow at Freedom of the Press', *Manchester Guardian*, 28 January 1941, p. 10; 'The Right of Public Criticism', *Manchester Guardian*, 4 February 1941, p. 10; 'Some Probable Effects', *Manchester Guardian*, 6 February 1941, p. 10.
[64] 'Risks of Stifling Criticism', *Manchester Guardian*, 1 February 1941, p. 4.

prevented advertisements in a London newspaper requesting two footmen, at least 5 ft 10 in tall, for 'a noblemen's establishment' and another two footmen to join a 'large staff' in London and Windsor. This, the writer, wrote was 'deeply shocking'.[65] Three days later another letter berated the sentence of 10 years handed down to two policemen for looting. 'I read the news with feelings of horror at the severe sentence', it read, 'and have since watched the press for some sign of charity and mercy, which I have failed to notice.'[66] On 30 December 1940 seven students wrote a letter about the conditions suffered by those who used London's tube stations as bomb shelters. 'Do the authorities really think that 12 sanitary buckets are sufficient for 2,000 people?' they asked.[67] These letters point to dissatisfaction among the *Guardian* readers at least, if not the general population, and hint at a lack of common purpose, but none was followed up with any determination by the press. This is more evidence of journalistic participation in the creation of the narrative desired by the government.

Home Intelligence reported that 'serious, long letters' were published only in *The Times*, the *Daily Telegraph* and the *Manchester Guardian*, and this was borne out by the *Manchester Evening News*. It comprised six broadsheet pages throughout the study period (compared to the *Guardian*'s 10), and averaged two readers' letters a week.[68] Hardly any criticism was contained in these letters and, what there was, referred to

---

[65] 'Service and Sahibs', *Manchester Guardian*, 16 December 1940, p. 8.
[66] 'Crime and Punishment', *Manchester Guardian*, 19 December 1940, p. 10.
[67] 'Shelter Conditions in Tube Stations', *Manchester Guardian*, 30 December 1940, p. 8.
[68] University of Sussex, Mass Observation Archive, FR 126.

the public shortcomings rather than those of the authorities.[69] No letter pertained to the Manchester Blitz until 2 January and the two published thanked a team of women voluntary helpers for their work in a rest centre and a Mr Eastwood, a greengrocer, who had given the keys of his shop to a local rector so that the homeless could have 'the run of the shop'.[70] There were only hints at social divisions, the first signed by 'Query', who articulated the class antagonism noted elsewhere when asking of a woman who employed two maids: 'Would she not be more patriotic if she were merely to do all her own housework and thereby release two women for whole-time national work?' In February 'Share Alike' from Levenshulme (south east Manchester) wrote that he was pleased to see the *Manchester Evening News* 'had the courage to criticise landlords who refuse to make a contribution towards the cost of long ladders to protect their own property'.[71] Given that the newspaper had neglected to confront the authorities over their lack of preparation for, and reaction to, the Blitz, it would difficult to back this alleged 'courage' with evidence.

The few readers' letters in the *Evening Chronicle* also eschewed criticism and some had an almost child-like belief in official communiqués, particularly a correspondent named as 'Chins Up', who wrote:

> Reading that Germans living in the much bombed Rhineland and Ruhr industrial towns don't bother to go to their shelter now in RAF raids because they have learned that British pilots stick to industrial targets, and that when the warning of an RAF raid is given factory workers quit

---

[69] The observation of December 1940 was typical: 'So, once more, even in time of war the mails are to be cluttered up with Christmas cards.' ('Letter', *Manchester Evening News*, 21 December 1940, p. 2.)
[70] 'Letters', *Manchester Evening News*, 2 January 1941, p. 2.
[71] Ibid., 5 February 1941, p. 2.

their jobs and move into residential districts for their safety, one wonders why, in the view of the Luftwaffe's methods, we should take such care to restrict the RAF to military targets. The only way to reply to the Nazi tactics is bombs and more bombs.[72]

There could have been other, less belligerent and believing, letters that did not make it to print, and 'Chins Up' could also have been a journalist asked to push the newspaper's point of view by an alternative means, but a publication would lose credibility if letters were consistently too far removed from the prevailing mood. On 1 January, for example, an un-named reader wrote: 'By far the largest majority of the public are indignant that we do not serve the enemies with similar raids to those suffered by our towns and cities.'[73] Ten days later 'Common Sense' wrote: 'They should have the same medicine.'[74] These letters pointed to a desire for retribution that Hastings claimed was fuelled by government propaganda:

> Only a limited number of British and American people gave much thought to the fate of Germany beneath air bombardment, partly because their governments persistently deceived them about the nature of the campaign: the reality of area bombing, the targeting of cities, was concealed beneath verbiage about industrial installations.[75]

The only suggestion of criticism in the *Evening Chronicle*'s letters column, came on 24 January when a reader questioned official assertions that bombed-out families had been adequately rehoused. The correspondent said he knew that one family had been moved into already crowded

---

[72] 'Your Own Opinion …', *Evening Chronicle*, 27 December 1940, p. 2.
[73] Ibid., 1 January 1941, p. 2.
[74] Ibid., 11 January 1941, p. 2.
[75] Hastings, *All Hell Let Loose*, p. 493.

accommodation, 'making a total of 10 in one house, with three small bedrooms'.[76]

4. A Template of Cheerfulness

The above evidence suggests that newspapers allowed their readers limited scope to criticise through their letters, although it could be argued these served to add to the newspapers' fictive 'fourth estate' mantle. If there had been allegations that they were too willing to voice the opinions of the powerful they could have offered this as evidence to the contrary. The attack on nameless landlords by the *Manchester Evening News*, for example, was a cheap assertion of the newspaper's independence that would not have cost it anything in terms of political approval or revenue but would have reinforced a notional position of independence.

Even before the war started the *Daily Mirror* was promoting a message of constancy. 'Cheerfulness was the keynote of Britain's people in the hours of crisis yesterday', it printed in August 1939. It added: 'We've always come smilin' through.'[77] This theme became the default position of the press, local and national, but among the wider newspaper reading public there was a more balanced reaction; people managed because there was no alternative. London was bombed heavily first and the 'Cheerful Cockney', precisely because this fiction was established by the press *ab initio*, became the template by which the populations in other cities would judge themselves. The hegemonic success of newspapers in persuading readers of this desired perspective was revealed when Home Intelligence, a government monitor of the public's mood, reported that people outside London had

---

[76] 'Your Own Opinion …', *Evening Chronicle*, 24 January 1941, p. 2.
[77] 'Britain Smiles and Prepares', *Daily Mirror*, 25 August 1939, pp. 16–17.

an exaggerated impression of the damage being inflicted on the capital but believed that 'if London can take it, so can we'.[78]

With such a determined effort to emphasise good news, it is not a surprise that no newspaper properly examined social tensions or the drift towards lawlessness by a significant number of people bombed out of their normal patterns of behaviour. While it would be overstating the case to say there was large-scale opposition to the war, the country had suffered deep divisions in the 1930s and it would have been remarkable if these merely evaporated under the threat of invasion. There were alternative views, but, an occasional letter to the editor apart, they were neglected by the newspapers. Marie Price, from Liverpool, remembered an atmosphere at odds with what she read in the press and saw in the newsreels:

> Churchill was telling us how brave we all were and that we would never surrender. I tell you something – the people of Liverpool would have surrendered overnight if they could have. It's all right for people in authority, down in their steel-lined dugouts, but we were there and it was just too awful.[79]

Surveys indicated that the lack of interest in the war rose from 10 per cent in spring 1940 to nearly a third by the end of that year.[80] Curran and Seaton summed up the mood in the civilian ranks not so much as all in this together as 'us' against 'them': 'The opposition was as much to the unbelievable bureaucracy of British administration as to the Nazis themselves.'[81] This harked back to pre-war social tensions and, as a consequence, Britons displayed a complex set of attitudes that

---

[78] University of Sussex, Mass Observation Archive, Box 1, *Propaganda*, 18 September 1940.
[79] Joshua Levine, ed., *Forgotten Voices of the Blitz and the Battle of Britain* (London: Ebury, 2006), p. 412.
[80] Ponting, *1940*, p. 171.
[81] Curran and Seaton, *Power Without Responsibility*, p. 126.

did not merely reflect the homogeneous and monolithic approval of the government and the war. Instead, the general reluctant assent to the conflict was sublimated into criticisms of the rich, the press and politicians, only a small amount of which was given a platform in Britain's newspapers.

CHAPTER EIGHT

THE AFTERMATH OF CHRISTMAS 1940

1. Observing the Masses

The impetus behind the launch of Mass Observation was provided by the Abdication Crisis in 1936. Three men, ornithologist and anthropologist Tom Harrisson, poet and *Daily Mirror* journalist Charles Madge, and film-maker Humphrey Jennings, were disappointed by the perceptions of public opinion being reported in the press and decided to collect more reliable data.[1] Their ambition was to construct 'an anthropology of ourselves' and monitor the effect of society on individuals.[2] This was provided by volunteers, who maintained diaries or answered questionnaires, and by paid investigators, who anonymously recorded conversations and monitored behaviour at work and on the streets. The subjects of the reports and the correspondents were not in positions of power, and, beyond their immediate family and local communities, had little influence. As a Mass Observation leaflet put it:

> Intellectuals find it hard to express themselves [but] observation comes naturally to people who are living in the thick of work-a-day existence. Among our best Observers

---

[1] Penny Summerfield 'Mass Observation: Social Research or Social Movement', *Journal of Contemporary History*, 20, 3 (1985), 439–52 (p. 440); Benjamin Jones, 'Mass Observation 75 Years On: The Extraordinary in the Everyday' (*The Guardian*, 2012) <http://www.guardian.co.uk/commentisfree/2012/apr/19/mass-observation-75-years> [accessed 1 April 2013].

[2] Simon Garfield, ed., *We Are at War: The Diaries of Five Ordinary People in Extraordinary Times* (London: Random House, 2005), p. 1.

are a mechanic, a coalminer, a waiter, a clerk, a housewife (middle class) and a housewife (working class).[3]

Looking from the context of the twenty-first century, this comes across as patronising, and it would be pertinent to question the criteria used to define middle and working class, but a modern perspective is not required to find voices for and against the project. Mass Observation also had its contemporary supporters and critics, some claiming it heralded a new form of social research while others complained it was simply snooping. Turner noted that Evelyn Waugh complained of 'pseudoscientific showmanship' and that during the war an official in the Ministry of Home Security described Mass Observation reports on Blitz morale as 'a most extraordinary mixture of fact, fiction and dangerous mischief emanating apparently from "the intelligentsia"'.[4] The sense of intrusion was reinforced when the MOI created the Home Intelligence unit at the outset of the Second World War, commandeering the Mass Observation reports and investigations by the Wartime Social Survey, an organisation established in April 1940 to investigate questions of sociological importance.[5] These became part of a network of sources who compiled material from shopkeepers, publicans, clergymen, shop stewards and others who regularly came into contact with the public. Crang of the University of Edinburgh said:

> Little did the people of Britain know that the government was secretly opening their letters and listening into their telephone conversations and, what I find most surprising, is that GPs were monitoring attitudes of their patients and

---

[3] Ibid., p. 2.
[4] E. S. Turner, 'Snooping', *London Review of Books*, 3, 18 (1981), pp. 23-24.
[5] Kathleen Box and Geoffrey Thomas, 'The Wartime Social Survey', *Journal of the Royal Statistical Society*, 107 (1944), p. 151.

reporting these to Home Intelligence. This was in effect the British government eavesdropping on the British people.[6]

Some on the political left felt they were being singled out for attention and on the same programme Bill Grave, a trade unionist during the war, expressed his anger:

> Those that knew were incensed. They said we are fighting a war for freedom and this stupidity is going on … It was the working class that were being picked on by these snobby people, from public schools. They picked on the little people and it was resented, very much so.[7]

If the reception was mixed, so was the reaction of the contributors. Some correspondents feared that, in a climate where people were being fined or threatened with prison for despondency, they might be laying themselves open to prosecution. For example, Christopher Tomlin, a writing paper salesman from Preston, wrote in July 1940: 'I must confess I'm nervous of this diary being in authorities' hands. It might get me a year or at least six months.'[8] A few months earlier, however, Tomlin had explained the appeal:

> The reason why I am keen on Mass Observation is because it wants to know and inform, tell all classes about the emotions, acts, thoughts and struggles of the ordinary or 'average' man and woman. Too many articles and books are on high-flown subjects, there are none about the prosaic things or everyday.[9]

Starting in Bolton, Lancashire, the first event that Mass Observation monitored was the coronation of George VI on 12 May 1937 when 12 observers were asked to move around

---

[6] *Secrets of the Blitz* (Channel 5).
[7] Ibid.
[8] University of Sussex, Mass Observation Archive, cited in Garfield, *We Are at War*, p. 1.
[9] Ibid., pp. 1–2.

during the day 'noting down what they saw and heard'.[10] The scope and the reach of the reports soon spread, however, so that the whole of Britain was covered when the Second World War began in 1939, although its claims that it had 2,000 amateur observers were an exaggeration. Calder and Sheridan stated that, excluding one-off replies, only 1,095 people joined the reporting panel between 1939 and 1945 and that very few of those did so without a break.[11] More typically, between 200 and 500 were reporting regularly so that the figure of 400 who replied to a questionnaire on 'class' in the summer of 1939 was not abnormal. Women accounted for a third of these respondents, another third was made up of unmarried men aged under 25, and 60 per cent of the total were aged under 35.[12] Calder and Sheridan wrote:

> The 'typical' male Mass Observer was a young clerk or student, the 'typical' female was a teacher or middle-class housewife. Unrepresentative of Britain's population as to age and sex, the Panel was also 'skewed' geographically, with a very heavy bias towards the South-East of England. Does this mean that the Panel was sociologically worthless? Certainly not. It gave ... access to the private opinions of hundreds of people.[13]

The government allied the Mass Observation reports to those being compiled by Mary Adams, in charge of the Home Information unit in the MOI, and Home Intelligence to monitor the mood of a population under fire. Initially, the government was reluctant to use Mass Observation, some detractors charging its members as being 'a bunch of dangerous pinkos',

---

[10] Summerfield, 'Mass Observation', p. 440.
[11] Angus Calder and Dorothy Sheridan, eds, *Speak for Yourself: A Mass-Observation Anthology 1937–1949* (Oxford: Oxford University Press, 1985), p. 73.
[12] Ibid., p. 74.
[13] Ibid.

and there was a preference for using the Secret Service instead.[14] Adams argued, however, that Mass Observation was more in touch with people's feelings than any official, writing:

> The results of Mass Observation are, not unnaturally, critical of certain social happenings and I do not think that criticism is subversive. The use to which criticisms may be put may lead to subversive actions. But it is our business to acquaint ourselves with criticisms and direct the attention of those in authority to the causes of discontent.[15]

The private opinions expressed in Mass Observation's reports showed that, contrary to the approved image, many were close to breaking point, something Harrisson confirmed in a report in the *British Medical Journal* in April 1941. In it he acknowledged he was a biologist rather than a doctor, but nevertheless he felt that the reports of low degrees of nervousness were faulty. There was evidence, he wrote, that people had left the bombed areas, found a refuge, 'and then caved in'. The report continued:

> In some cases they have simply taken to bed and stayed in bed for weeks at a time. They have not shown the marked trembling of hysteria, but an extreme desire to retreat into sleep and be looked after, as if chronically ill. We have found such cases mainly among women but also among men and children.[16]

One of Harrisson's Mass Observation reporters, L.E. in Streatham, south London, reported in January 1941 that morale was 'lower than ever before' and that there was a

---

[14] Gardiner, *The Blitz*, p. 169.
[15] Ibid.
[16] *British Medical Journal*, 12 April 1941, cited in Gardiner, *The Blitz*, pp. 190–91.

strong feeling of 'how futile it all is'.[17] L.E. added: 'This for the most part has not developed into a Stop-the-War feeling, though one local rumour (unfounded as far as inv [investigator] can see) reports a Stop-the-War meeting in a local road.' This wholly contradicted the newspapers, *The Times* being typical. On the same day it reported that the Minister for Labour Ernest Bevin had told the Transport and General Workers Union: 'I sincerely trust that this year will bring us victory.'[18] The tone could hardly have been more different. L.E. also recorded a 'typical' conversation: 'I don't think I can stand it if it goes on much longer like this, night after night, coming down all around us. I must go away.'[19] Kathleen Box's report of a conversation in Fulham at the height of the London Blitz on 14 October 1940 was also pessimistic: 'Sleep! You can't sleep. We can't go on like this can we? It can't go on ... They'll have to do something about it soon or there'll be a revolution.'[20]

The newspapers did not print these cries of helplessness or mutinous belligerence, but Home Intelligence did report on the newspapers. Earlier it was noted that a survey in May 1940 reported that distrust in the press had increased and a year later Stephen Taylor, in an appendix to a regular Home Intelligence report, *Home Morale and Public Opinion*, wrote that Fleet Street exercised considerable influence when it came to foreign news 'as the public as a whole has no means of cross

---

[17] Many correspondents preferred to use initials rather than their full names; University of Sussex, Mass Observation Archive, Box 1, *Propaganda*.
[18] 'Mr Bevin on the Work of Reconstruction', *The Times,* 14 January 1941, p. 2.
[19] University of Sussex, Mass Observation Archive, Box 1, *Propaganda*.
[20] Calder and Sheridan, *Speak for Yourself,* p. 85.

The Aftermath of Christmas 1940

checking', but at home it was less powerful.[21] 'The public often makes up its mind on its own experience before the press knows anything about it.' Taylor added:

> So far the most calamitous events have been turned to mental profit by the British public. Thus, the collapse of France was treated along these lines:– 'At last, we're on our own and there's no-one else to let us down; now we've really got to get on with the job.' Again, the Blitz was converted from a thing of terror to a symbol of pride and toughness. 'Our Blitz was worse than yours – and look at us.'[22]

Taylor drew a distinction between the national and local press, regarding the latter as a more reliable indicator, and creator, of public opinion. The reporters, he argued, came from the community and therefore were more aware of the pulse beating in the surrounding streets, and that the newspapers could devote a greater share of its space to local happenings and news, which influenced opinion. Taylor's perception of the local press was generous. Haley, the editor of the *Manchester Evening News,* wrote about his journey to work in the post-Blitz city in his diary on 29 December 1940: 'For four days afterwards one walked through a line of soldiers with drawn bayonets down Piccadilly.'[23] That alarming entry not only evokes a striking visual image at odds with the propaganda of the time but also implied that the troops were there to prevent lawlessness breaking out in the bombed out centre of Manchester. Not a word, or even a hint, of this appeared in Haley's newspaper and nor did it appear in other local or national newspapers.

---

[21] University of Sussex, Mass Observation Archive, FR 126; Mass Observation Archive, Box 1 *Propaganda*, 1 October 1941.
[22] Ibid., Box 1 *Propaganda*, 1 October 1941.
[23] Churchill Archives, Sir William John Haley, 29 December 1940.

While L.E. and Kathleen Box were writing diary entries in or close to the capital, Bill Naughton was compiling reports for Mass Observation from Manchester. Not to be confused with the Bolton-born playwright of the same name who also reported from London for Mass Observation in the war, Naughton was described as a 'very intelligent lorry driver' by an anonymous official.[24] He lived on Wilbraham Road, Fallowfield, three miles south of the city centre, and wrote of a 'Blitz complex' in January 1941 in the days after the Manchester bombings that was exposed by absenteeism. His own workplace, a fruit and vegetable distributor, was operating at 20 per cent of pre-Blitz levels, he reported, partly because of the disruption to transport caused by the bomb damage but principally because of the attitudes of the employees.[25] He wrote that 'sharp extremes of mental and moral feelings were manifest' and, while those who lived outside Manchester were philosophical about the damage to their city centre, those whose homes were closer to the blitzed areas were near to total dejection. Naughton reported: 'In the bombed areas where homes, personal belongings and relatives were lost, the morale was shockingly low. I visited three rest centres ... the misery and despair of the people were past description.' This evidence of contrasting moods set by the geographical proximity to the bombing coincided with the response of the *Manchester Evening News* editor, Haley, who, 13 miles away in Disley, Derbyshire, reacted in wonder as well as horror to the first night of bombing. Haley wrote in his diary:

> The whole Manchester part of the horizon was amazingly lit up by hundreds of flares. It was so remarkable a sight that

---

[24] University of Sussex, Mass Observation Archive, FR 839, *Manchester Industrial Atmosphere*, August 1941.
[25] Ibid., FR 620, *Manchester Air Raids*, March 1941.

The Aftermath of Christmas 1940

we took all the children up to our bedroom to see it, then hurried them back to shelter.[26]

Compare Naughton's observations with what was appearing in the local newspapers – The *Evening Chronicle* reported on 27 December 1940: 'Manchester is rapidly assuming its normal workday aspect after the Blitz. Its countenance may be scarred and in some parts battered, but the people, after the Christmas respite, returned to work with determination.'– and there was little wonder that the public began to lose faith in what they were reading.[27] Two months later, on 19 March, Naughton recorded conversations in Manchester about the bombing of Merseyside and Clydeside:

> People were shocked by the high death toll. I repeatedly heard the expressions: 'It's not war, just wholesale murder', 'it can't go on long this sort of thing, there's going to be nothing left fighting for', 'if they admit 500 dead you can bet it's nearer 5,000'.[28]

In his Manchester Industrial Survey, Naughton gave an insight into how he and other Mass Observation reporters gathered their information. On a week's holiday in 1941 he moved to parts of Manchester and the North where he was unknown and had to earn the trust of the locals:

> If one spoke different; wore better or unusual clothes; was alone; a stranger; or kept silent (this instantly creates a 'taking it all in' impression) or even asked for a Worthington Bass or glass of whisky, instead of a mild, then somebody became suspicious … In Manchester it is necessary to display a facile use of the only two swearing adjectives, and it was my correct use of 'Fuckin' and 'Bleedin' that gave me the hospitality of the conversation in the somewhat esoteric

---

[26] Churchill Archives, Sir William John Haley, 29 December 1940.
[27] 'Manchester Gets Down to Work Behind Boards', *Evening Chronicle,* 27 December 1940, p. 1.
[28] University of Sussex, Mass Observation Archive, FR 620.

locals. In transport cafes and works canteens, I always wore a greasy boiler suit and grubby hands ... I never ask a question, but often start an argument.[29]

His report also gave an insight into how behaviour was changing in the war-time conditions. More beer, Guinness in particular, he reported, was being consumed and quoted one licensee as saying: 'I sell more beer in a dinner hour in one day than I used to do in a week.' Moral and personal values, too, may have been affected by the potential of imminent death and Naughton wrote that munitions factories had a 'bad name' in the North for illicit intercourse during night shifts. 'Most girls are ashamed of admitting they work at Risley or Euxton munition factories.' It is not possible to corroborate these claims, the drinking might be an exaggeration and the latter mere gossip, though both are indicators of stress and symptoms of suffering that went unreported in the press.[30] Hylton wrote:

> The relationship between warfare and heightened sexual activity had been understood long before the Second World War. In his 1917 work *Reflections on War and Death*, Sigmund Freud talked of 'war aphrodisia' – the link between violence and eroticism. Originally it applied only to those in the armed forces who were directly involved in conflict, but the age of total war brought soldier and civilian alike into the front line ... The sense of living for today, lest there were no

---

[29] Ibid., FR 839.
[30] Goodman has suggested that the process of sexual harassment reinforced the power and authority of men and that women were constructed as sexually available whether or not they were. (Phil Goodman, '"Patriotic Femininity": Women's Morals and Men's Morale During the Second World War', *Gender and History*, 10, 2 (1998), p. 284).

The Aftermath of Christmas 1940

tomorrow, found its way equally into the civilian population.[31]

2. Report on Manchester and Liverpool

The bombings of Liverpool and Manchester in the pre-Christmas period of 1940 provoked a quick reaction from a government anxious to monitor morale in blitzed cities. Liverpool was visited by four Home Intelligence observers in late December and three of that quartet began working in Manchester on 4 January. The inspectors reported that they received an 'exceptional degree of other voluntary observational help' from Manchester's social workers who were described as 'high quality' but whose services were 'practically unused and completely uncoordinated in relation to Blitz problems'.[32] The contrast between Liverpool and Manchester hit the inspectors immediately:

> Going from Liverpool to Manchester was like going from an atmosphere of reasonable cheerfulness into an atmosphere of barely restrained depression. Directly investigators got into the town, only an hour away from Liverpool by road, they felt themselves back in the Blitzed town atmosphere with which they had grown familiar in the south.

This clearly contradicted what was appearing in the newspapers, but the report was headed by 'MORALE IN LIVERPOOL IS APPRECIABLY HIGHER THAN in any other Blitzed town' (the capitals the observers' own), which also revealed that other blitzed towns and cities had also suffered sharp, and unreported, drops in morale. The good mood on Merseyside, the Home Intelligence report noted, showed itself in many ways, the most obvious being the bustling night life and the large amount of singing and whistling in the streets,

---

[31] Hylton, *Their Darkest Hour*, p. 115.
[32] University of Sussex, Mass Observation Archive, FR 538.

the most popular tune being 'Bless 'Em All'. Liverpool's young, those aged under 20, were described as the most cheerful, while the most gloomy were the upper and middle classes, who had most to lose. The knock-on effect of that, the report noted, was a shortfall in the Women's Voluntary Service, typically staffed by females from the top end of society, upon which rest centres and other emergency services largely relied. The reasons for this generally good morale on Merseyside were cited as a toughness derived from the harsh economic climate of the 1930s and the city's strong religious background, particularly Roman Catholicism. If people were down, they could visit vicars and priests to find solace. The report noted that only one section of Liverpool's population came in for sustained criticism: the dock workers, who were believed to be evading work and exploiting overtime rates. Given that the dockers comprised 11 per cent of the city's workforce, this was a matter that required 'action and propaganda'. The report added:

> Undoubtedly, a considerable proportion of dockers are showing very little interest in winning the war or working hard to win it. It should seem that there are numerous ways in which the optimum transport of goods from the ship to the consumer are delayed.

If the report on Liverpool singled out one profession and the upper echelons of the city's society, Home Intelligence stated that Manchester's gloom spread to all classes and all sets of workers. The full point-by-point list of symptoms read:

I. Plenty of rumour including Haw-Haw rumours, which were common. Some of these rumours are very alarmist, eg. That a female parachutist had landed dressed as a nurse and was now working in one of the hospitals.

II. Consistent talk about air-raids and endless discussion of air-raid damage.

The Aftermath of Christmas 1940

- III. Visible alarm when sirens sounded, people running, hurrying out of pubs and dance halls, etc.
- IV. Much staring at burnt-out buildings, etc.
- V. Practically no singing or whistling in the streets
- VI. Night transport difficulties, and no taxis after an alert. Many clubs closing at 7 pm, film show failing to come off when advertised, despite absence of raid. Open pubs only doing a quarter usual business. Only one dance hall open anywhere central, and that containing 60 people as compared with 500 in a similar hall in Liverpool.
- VII. No night entertainment.
- VIII. Little laughter and joking in the streets, much silence, and at night great silence. Overheards on Ypres, peace, rottenness of war etc.
- IX. Dance halls nearly empty – see above.
- X. Higher degree of gasmask carrying.
- XI. Considerable evacuation, though still large number of children left. Reported to be a very serious increase in juvenile crime.

The report did acknowledge that plenty of Mancunians were 'determined and courageous' but conversations with senior sociologists and social workers also indicated there was 'real depression and despair' in the city. It added: 'Manchester people are definitely on edge, are afraid of the next raid, are beginning really to worry about the future with a feeling of crime semi-despair [sic]. All this is under the surface.' The report said that this could be remedied by adequate leadership and encouragement but could find little of either, commenting that the 'atrophy of local leadership' caused by the war-time relationship between local and central government led to a weakening of the 'solidarity of the bigger cities'. This was not reported by local or national newspapers.

As this book noted earlier, Home Intelligence's reporters speculated on why Manchester had not reacted in a similar manner to Liverpool, quoting 'selfishness' and 'softness'. This did not put Manchester in a favourable light, but the report did concede that, paradoxically, Liverpool benefitted from being raided more frequently:

> A steady stream of small raids actually helps many people to overcome their anxieties and make their adjustments. Then, when a big raid does come, it is only a bigger raid than the previous ones. But a big raid on a town which is mentally unprepared, which is not in training for the Blitz, is a knockout drop. In Manchester, Coventry and Southampton, there has been no such conditioning.

This lack of conditioning was exacerbated because the pre-Christmas raids were concentrated mainly on the city centres of Manchester and Salford, which had a profound effect on the area's infrastructure. Transport was more severely damaged than in Liverpool and led to a virtual close-down of the city's hub. 'The importance of transport in keeping up morale cannot be overemphasised', the Home Intelligence inspectors noted. The observers also reported that the timing of the raids, just before Christmas, 'gave a tragic bitterness to the whole affair' and was unfortunate because many of the voluntary helpers who staffed the rest centres had taken time off for the festivities. After the bombing, those volunteers often had no means of getting back into the city centre. The holiday period also meant that there were no newspapers on 25 and 26 December, a period, the report noted, when 'the local press can do so much to rally morale'.

The report accused Manchester of 'over-complacency', pointing its fingers at the 'upper classes' but in particular those responsible for preparing for blitzed conditions. It highlighted several deficiencies, including a breakdown in information that led to 'extraordinary confusions and unnecessary

The Aftermath of Christmas 1940

hardships'. As a consequence, 90 per cent of bomb victims failed to apply for help that they should have received from the Assistance Board and, when the Lord Mayor of Manchester announced another aid scheme, only four people applied in the first two days. The chief problem, however, was bad organisation on a widespread basis. The report noted that actions taken in the first 36 hours after a raid had beneficial effects on morale, but rest centres in Manchester were 'unsatisfactory and unprepared'.

One of the self-proclaimed main functions of the press is to hold authority to account and no Manchester newspaper reported these deficiencies. They also ignored what conventional news values would regard as an even stronger news story: that the city's lack of preparation was a direct result of the interference of Manchester City Council. The city had been unprepared, according to the Home Intelligence inspectors, partly because the local authority had attacked the city's emergency committee, which had led to the resignation of the chairman and other changes in personnel. When Manchester was bombed the new committee had been in place just a few weeks and the lack of experience was telling. The report read:

> The delay in taking elementary measures, such as the provision of rest centres with bedding and beds, seems incredible to the observer of London or Coventry. It is connected, of course, with the general morale of Manchester before the Blitz, which infected all groups; with a particularly striking lack of co-ordination, and several notorious local jealousies.

The report also quoted several examples of incompetence, stating: 'Many cases of errors of judgement and inefficiency which could not be tolerated in a tank or battleship, were revealed.' An example included the largest rest centre running out of registration forms for rehousing on the first morning after the Blitz. Manchester Town Hall could provide only five more of these forms when 1,000 people were in this main centre. 'The consequence of this trivial omission, which impacts on hundreds of homeless families, adds up in terms of morale to an influence on many thousands of people.'

Manchester newspapers might have wished to gloss over or ignore 'local jealousies' because highlighting them would have been seen as an attack on its target audience, but failing to pursue incidences of local authority incompetence contradicted a basic tenet of news reporting, the public watchdog. [33] By comparison, newspapers in Manchester and elsewhere in Britain quickly asked questions about the adequacy of the fire warden system, that was the duty of private firms to provide and could save buildings hit by incendiary bombs, yet ignored the other manifest inadequacies of local and central government. Whether this was fuelled by patriotism or fear of government censure, the consequence was a widespread mistrust of the media. So great was this that in 1941 the Home Intelligence inspectors were moved to criticise the local and national media, including the BBC, whose news bulletins on the Manchester Blitz were described as 'clumsy' and providing an impetus to the darker rumours sweeping the city. The report added:

> There was violent feeling among the middle class and others about the way the Manchester raids were handled on the news, and Manchester felt that they ought to have been given much more praise and much more emphasis. This is really a point which has not been sufficiently considered;

---

[33] James Curran, 'Press Reformism 1918–98: A Study of Failure', in H. Tumber, ed., *Media Power, Professionals and Policies* (London: Routledge, 2000), p. 35; Randall, *Universal Journalist*, p. 22; Cottle, *Mediatized Conflict*, p. 3.

The Aftermath of Christmas 1940

how far do the morale effects of Blitz censorship outweigh the military necessities of suppression?[34]

The next chapter will show that newspapers, even those based and printed in Manchester, moved on to other news items within days of the city's bombing, but the report noted that even what was printed could have had a negative effect. The Home Intelligence observers agreed that they had dwelt on the 'darker side of the picture' but were unapologetic because the authorities had adopted an attitude of complacency and 'we put up a fine show', and the local and national press painted a happy picture. Individual mention was made of the *Manchester Guardian,* which, as this book stated earlier, reported that every rest centre had its turkey as part of the Christmas Day celebrations. The observers wrote:

> Had there been turkey for everyone in the rest centres, and a turkey atmosphere in Manchester on Christmas day, the morale of this town might have been in a much better condition to face any trials which may lie ahead.

The rest centres were a persistent concern for the inspectors. Quoting another report, written by an 'expert' social worker, it was noted that people arrived in Manchester's 'show' centre at 11 pm on Sunday, 22 December 1941, and did not receive their first cup of tea until more than 12 hours later, at 11.30 am. Bread and jam was the lunch and dinner arrived at 5 pm on 23 December but consisted of only potatoes and gravy. 'Tea was expected in the evening but never came.' The report conceded that the meals improved but 'ran out' prematurely; noted that there were no cooking facilities 'not even a primus stove'; and that milk was provided for babies but there was no distribution of milk to children even though there was surplus caused by people who had fled the city. The

---

[34] University of Sussex, Mass Observation Archive, FR 538.

inspectors wrote that there were no medical services in the centres, adding:

> Old and infirm people suffering from shock, cripples and blind people, had to sit all night in the crowded hall. There was no-one to look after them, and it was difficult for even an able person to pick his way in and out of the room. The lavatories were up steps, which were very dark.

The report also commented on a lack of bathing facilities – many people did not have a bath for a week – room cleaning and ventilation, the last of which was pointed out to a representative of the local Welfare Department, who replied: 'This is a rest centre, not the Ritz.'

The report's conclusion listed 13 reasons why Manchester's morale had suffered more than Liverpool's. It noted the latter had a 'general conditioning of toughness' and that the former exhibited an 'astonishing lack of real preparation' and a failure to co-ordinate and harness 'all the available resources of good will and social consciousness'. Its final reason was the most damning: 'A major factor in Manchester was the lack of mental preparation, which was surely the responsibility of local leadership and central authority.' A local reporter in different circumstances would have noted that Manchester was singled out because this mental preparedness was 'undoubtedly operating, often subtly, in many other towns'.

A subsequent report, written for Home Intelligence by the Mass Observation founder Harrisson, reported that the raids on Manchester had definitely weakened the morale of the people.[35] His main target was not the local authorities, however, but the press and what he described as its 'superficial observations', underlining that the Manchester press was more culpable than most in the creation of myth. He added:

---

[35] Ibid., FR 568.

'Journalists, who are not of the working classes and who have little economic or personal experience of the masses, have produced a picture of complete courage, determination, carryonism [sic]; a vast press propaganda of "everything is OK with civilians".' The effect of this reporting, he wrote, was that it made it 'practically disloyal to suggest that morale is not perfect' and that the 'rosy atmosphere of 100 per cent morale' had been so pronounced that Home Intelligence inspectors had begun to doubt their findings about weak morale in Manchester, Portsmouth and Bristol. He added: 'Confidence in news and official statements, which are vital in keeping morale steady and people wide awake, has strikingly declined.'

3. Contemporary Reaction

The Home Intelligence report on morale in Manchester and Liverpool concluded with an appendix, a subjective account from a Mass Observation diarist, Rita Maloney, a 20-year-old female clerical worker in Manchester whose husband was a soldier serving overseas.[36] She wrote that the attack on the city had been unexpected because people had come to believe that the Luftwaffe merely passed over Manchester on the way to Liverpool. Such was the complacency that she and most of her neighbours had abandoned going to shelters when the sirens sounded. This lack of real concern continued through the two nights (Sunday and Monday) of the Manchester Blitz until she had to walk to work. She wrote:

> I must have been foolish to imagine after such a raid that I would be able to catch a bus as usual. The few that were running were full long before they came in sight, and the trams were not running at all.

---

[36] Ibid., FR 538.

She noticed the reluctance of drivers to give bus-less commuters a lift. 'I was appalled by the lack of co-operation from car drivers', she reported, contradicting the *Manchester Evening News*'s cheerful assertion that motorists 'entered into the spirit of the free "lifts" scheme this morning'. [37] Mrs Maloney added:

> There were hundreds of us all walking over pavements littered with broken glass from the broken shop windows on either side of the road. It was curious that we saw these broken windows for a mile, but no sign of any other damage.[38]

It was not until she cycled to work the following day to find Piccadilly, one of Manchester's main squares, cordoned off and saw local landmarks on fire, that the full impact of the bombing hit her. She wrote:

> I didn't realise the sight would affect me so much that I was near to tears. We were all quiet at work, shaken by the sight of so much damage ... None of us worked again, and early in the afternoon we were paid and sent home ... I was glad to get away from town.

She then deconstructed the tales of defiance that were being broadcast by newspapers and the radio and articulated a distrust of the media:

> You will hear a lot of talk of Manchester carrying on. I suppose we are, as well as any other town at any rate, but as one who lives here, it's a rather weary carrying on. When we heard the BBC's summing up of our Blitz, making it sound rather like a village which had had a stick of bombs dropped on it, along with many others, we wondered how true the reports on Coventry and Liverpool were, and all the other

---

[37] 'Buildings Dynamited in Lancashire Town', *Manchester Evening News*, 24 December 1940, p. 1.
[38] University of Sussex, Mass Observation Archive, FR 538.

towns. We are carrying on and 'taking it' because we've got to, but we aren't very happy about it.

The *Evening Chronicle* had reported that Manchester 'may be scarred and in some parts battered, but the people, after the Christmas respite, returned to work with determination.'[39] Weary, untrusting and unhappy would have been a more accurate description.

Other Mass Observation diaries underlined the sense of destruction and helplessness in the city. G. W. Shipway, the railway draughtsman referred to earlier in relation to the League of Nations, wrote: 'On reaching Piccadilly a terrible scene confronted me – streets of burning buildings. Water was being played on some, but it seemed hopeless.'[40] He added that soldiers had cordoned off a half-mile zone and, even on Christmas Day, he noted that 'soldiers were much in evidence'. Another diarist, Mrs M. Woodside from Northern Ireland, recorded that an acquaintance had just returned from bombed Manchester. She reported that the blackout was a 'farce', stating that the Luftwaffe released incendiary bombs until the city was lit up and then proceeded 'to pick their targets with HE [high explosive] bombs practically unhindered'.[41]

Even 18 months later the city had not recovered, a story at odds with what was being reported in Manchester's newspapers. Mr G. F. Sedgwick, from Glasgow, visited Manchester on holiday for a fortnight on 29 July 1942 and described what greeted him as 'depressing'. He wrote that he did not want to be over-sentimental, but added: 'It was heartrending

---

[39] 'Manchester Gets Down to Work Behind Boards', *Evening Chronicle*, 27 December 1940, p. 1.
[40] University of Sussex, Mass Observation Archive, D5199, Shipway, 17 January 1941.
[41] Ibid., D5462, M. Woodside, 2 January 1941.

to see the smashed shells of such notable buildings as the Royal Exchange, the Free Trade Hall and the Central Hall.'[42] His greatest impression was the general deterioration of the city, writing:

> It had been going down hill for some time and strenuous efforts [are] required to be made to eradicate the mess which industrialism had made of the place in the nineteenth century. Proposals were on hand to rebuild the derelict belt of slums ... around the city but progress has been sadly interfered with by the war and the place looks a ruin. I have never, for instance, seen so many empty shops and dilapidated buildings. Why private shops should have gone out of business in Manchester and not in Glasgow is impossible for me to explain.

4. Looking Back on Manchester's Blitz

The reports from Mass Observation and Home Intelligence on the Manchester Blitz were contemporary, or recorded soon afterwards. There were later accounts, including books referred to earlier, many of which were published after the myth had been fixed as how things really were. Read, a schoolboy in Manchester in the Blitz, was among them:

> Although, according to the Mass Observation reports, morale in parts of Manchester was very low after the December raids, in Burnage I never heard any complaints from my parents or at school. The Fairey Aviation works were only half-a-mile from our house, where warplanes were made, so we accepted that we were in a target area. Perhaps this even raised our morale subconsciously, letting us feel that we were more than simply a target for indiscriminate bombing, that we were on the front line, and in the phrase of the time, we could 'take it'.[43]

---

[42] Ibid., D5196, G. F. Sedgwick, September 1942.
[43] Read, *A Manchester Boyhood*, p. 79.

Read's predominantly defiant memory was not universally shared. Henry Abraham from Salford wrote: 'It was really frightening, and anyone who said he was not frightened was lying.'[44] Brenda Lees, who lived in Old Trafford, two miles south-west of the city centre, wrote a letter to her husband describing a scene of chaos in the immediate aftermath of the Manchester Blitz, with no gas, electricity or a wireless to let her family know what was happening. 'Many a time we thought the house was caving in on us … We were cramped in the cellar for 12 hours, with our limbs trembling with fright.'[45] Kathleen Fox (nee Shell), a volunteer nurse in the St John Ambulance, recalled running from Manchester Royal Infirmary to a first aid post through Seymour Park at the height of the raids. She told of the noise of the detonating bombs, chains of shells from the ack-ack guns exploding in the sky and 'the terrifying screams of bombs falling made my dash to the shelter a complete horror. Manchester was a raging inferno, encircled by a wall of fire, the sky for miles illuminated'.[46] Jean Slater, who was five when the war started, spoke of her mother, who was so scared by the sirens as she sheltered with 300 other people in Oxford Hall in Oxford Road, she had 'many a personal accident'.[47]

---

[44] Simon Wright, *Memories of the Salford Blitz. Christmas 1940* (Manchester: Richardson, 1987), p. 16.

[45] Brenda Lees, *Letter to my Husband Christmas 1940* (BBC, *People's War*, 2004) <http://www.bbc.co.uk/ww2peopleswar/stories/96/a2875296.shtml> [accessed 4 September 2009] (para. 3).

[46] Kathleen Fox, *Manchester Blitz 1940: The Worst Night* (BBC, *People's War*, 2004) <http://www.bbc.co.uk/ww2peopleswar/stories/90/a2396090.shtml> [accessed 4 September 2009] (para. 11).

[47] Jean Slater, *My Memories: A Childhood in Manchester* (BBC, *People's War*, 2003) <http://www.bbc.co.uk/ ww2peopleswar/stories/99/a2062199.shtml> [accessed 4 September 2009] (para. 11).

Tony Bryan's memory was of his last words to his mother, who would not go to a shelter in south Manchester because she was recovering in bed from an appendectomy. When she would not listen to his words of encouragement he retorted: 'It'll serve you right if you get killed.' A German bomb ensured this was a dreadful prophecy and provided him with a lifetime of self-recrimination.[48] People with relatives in the armed forces had fears beyond the Blitz. Mancunian Margaret Gittins, who was 15 in 1941, lost two of her brothers, Arthur and Ralph Stringer, and the day her family was informed the first had been killed was so impressed on her memory she could remember the weather (crisp and bright), the time (late afternoon) and the date (26 October 1941). She wrote:

> I saw my father weeping. I did not realise that men could weep. Nothing in my life had prepared me for this sorrow. My father's silent weeping shocked me into thinking I must not weep, in case it made it worse for my parents, and it was quite some days before my tears came too.[49]

5. Lingering Suspicion and Rumours

Women, trembling and wetting themselves, people nearly petrified with fears for themselves and loved ones, years of regret. These stories were from Mancunians but similar tales would be repeated wherever the bombs fell heavily. They did not make contemporary newspapers because they would have contradicted the myth that Britain 'could take it'. Questions

---

[48] Tony Bryan, *Everlasting Words: Childhood Memories during War* (BBC, *People's War*, 2003) <http://www.bbc.co.uk/ww2 peoples war/stories/90/a2009990.shtml> [accessed 4 September 2009] (para. 4).

[49] Margaret Gittins, *The Day the Telegram Came* (BBC, People's War, 2005) <http://www.bbc.co.uk/ww2peopleswar/stories/92/a3607292.shtml> [accessed 4 September 2009] (para 5).

The Aftermath of Christmas 1940

could be asked as to whether the number of Mass Observation reports represented a significant sample, and that their concerns might be as misleading as to the true mood as the forced optimism of newspaper columns, but their evidence is reinforced by the Home Intelligence reports and other contemporary accounts. From these it is clear that instead of maintaining the normal reporting conventions as listed by Curran, namely informing the public, scrutinising government, staging a public debate and expressing public opinion, newspapers in 1940 and 1941 became publishers of propaganda, ignoring official incompetence and the senses of panic and desolation felt by many of their audiences.[50]

Journalists did not report that people were not always resilient when their houses were destroyed and their loved ones killed and that there were Mancunians openly questioning whether the war was worth pursuing. The consequence was a lingering resentment against the media and the spread of dark rumours because people could see what had been reported bore little relation to what had happened. Harrisson reported for Home Intelligence that the 'intense ballyhoo' about wonderful morale after each town has been blitzed had been a formula that 'infuriated each place in turn'.[51] He stated that the BBC had suffered most because it was most reliant on official reports but extended his criticism to the media at large, writing 'Confidence in news is therefore, at present, only moderate. There is much underlying scepticism about the news.'

That became apparent within weeks of Manchester's Blitz when the relative good shape of Liverpool's morale disintegrated in May 1941. Repeated bombings stripped away the optimism of the previous Christmas and Home Intelligence

---

[50] Curran, 'Press Reformism 1918–98', p. 35
[51] University of Sussex, Mass Observation Archive, FR 568.

reported a very different picture. An inspector, whose local knowledge was bolstered by his growing up in the city, made a follow-up visit and reported that the vehemence of the discontent about the local authorities was stronger there than in any city he had visited. He noted an 'atmosphere of ineptitude' and 'lack of energy'. He added: 'Residents spoke of 'no power or drive left in Liverpool to counter-attack the Luftwaffe' ... For the first time in any town or place a conversation was heard in which one side argued in favour of our surrender.'[52]

The inspector reported that rumours were rife of peace demonstrations in Liverpool, a suggestion that was verified by a Mass Observation diarist, a Women's Auxilliary Air Force member in Preston, writing on 10 May 1941. She reported a woman named Jean saying: 'Everyone's talking about Liverpool ... They say the people there want to give in.'[53] Later that day the diarist accepted a lift in a lorry and was told more about Liverpool: 'There's 50,917 dead and God knows how many wounded, just walking the streets, with their bandages on ... There is a lot of military with bayonets – they've more or less taken it over.'[54] Seven days later an observer in Leek, Staffordshire, also reported rumours of severe disruption in Liverpool, describing: train loads of unidentified corpses being sent from Merseyside for mass cremation; martial law being imposed in heavily bombed industrial areas; homeless and hungry people marching with white flags; and food riots. On this occasion, newspapers were correct to ignore such reports because the rumours were mainly false, but the reaction is an indictment of the press. It is indicative of the mood of the British public that the rumours were believed

---

[52] Ibid., FR 706, *Liverpool*, May 1941.
[53] Ibid., Box 1, *Propaganda*, 5 May 1941.
[54] Ibid., 17 May 1941.

The Aftermath of Christmas 1940

because people knew from their own experiences that the press had abdicated its responsibility to report objectively. Knowing that newspapers and other media would never report anything negative in respect of the fight-ing of the war, imaginations went on wild sorties towards pessimism. In terms of Manchester, Rita Maloney articulated the general lack of trust in this chapter, but there were other Mass Observation observers in the city who also questioned what news and entertainment outlets were printing and broadcasting. A 17-year-old Mancunian wrote: 'People now turn from the BBC news to the German quite automatically', while R. South, a journalist working in the city, encapsulated the generic feeling that attempts were being made to sway public opinion.[55] After watching *Confessions of a Nazi Spy*, he wrote: 'We were left with the impression that it is a good propaganda film.'[56]

---

[55] Ibid., D5081, Manchester Teenager, 17, 4 December 1939.
[56] *Confessions of a Nazi Spy*, dir. by Anatole Litvak (Warner Bros., 1939), cited in University of Sussex, Mass Observation Archive, D5204, R. South, 1 January 1940.

CHAPTER NINE

ESCAPE AND THE MOVING NEWS AGENDA

1. Satisfying the Audience?

While the previous chapter showed disenchantment towards the media, the number of newspapers bought by the public increased between 1937 and 1947, the daily figure for the national press rising from 9.9 million to 15.4 million.[1] This seems contradictory, but also implies that the press, for all its perceived shortcomings, was satisfying some of the needs of the audience. Fussell argued that one was a desire for entertainment because the British public were looking for an escape from the grimness of life during the war and McNair pointed out that news values in Western democracies are flavoured by the requirement to 'win audiences with entertainment as well as information'.[2] This was borne out by other forms of entertainment that also boomed between 1939 and 1945: cinema audiences grew 58 per cent; the number of people listening to the radio increased; and more people read books from the library.[3]

If newspapers were not selling then their contribution to a myth of unrelenting fortitude would have been negligible, so the non-news reports and features had an important role to play in satisfying an audience who, evidence suggests, grew

---

[1] HMSO, *Royal Commission*, p. 195.
[2] Fussell, *Wartime*, p. 189; McNair, *News and Journalism*, p. 40.
[3] Political and Economic Planning, *The British Film Industry* (London: PEP, 1952); A. Briggs, *The War of Words, 1939–45* (Oxford: Oxford University Press, 1995), p. 18; Library Association, *A Century of Public Libraries: 1850–1950* (London: Library Association, 1950).

increasingly sceptical of what they were reading about the war. A quantitative analysis on the proportions of hard news, war and non-war, to comment, business and entertainment, was applied to the eight Tuesday editions of the three Manchester newspapers beginning 17 December 1940 and the findings were considered alongside research undertaken by the 1947–49 Royal Commission on the Press that analysed newspaper coverage in *The Times*, the *Daily Mail* and the *Daily Mirror* in 1927, 1937 and 1947.

The previous chapter indicated that there was an element within the Manchester public who believed their suffering did not get the media attention it merited and the newspapers' inclination to move on contributed to the mythology of the Blitz because they did not report the mood of the people over a longer period. In addition to the analysis of the proportions of war news, this chapter examines whether Mancunians had grounds for their grievance with an analysis of the three Manchester newspapers to chart the Christmas Blitz's fall down the news agenda. This was done by enumerating the references to the air raids on the seven subsequent Tuesdays.

To ensure that the *Manchester Guardian*, *Manchester Evening News* and *Evening Chronicle* were not exceptional, they were compared to the coverage that appeared in other newspapers: two nationals, *The Times* and the *Daily Mirror*, and the local weekly, the *Salford City Reporter*. These newspapers were chosen for their contrasting audiences. The *Mirror* was a left-leaning paper that was targeted at the working class, while *The Times*, described by Gannon as 'incomparably the most important British newspaper of the 1930s', was conservative (and Conservative) in nature, regarded as the newspaper for the establishment and had in its editor from 1929 to 1941,

Geoffrey Dawson, a lifelong friend of Lord Halifax.[4] The *Salford City Reporter* had a narrowly defined, and largely working class, audience and its coverage rarely strayed even into other parts of Greater Manchester. Formed in 1879 by Peter Hampson, it remained in his family and in the 1940s was owned and edited by Capt. Stuart Hirst Hampson.[5] A weekly paper published on Fridays, it merged with the *Salford Chronicle and Telephone* in 1926 but never threatened the dominance of its Manchester neighbours and the city's only mention in the 1949 Royal Commission on the Press was its distinction as the largest conurbation outside Greater London with no daily paper.[6] Nevertheless, in the terms of this study, it provided an appropriate counterpoint to the above national newspapers and another example by which to weigh the reporting in Manchester's newspapers.

2. Entertaining the Masses

The mass evacuation of children from cities at the start of the war and the nightly journeys into safer, rural, areas provided physical means to escape the bombing, but there were intellectual ways too. Mancunians, like most Britons, suffered a variety of negative emotions from fright to war-weariness, and many took refuge in the diversions provided by newspapers and other media. The press had long realised that providing news was not its only role and Conboy identified that, early in

---

[4] Bingham and Conboy, 'The *Daily Mirror*', p. 643; Gannon, *The British Press*, p. 56; University of Sussex, Mass Observation Archive, FR 126, described *The Times* as a 'purely class A-B' newspaper, while the *Daily Mirror*'s readers were 'predominantly working class', but with a larger sample than expected of 'A-B women'.

[5] 'S. H. Hampson', *The Times*, 13 Jan 1956, p. 11.

[6] HMSO, *Royal Commission*, p. 11.

their development, English newspapers, journals and periodicals had become 'part of a generic hybrid between public information source, topical entertainment, communal identity and profit that together constituted journalism'.[7] This manifested itself in the nineteenth century partly in the publication of novels and short stories that promoted the careers of successful novelists like Charles Dickens and Arthur Conan Doyle, and by the 1930s in a myriad of features that included cookery tips, crosswords, film reviews and gossip, problem pages and sport reports.[8] Indeed, the proliferation of sport, which Bingham described as a 'central ingredient in the development of the popular newspaper', was a source of concern for the Royal Commission on the Press in 1949, which noted there was more space devoted to sport in *The Times*, *Daily Mail* and *Daily Mirror* of 1927 and 1937 than to political, social and economic news.[9] On the subject of celebrity the Commission lamented that the popular press reported 'the matrimonial adventures of a film star as though they possessed the same intrinsic importance as events affecting the peace of a continent'.[10]

Despite the Commission's misgivings, Gannon stated that the new mass literate newspaper-buying public preferred 'entertainment to information' and, with the audience demanding to be diverted, newspapers responded and even editions reporting the Manchester Blitz contained large amounts of

---

[7] Martin Conboy, 'The Print Industry – Yesterday, Today, Tomorrow', in Richard Keeble, ed., *Print Journalism: A Critical Introduction* (London: Routledge, 2005), 4–20, p. 5.

[8] Claire Tomalin, *Charles Dickens: A Life* (London: Viking, 2011), p. 63; Arthur Conan Doyle, *Memories and Adventures* (Cambridge: Cambridge University Press, 2012), p. 96.

[9] Bingham, *Gender, Modernity and the Popular Press*, p. 219; HMSO, *Royal Commission*, p. 250.

[10] HMSO, *Royal Commission*, p. 131.

newsprint devoted to non-war items. For example, only 43 per cent of the combined war, non-war and business copy in the *Manchester Guardian*'s eight broadsheet pages on the 24 December 1940, the first edition with at least 24 hours to report the Manchester Blitz, was taken up by war-related material. This seems extraordinary in the light of the world events happening on the *Guardian* readers' doorsteps, but with the censor ensuring that details of the Manchester bombing, even that it had happened at all, were kept to a minimum, the newspaper was faced with either filling its pages with non-war items or with reports of bombing elsewhere that would have alienated its audience needing recognition of its suffering.

The *Manchester Evening News*, as a local paper, had a greater freedom to report the Blitz, but still devoted large amounts of space to non-news items. This could be used for a variety of purposes and on 1 January 1941, a week after the Manchester Blitz, the *Evening News* used an entertainment report and picture on the front page as a propaganda tool, emphasising a return to normality after the Manchester Blitz with the headline: 'Morning Panto is crammed'.[11] Inevitably, the war played prominent parts in plenty of entertainment elements, the letter on page four of the 19 December issue, headlined 'He writes: I have met someone else', being typical. 'My sweetheart, who is in the army, has just written to tell me he has just met another girl', the letter, signed 'Heartbroken', read.[12] How this would have played to the many wives and girlfriends left alone because of enlistment is not recorded, but

---

[11] 'Morning Panto is Crammed', *Manchester Evening News*, 1 January 1941, p. 1.
[12] 'He Writes "I Have Met Someone Else"', *Manchester Evening News*, 19 December 1940, p. 4.

'Useless to Buy Newspapers'

it was part of the popular newspaper strategy of reporting melodrama to which its readers could relate.

Most days in the study period the *Evening Chronicle* carried a short piece of fiction, usually with only a slight reference to the war, and every day there was a light-hearted entertainment/comment piece headed 'The Northern Window' by 'Denys'. There was also significant entertainment coverage, the 13 January edition carrying three advertisements for Charlie Chaplin's film *The Great Dictator*, one for pantomime *Cinderella*, and one for Belle Vue Circus.[13] The 15 January edition devoted a quarter of page three and half of page four to the January Sales, with page five supplementing the paid-for centimetres with a promotional piece headed 'Wartime Bargains'.[14] There was also a diminished amount of space devoted to sport, including a display of dark humour on 20 January when page three reported that Lancashire had posted a message outside its Old Trafford cricket ground reading 'No play today, bad ground'.[15] Quite apart from it being outside the normal season of April to September, two bombs had blasted the Test pitch. The most insensitive advertisement also appeared on the front page of the *Evening Chronicle* in January 1941 under large type reading: 'Lost in Manchester'.[16] The absent article in question was Cinderella's glass slipper, but less than a fortnight after the Blitz, with Mancunians mourning and some looking for the bodies of relatives, the inclusion could be described as ill-timed at the very least and said something about the separation between newspapers and their audience.

---

[13] *Evening Chronicle,* 13 January 1941, p. 2
[14] 'Wartime Bargains', *Evening Chronicle,* 15 January 1941, p. 5.
[15] 'Pitch Hit', *Evening Chronicle,* 20 January 1941, p. 3.
[16] *Evening Chronicle,* 3 January 1941, p. 1.

Weather, normally a staple of national and local newspapers, proved to be a thorny issue for newspapers, as has been seen earlier. The *Evening News*'s worries about revealing details of the weather to the enemy led to the Pilgrim Papers column giving false information when it announced the weather had been so good a cricket match had taken place between Kent and Lancashire in January:

> The cricket was bright enough to make us forget the war. True, enemy aircraft were sighted high over the pavilion about noon, and during lunch a Heinkel was brought down near the ladies enclosure, but it was a grand catch that got rid of Ames at extra cover.[17]

The report was intending to demonstrate the absurdity of a country that 'has no weather' but it did not prevent the columnist, writing under the pseudonym Mr Dare Not Lie, from being upbraided by a reader for suggesting Lancashire's bowling attack was so feeble that Kent had scored 509 for 2 on the first day. 'Were Kent playing Bootle Boys Brigade or Oldham Old Age Pensioners?', Albert from Oswaldtwistle asked. 'I strongly suspect you are a man of Kent or a Kentish man, or both.'[18]

The press was not alone in being able to point to improving figures, as there was a parallel rise in the consumption of all literature. Book sales, particularly paperbacks, rose and borrowing from libraries increased, going from 247 million in 1939 to 359 million in 1953.[19] The *Manchester Guardian* reported that the number of books borrowed by young people in Manchester in November 1940 rose to 79,020,

---

[17] 'Phew! Mr Censor', *Manchester Evening News*, 22 January 1940, p. 3
[18] 'Not Out, Sir', *Manchester Evening News*, 29 January 1940, p. 4.
[19] Clarke, *Hope and Glory*, p. 212; Butler and Sloman, *English Political Facts*, p. 313.

an increase of 25,790 compared to November 1939.[20] The total number of books issued in the city was 422,113, a rise of 49,150 on the previous year and a record for any November. The most significant increase, however, came in the radio audience. The BBC, the only home-based broadcaster in Britain during the war, expanded its staff from 4,800 in September 1939 to 11,663 in March 1944, trebled its output in terms of hours, increased its transmitter power five times, and expanded its foreign language services from 10 to 45 in 1943.[21] By 1944 the BBC's 9 pm news programme was estimated to reach 43 to 50 per cent of the population and the BBC recorded its audience at 34 million (out of a population of 48 million).[22]

This success emerged from an inauspicious start because the BBC's output at the start of the war lacked popular appeal and the first radio personality of the conflict was Germany-based. In the autumn of 1939 as many as six million Britons tuned in regularly to Lord Haw-Haw's broadcasts from Berlin and by January 1940, 25 per cent of the population said they had listened to his programme the previous day.[23] This failure to engage with the audience was not entirely the BBC's fault because measures to protect the print industry had handicapped its news-gathering in the build-up to the war and, once the war had started, the scrutiny of the MOI ensured bland and dated programmes.[24] Mass Observation also reported that

---

[20] 'Manchester Reading More Books', *Manchester Guardian*, 19 December 1940, p. 3.
[21] Briggs, *The War of Words*, p. 18.
[22] Ibid., p. 43. The scale of licence evasion meant the true figure could have been as high as 40 million (S. Nicholas, *The Echo of War: Home Front Propaganda and Wartime BBC* (Manchester, Manchester University Press, 1996), p. 12.
[23] Williams, *Get Me a Murder!*, p. 126.
[24] Pronay, 'The News Media at War', p. 182. The output from the BBC in the initial months of the war was dominated by official

the public had little trust in what it was hearing on the BBC.²⁵ Nevertheless, by the end of the war 'it was radio, not newspapers, which assumed greatest prominence as purveyor of wartime news'.²⁶

Like the BBC, cinemas showed a significant increase in numbers. *Gone With The Wind* was the 'box office phenomenon of the war years' and other, hugely popular, films included *Mrs Miniver* and *Random Harvest*, which topped the UK box office numbers in 1942 and 1943 respectively.²⁷ Cinemas were closed in Britain as soon as war was declared in an inauspicious over-reaction that was reversed a week later in non-urban theatres and even London (until 6 pm) by 15 September 1939. On 4 October all cinemas were allowed to stay open until 10 pm and from 4 November 1939 until 11 pm.²⁸ Bomb damage, shortages of equipment and staff and a lack of new films caused problems but of Britain's approximately 4,800 cinemas in existence at the start of the war, it has been estimated that 'the maximum number closed at any one stage of the war was probably never more than 10 per cent of the total'.²⁹ Seat prices also had to rise thanks to increased taxation in the form of the Excess Profits Tax and an

---

broadcasts, talks by civil servants and experts on topics such as the blackout and making the most of rationed food (Williams, *Get Me a Murder!*, p. 136).

[25] University of Sussex, Mass Observation Archive, FR 126.
[26] Carruthers, *Media at War*, p. 81.
[27] *Gone With The Wind*, dir. by Victor Fleming (MGM, 1939), *Mrs Miniver*, dir. by Wiliam Wyler, (MGM, 1942), *Random Harvest*, dir. by Mervyn LeRoy, (MGM, 1942); Aldgate and Richards, *Britain Can Take It*, p. 16.
[28] University of Sussex, Mass Observation Archive, FR 24, *The Cinema in the First Three Months of the War,* January 1940.
[29] PEP, *British Film Industry*, pp. 80–81, cited in Aldgate and Richards, *Britain Can Take It*, p. 2.

Entertainments Tax, which was raised three times during the war and by 1945 amounted to 36 per cent of gross receipts.[30] Nevertheless, there was a dramatic increase in average weekly attendance, which rose from 19 million in 1939 to more than 30 million in 1945.[31]

3. War and Non-War News

This section will examine how much space was allocated by Manchester's newspapers to non-war news and other, lighter, items with a quantitative analysis over the eight weeks of the study. The war was the pre-eminent story in 1940 and 1941, particularly after Manchester was bombed in the Christmas Blitz, and this was duly reflected in the coverage but other subjects intruded on the news agenda. This study divided them into six other categories, five of which were: crime and other non-war news; comment, including editorials and leaders; business; photographs and cartoons; and advertisements. The final category was loosely combined as entertainment. Harcup and O'Neill identified five sub-categories making up entertainment – picture opportunities; reference to sex; reference to animals; humour; and Showbiz/TV – but their news values were framed 60 years after the Manchester Blitz and bore little relation to those of the 1940s.[32] Sex, for example, was barely mentioned outside court reports and instead, for this study, the category comprised: pools coupons; puzzles; gardening and other advice columns; film, book and theatre reviews; short stories; and sport. Humorous columns were included in the entertainment category, while readers'

---

[30] Ibid.
[31] Ibid.
[32] Harcup and O'Neill, 'What is News?', pp. 274–75.

letters, many of which referred to the war, were included in the figures for comment.[33]

The *Manchester Guardian* comprised 10 pages in seven of the eight editions, the exception being 24 December 1940 that had eight. This might have been due to the Christmas holiday or it might reflect the difficult circumstances in which the newspaper was published, as the night of 23/24 December was the second of the Manchester Blitz. Only advertisements, mainly classified, were on the front page, and at least 21 per cent of the content was paid for in all eight editions of the *Guardian*. In the 31 December edition that proportion rose to 28 per cent. This commercial input was vital for all newspapers during the war because the price of newsprint rose from £11 10s. (£11.50) per ton in 1938 to £45 ten years later, yet profits rose.[34] The *Manchester Guardian* benefitted from the drift of advertising to the provinces reported earlier, and the newspaper, appropriately, paid great attention to commerce, devoting at least one page and frequently two to news from the City of London and Manchester's Stock Exchange, averaging 13 per cent of the newspaper, and 18 per cent of the journalistic copy, over the study period. The proportion of business news rose to 25 per cent of the journalistic copy in the 24 December 1940 newspaper, amounting to 534 centimetres (out of 2,150 centimetres) in an edition that could report the aftermath of the first night of the Manchester Blitz and had the running story of the second night of the bombardment. War news, most of it from outside Manchester, amounted to only 594 centimetres of the 24 December edition, making it the second largest contributor to the edition after advertising, but

---

[33] Measurements were taken from copies of the newspapers on microfilm in Manchester Central Library, so, while the figures might be affected by magnification, the proportions were not.

[34] HMSO, *Royal Commission*, p. 5.

'Useless to Buy Newspapers'

still a small amount given the context of the local news available.

Over the study period, war news comprised 20 per cent of the *Manchester Guardian* and even when non-journalistic elements – cartoons, photographs and advertisements – were excluded, the percentage was 28 (Table 1). The editions in which war news was most prominent were 7 January and 4 February 1941 in which they filled 28 and 26 per cent of the newspaper (45 and 41 per cent of the written copy) respectively, but the work of the censor may be detected here because these newspapers came more than 20 days after the raids on Manchester on 23 December and 10 January. Typically, nearly three-quarters of the journalistic copy was devoted to news other than the war, with entertainment forming 18 per cent of the total. A short story appeared in every edition on the back page, alongside the readers' letters, and a crossword and the radio listings were printed on page two. Sport was severely restricted during the war and this was

Table 1. The *Manchester Guardian:* Analysis of the different proportions allocated to each category in the newspapers on Tuesdays from 17 December 1940 to 4 February 1941.

	Total column centimetres	%	% of journalistic copy
War	5,802	20	28
Non-war	4,086	14	20
Comment	3,320	11	16
Entertainment	3,640	12	18
Business	3,670	13	18
Cartoons/ Photographs	1,779	6	–
Advertisements	7,003	24	–
Total	29,300	100	100

reflected in the amount of space it filled in the *Guardian*, 400 centimetres over eight editions, or 1.4 per cent of the newspaper. Its peak contribution to the news space was 3.5 per cent of the 21 January edition. By comparison, *The Times* devoted 18, 21 and 16 per cent of its news space to sport in its 1927, 1937 and 1947 newspapers.[35] The figures for the equivalent editions of the *Daily Mail* and the *Daily Mirror* were 27, 36, 33 and 37, 36, 24 per cent respectively.

The *Manchester Evening News* comprised six broadsheet pages throughout the study period, pages four and five of which were made up entirely of advertisements and births, marriages and deaths in every edition except 24 December. The importance of the *Evening News* in terms of financing the group was mentioned earlier in the book and advertising in the evening paper was critical for both the newspaper and the poorer sister publication, the *Manchester Guardian*. Paid-for content comprised an average of 56 per cent of the newspaper, never falling below 40 per cent and rising to 60 per cent of the 7 January edition. War news averaged 15 per cent of the newspaper over the eight Tuesdays, reaching its peak on 31 December when the censors were relaxing the restrictions on what could be reported about the Manchester Blitz (Table 2). War reports comprised 35 per cent of the journalistic copy (excluding pictures/cartoons and advertising) for the eight weeks and, as business reports made up only three per cent, this meant that more than 60 per cent of the written content was filled by non-war, comment and entertainment items, though the last was a surprisingly low 10 per cent.

---

[35] Ibid., p. 250.

Table 2. *Manchester Evening News:* Analysis of the different proportions allocated to each category in newspapers on Tuesdays from 17 December 1940 to 4 February 1941.

	Total column centimetres	%	% of journalistic copy
War	2,684	15	35
Non-war	2,892	16	38
Comment	1,046	6	14
Entertainment	734	4	10
Business	229	1	3
Cartoons/Photographs	377	2	–
Advertisements	9,990	56	–
Total	17,952	100	100

The *Evening Chronicle* was also a six-page newspaper throughout the study period but it laid greater emphasis on entertainment, devoting 18 per cent of the newspaper to lighter elements including gardening advice, show business news, the Northern Window column and the crossword (Table 3). This meant entertainment filled more of the *Evening Chronicle* than any other category but Tuesday was the edition that included pools coupons, so the figure might have been slightly inflated from the norm. Sports news averaged 1.5 per cent of the paper, rising to 5 per cent of the 24 December edition in the build-up to the Christmas holiday period. War news comprised 17 per cent of the editions, rising to 36 per cent of the Christmas Eve newspaper, making up nearly half the journalistic copy.

Table 3. *Evening Chronicle:* Analysis of the different proportions allocated to each category in newspapers on Tuesdays from 17 December 1940 to 4 February 1941 (variations in percentage due to rounding up and down).

	Total column centimetres	%	% of journalistic copy
War	3,535	17	31
Non-war	2,399	11	21
Comment	1,079	5	9
Entertainment	3,677	18	32
Business	673	3	6
Cartoons/ Photographs	524	3	–
Advertisements	9,057	43	–
Total	20,944	100	99

The key statistic that can be drawn from this analysis is that the war on average filled only 20 per cent or less of Manchester's newspapers. This might seem surprising given that it was by far the most important story in 1940 and 1941, particularly after the Christmas Blitz, but it tallied with a survey undertaken by Home Intelligence that revealed 60 per cent of interviewees read newspapers for items other than war news.[36] The same report discovered that readers felt there was too much propaganda, which was making them feel apathetic about the war. Rising numbers for other forms of entertainment suggested the audiences wanted a distraction and this was reflected in newspapers' news values. Fuller wrote:

> Every newspaper, from the most cosmopolitan national daily to the smallest rural weekly, is provincial. To survive, a

---

[36] University of Sussex, Mass Observation Archive, FR 126.

newspaper must reflect a specific audience, usually by holding up a mirror to a particular place. It must share with its readers a sensibility and a set of interests, tastes and values.[37]

There were other imperatives. Even without the restrictions on reporting the effects of the bombing, weather and so on, the censor's work elsewhere encouraged newspapers to report non-war items. Entertainment and lighter news, like crime, gave Manchester's editors, who were restricted in what they could publish about the war, an opportunity to make their newspapers distinctive. The evidence suggests they grasped that opportunity.

4. Piccadilly, Manchester, or Piccadilly, London?

Wars are exceptional in that events move quickly and incidents that would remain in the news agenda in normal times are swiftly overtaken. In the Second World War Germany launched bombing raids on Britain, to a lesser and greater extent, for five years, so even hugely significant local events, such as the Manchester Blitz, expeditiously descended the news agenda. Within a week of the Christmas raids on Manchester, London suffered the big raid on 29 December and what was happening in Piccadilly, Manchester, was superseded by Piccadilly in the West End. For national newspapers news priorities moved 200 miles south very quickly; what was surprising was that Manchester's newspapers followed just as rapidly.

The censor was partly to blame. Randall noted that timing is important:

> News, unlike wine, does not improve with keeping. Elapsed time, however, is not the most important of factors in itself.

---

[37] Jack Fuller, *News Values* (Chicago, IL: University of Chicago Press, 1997), p. 69.

> If you learn of a major development three weeks after it has occurred, the crucial factor is not the delay, but how many people have learnt of the development in the meantime. If the story is still not public knowledge, the three-week interval will not significantly reduce the news value ... Timing is more often a negative factor, subtracting value when there are delays which allow the story to become widely known.[38]

With the censor insisting that national newspapers could not name bombed cities until it was certain the Germans knew where they had raided, normally meaning a delay of two days, and restrictions on identifying localities and damage to buildings for 28 days, the news value was diminished, particularly when the local population could witness the damage with their own eyes. There was also an eagerness to subsume the Manchester narrative into the national one constructed around St Paul's, the City and the East End.[39] This meant that even in late December 1940, when the city and its people were at their lowest, there was no distinctive northern voice recorded in Manchester's newspapers.

The way the news focus moved quickly away from Manchester was best illustrated by *The Observer*, a national Sunday newspaper whose first opportunity to report and reflect on what had happened in the city on 22/23 and 23/24 December was in its 29 December issue. Sunday newspapers, according to Hamilton, should analyse and amplify the news – 'On a busy weekday, people wanted newspapers with well-organised, instantly accessible information. But on Sundays they wanted something more.' – yet only three reports contained the word 'Manchester' in *The Observer* on 29 December and one of those was on the sports page about football

---

[38] Randall, *Universal Journalist*, p. 26.
[39] Calder, *The Myth of the Blitz*, p. xiv.

'Useless to Buy Newspapers'

results.[40] The principal story was on page two and comprised only nine short paragraphs and 17 centimetres of print on the previous day's mass burial at Southern Cemetery.[41] Given that *The Observer* was printed too early to report on the previous night's attack on the capital when the Luftwaffe dropped 10,000 incendiaries – a headline read 'Quiet day in London' – such neglect reflected the eagerness of all editors to report the latest news rather than reflect on past events.[42]

The Observer was and is a national newspaper and had to satisfy an audience that was far wider than Manchester. Yet, surprisingly, both the *Manchester Evening News* and the *Evening Chronicle* also failed properly to report the aftermath of the city's Blitz, neglecting to highlight the deficiencies listed by Home Intelligence, to report the plethora of human interest stories, or to examine the restoration to normality or the rebuilding of the transport and utility infrastructure. By 30 December, eight days after the first night of the raids, the concentration of the *Evening Chronicle* was on London. The main headline read: 'Guildhall and other famous buildings damaged', while the strap line was 'Nazis' deliberate attempt to fire city of London'. This was complemented by a picture of the wrecked Guildhall, with a headline 'Nazis chose this as a target'.[43] The only Manchester reference on page one was a small article reporting a message to the city's people from the chairman of the Manchester Emergency Committee.[44]

---

[40] Hamilton, *Editor-in-Chief*, p. 86; 'Football: Yesterday's Results Rugby Union, *The Observer*, 29 December 1940, p. 10.
[41] 'Mass Funeral in Manchester: Air Raid Victims Buried', *The Observer*, 29 December 1940, p. 2.
[42] 'Quiet Day in London', *The Observer*, 29 December 1940, p. 7.
[43] 'Guildhall and Other Famous Buildings Damaged', *Evening Chronicle*, 30 December 1940, p. 1.
[44] 'Tribute', *Evening Chronicle*, 30 December 1940, p. 1.

Looking at the *Evening Chronicle* editions published on Tuesdays from 24 December 1940 to 4 February 1941 there is a clear pattern of diminishing coverage of the Manchester Blitz. On 24 December there were six stories about the attacks on the front page and on the back page there was a report headlined: 'Manchester is keeping its chin up.'[45] Seven days later, the number of front page reports had fallen to four, but the lead story had no reference to the city at all, and concentrated on the battle in the north Atlantic.[46] This was a surprising choice in news terms because the second lead was headlined: 'City had fewer than 500 dead'.[47] The figure was a fiction, but normative news values would have concentrated on what was still a huge number of fatalities, with a headline emphasising the rising death toll. These values were contemporary: Henry Wickham Steed, a former editor of *The Times*, was quoted by Home Intelligence in May 1940 defining news as 'something exceptional, something out of the ordinary run'.[48] The death of 500 local people was unprecedented.

If the coverage on 31 December was clearly affected by the censor, by 7 January 1941 the editorial judgement of the *Chronicle* was becoming clearer because there was not a single report on the Manchester Blitz, a surprise omission given that the city was only just beginning to recover. Only the advertisements on the back page indicated that something extraordinary had happened to the city. One read: 'Manchester carries on and so do the Fifty Shilling Tailors', while another,

---

[45] 'Manchester is Keeping its Chin Up', *Evening Chronicle*, 24 December 1940, p. 6.
[46] 'Nearer to Beating U-Boat', *Evening Chronicle*, 31 December 1940, p. 1.
[47] 'City Had Fewer Than 500 Dead', *Evening Chronicle*, 31 December 1940, p. 1.
[48] University of Sussex, Mass Observation Archive, FR 126.

'Useless to Buy Newspapers'

from a shoemakers, told customers that its St Mary's Gate shop would be restored but asked customers to 'kindly make use of the other Manchester branches'.[49] There was no reference to the Blitz in the 14 January edition, two in the 21 January newspaper, one on 28 January and none on 4 February (see Table 4, on page 217).

The attention of the *Manchester Evening News* moved even more quickly than the *Evening Chronicle* and there was no reference to the city on the front page of 27 December, only the third edition after the Manchester Blitz. By 6 January 1941 there was not a single domestic report on page one, with every story referring to foreign news. Paradoxically, the following day the *Evening News* led on a follow-up story to London's raid on 29 December, something they neglected to when it came to its own city. Reporting the bombing of the BBC, the report began: 'Today it can be revealed that Broadcasting House has twice been hit during raids and has been seriously damaged.'[50] The BBC was the national broadcaster so the report would have had impact on the *Evening News*'s readers, but the contrast is still stark.

This reflected the *Evening News*'s news agenda, no doubt influenced by its editor Haley, who was reported as saying that the capital was of prime importance, adding: 'Nothing in the North signified.'[51] This was a clear departure from the usual framing of local news and was borne out by a quantitative analysis of the references to the Manchester raids. The 24 December edition carried three large reports on page one and seven days later there was only one reference on the main news

---

[49] *Evening Chronicle*, 7 January 1941, p. 6.
[50] 'BBC Staff Killed, but Programmes Went On', *Manchester Evening News*, 7 January 1941, p. 1.
[51] Koss, *The Rise and Fall*, p. 388.

page, highlighting the need for more firewatchers.[52] This edition proved to be a high point, however, because the eight reports in total had fallen to one on 7 January 1941 and on 14 January there was only an advice column on the back page, headlined: '11 tips for Blitz victims who have a claim.'[53]

As the raids on the city became more sporadic later in 1941, this attention wandered even further and an attack on Chorlton-cum-Hardy, an area to the south of the city centre, not only failed to make the front page but was relegated to a short single-column story on page six.[54] A heavier raid received more coverage but the emphasis was on Manchester's air defences rather than the bombers, and any sense of objectivity had been surrendered. Indeed, the report could have come from a novel or a boys' comic. It read:

> Twenty three German bombers – a grand new record – were destroyed during widespread attacks on Britain last night. Twenty-two fell to our ever-deadlier night fighters. AA gunners blasted the 23rd out of the sky, and a number of others were damaged. One night fighter pilot chased his quarry 40 miles before sending in a deadly burst.[55]

The *Manchester Guardian,* as a national newspaper, had a greater interest in reflecting the national picture and it, too, quickly, switched its focus. On 27 December, the first edition when reporters could reflect on the damage to the city, the lead story on the main news page was the battle for a town on the

---

[52] 'Extend the Watch', *Manchester Evening News,* 31 December 1940, p. 1.
[53] '11 Tips for Blitz Victims who have a Claim", *Manchester Evening News,* 14 January 1941, p. 6.
[54] 'Short, Swift Raid in N-W', *Manchester Evening News,* 2 May 1941, p. 6.
[55] '23 Down in One Night: 22 by Fighters', *Manchester Evening News,* 8 May 1941, p. 1.

'Useless to Buy Newspapers'

Libya-Egypt border, and the aftermath of the Manchester Blitz did not even make the top of the page.[56] Instead it appeared below a separate report headlined:

CHRISTMAS LULL IN AIR WAR
No Bombing Attacks on Britain or on Germany.[57]

The work of the censor can be detected here because it is a non-story and even the report on the city's bombing, the bulk of which was below the fold, lacked human interest in that its headline focused on a bureaucratic exercise: a survey.[58] This avoidance of the 'human angle' was contrary to accepted reporting norms as defined by a Home Intelligence report seven months earlier. It read:

> After news of a battle has been printed and become stale, it is usually followed up by accounts of interviews with those who took part in it, what they said, what they felt, etc. ... Getting the 'human angle' on news has the advantage of making events come alive to the reader, of stirring him by personal detail.[59]

This anxiety to move on was reflected elsewhere in the *Guardian* and within a week, the main headlines on consecutive editions were: 'Last night's heavy bombing of London', 'Night fighters in action over London' and 'Guildhall destroyed: City churches suffer'.[60] This was in line with the

---

[56] 'The Siege of Bardia', *Manchester Guardian*, 27 December 1940, p. 5.
[57] *Manchester Guardian*, 27 December 1940
[58] 'A Manchester Survey After Attack', *Manchester Guardian*, 27 December 1940, p. 5.
[59] University of Sussex, Mass Observation Archive, FR 126.
[60] 'Last Night's Heavy Bombing of London', *Manchester Guardian*, 28 December 1940, p. 7; Night Fighters in Action over London', *Manchester Guardian*, 30 December 1940, p. 5; 'Guildhall

number of references to the Manchester Blitz over the study period. On 24 December 1940 the most illuminating aspect of the edition was the warning to boil drinking water referred to earlier in the book. There were four reports on the raids and that increased to five by 31 December and six by 7 January as the censor allowed more to be reported. That proved to be the peak in terms of coverage, because there were only three references to the Manchester Blitz in the 14 January 1941 newspaper, one on 21 January and two on 28 January, an extraordinary neglect in view of the scope for stories. Visually, the largest coverage of the Manchester Blitz in all the Tuesday editions came on 4 February 1941 when page three carried five photographs, comprising 182 centimetres, of Wendell Willkie's visit to Manchester. The previous chapters have highlighted that Mancunians felt their suffering had been underreported and it is perhaps a reflection of their need to share the news of the city's plight that a *Guardian* advertisement offered readers the opportunity to order reprints of the 14 January edition with a particular story, 'They came to Manchester', the principal attraction.[61] 'In many cases readers wanted copies to send to relatives and friends at home or abroad', the advertising copy read.[62] The article in question, a single column 65 centimetres long, was narrative in tone, the introduction being typical:

> Do you remember Manchester? The rain, the soot, the businessmen with their bowler hats and their neatly rolled umbrellas, and the trams. Do you remember those narrow alley-ways, paved with rough cobbles and perpetually

---

Destroyed: City Churches Suffer', *Manchester Guardian*, 31 December 1940, p. 5.
[61] 'They Came to Manchester', *Manchester Guardian*, 14 January 1941, p. 10.
[62] *Manchester Guardian*, 28 January 1941, p. 4.

running with muddy water which were so proudly and so mistakenly described as streets?[63]

The report was full of stereotypes – 'Every self-respecting Manchester man carries an umbrella' – and propaganda and skirted over much of the damage, yet the initial print could not meet the demand. A week later a second reprint was announced because 'the first supply was exhausted within a few hours'.[64]

Table 4. News stories on the Manchester Blitz on Tuesdays from 24 December 1940 to 4 February 1941.

	Manchester Guardian	*Manchester Evening News*	*Evening Chronicle*
24/12/1940	4	4	7
31/12/1940	5	8	7
07/01/1941	6	1	0
14/01/1941	3	1	0
21/01/1941	1	5	2
28/01/1941	2	2	1
04/02/1941	2	0	0

The hunger for news about the Manchester Blitz was clearly there, making the decision to leave the aftermath largely unreported more inexplicable.

5. *The Times*, the *Daily Mirror* and the *Salford City Reporter*

The above suggests there was demand for news of the Blitz, but Manchester's newspapers did not linger over their own

---

[63] 'They Came to Manchester', *Manchester Guardian*, 14 January 1941, p. 10.
[64] *Manchester Guardian*, 4 February 1941, p. 4.

city's attack. Were they atypical? Analysis of two national titles and the weekly newspaper in neighbouring Salford over the same period shows they were not. *The Times*, typically, comprised 10 broadsheet pages over the study period and cost 2*d*. (less than one penny). Of those, only five contained foreign and domestic news, two were devoted to finance, one was filled with births, marriages and deaths and two contained only small advertisements. In terms of space, news made up 50 per cent of the newspaper, but war news made up only 30 per cent of the entire edition. The main difference between *The Times* and Manchester's newspapers was the amount of space given to entertainment, just a quarter of a page, with sports news amounting to just four shorts that filled eight centimetres of newsprint. Closer analysis of the copy showed that news travelled slowly to London where the offices of *The Times* were based, so while the *Guardian* gave extensive reports on the first night of the Manchester Blitz, albeit cloaked as a North-West inland town, the only mention of that raid in *The Times* came in a report headed 'Raids again on Merseyside' and even that was only in passing: 'For the third successive night enemy aircraft were over Liverpool last evening as well as another town in the North-West.'[65] The censor's work was evident but the following night restrictions had clearly been lifted because *The Times*'s lead story was:

SEVERE RAID ON MANCHESTER

Many Buildings Burnt Down

ALL-NIGHT ATTACK[66]

The report referred to the raid on the Sunday night, rather than Monday, which is why the target could be named, but if the censor was relaxing his grip over the use of Manchester, there

---

[65] 'Raids Again on Merseyside', *The Times,* 23 December 1940, p. 4.
[66] 'Severe Raid on Manchester', *The Times,* 24 December 1940, p. 2.

'Useless to Buy Newspapers'

was plenty of evidence of propaganda in the copy in that it emphasised civilian targets. The report listed the damage to a large block of shops, a clothing store, a theatre and a hotel, while, lower down, it reported: 'Bombs fell on two public shelters, one accommodating nearly 500 people, and casualties were caused.'[67]

If that suggested to *The Times*'s readers that things were dire in Manchester, readers were reassured in the paper's next edition, 27 December. Under the headline 'Restoring order in Manchester' a report read: 'It is serious enough but not as much as one would have expected after seeing flames which, besides eating up buildings, acted as beacons for the raiders.'[68] By it were the headlines: 'A raid-free Christmas' and 'Merry-making in the shelters', neither of which referred to Manchester. With that optimistic postscript, Manchester virtually disappeared from *The Times*'s news agenda and there were passing references to the raids on the city in only nine more reports until 4 February 1941, and one of those was a single sentence announcing the abandonment of the New Year's Day meeting at the local horse-racing track.[69] There were suggestions of criticism of Manchester's preparation but only hints, the most obvious being a report on 9 January which had the headlines:

LESSONS OF THE BOMBING
GATE-CRASHING OF REST CENTRES
MANCHESTER CRITICISMS[70]

---

[67] Ibid.
[68] 'Restoring Order in Manchester', *The Times*, 27 December 1940, p. 2.
[69] 'Manchester Meeting Abandoned', *The Times*, 28 December 1940, p. 2.
[70] 'Lessons of the Bombing', *The Times*, 9 January 1941, p. 2.

The copy, as so often, was less damning. The council agreed that 'an obvious precaution should be to send representatives to learn lessons from cities already bombed' and a councillor reported that too many people had turned up at a shelter designed for 700. 'Over 1,500 persons claimed admittance as having been bombed out and all were admitted and given breakfast, the truthful and the untruthful.' Both elements had the potential for news reports but neither was followed up.

If the Manchester public felt that their suffering was largely ignored by *The Times*, the sense of neglect would have been greater in readers of the *Daily Mirror*, a newspaper that would have had a far larger circulation in a city based on manufacture and particularly so in the largely working class areas that felt the brunt of the bombing. The *Mirror*, made up of 12 tabloid pages and costing 1*d*. throughout the study period, did not acknowledge that Manchester had been attacked until 24 December 1940, an edition later than *The Times*, and the front page story comprised only three short paragraphs at the bottom of the page that displayed unusual news values.[71] The introduction concentrated on the reported shooting down of an enemy aircraft – the word 'reported' suggests there has been no official confirmation, thus weakening the story – yet the second paragraph, which was the obvious news peg, read: 'During a raid on a N-W town a number of people were trapped in cellars. Some houses were demolished and some people were killed.' Even that paragraph had a surprising order of information because the deaths should have come before those trapped in the cellars and the demolished houses. On page two there was an indication of the scale of the bombing that had hit the city on the night of

---

[71] 'Raider Down at Manchester', *Daily Mirror*, 24 December 1940, p. 1.

'Useless to Buy Newspapers'

22/23 December. Under the headline 'Manchester gets its first big bombing', the report read:

> Seventeen hours after the start of Sunday night's Blitz on Manchester, rescue squads were still working to free people trapped under damaged buildings in various parts of the city.[72]

The timescale, the word 'Blitz' and the fact that the bombing was not confined to a single area would have been an indicator of the size of the raid. The reporting was inadequate given that around 1,000 people died in Manchester, Salford and Stretford but from 24 December until the end of the study period the *Daily Mirror* made only one more reference to Manchester's Blitz and that was in a comment piece in the 'Tin Hat Tales' column of the 1 January edition. Even that was by way of an introduction to a reader's letter and began:

> You probably heard the reference in a recent BBC news bulletin to a Manchester appeal urging people not to crowd into the bombed part of the town to 'view the damage'.[73]

That would suggest there was something to see but the *Mirror* did not report it and the main references to Manchester from Christmas were in the football results.

The *Mirror* in the study period carried news on five of its 12 pages, and displayed the characteristics shown in other newspapers studied in this book in its determination to downplay German success and overrate British triumphs. For example, on 17 December, the RAF was reported as hitting railways, munitions factories and power plants in Berlin while, in the story next to it, a 34-year-old woman was described as 'The angel of the shelter' for her work in Stratford,

---

[72] 'Manchester Gets its First Big Bombing', *Daily Mirror*, 24 December 1940, p. 2.
[73] 'Tin Hat Tales', *Daily Mirror,* 1 January 1941, p. 4.

London.[74] It carried far more photographs – averaging six an edition – and put even greater emphasis on entertainment than its rivals, pages nine and 10, for example, carrying a short piece of fiction and a near full page of cartoons. This was apart from 'Jane', a daily cartoon pin-up that was considered such a circulation booster it appeared with the paper's main commentator, 'Cassandra', on page four. Jane 'was the heroine of the British Army', her contribution to the war effort being 'to take off an unprecedented number of clothes'.[75] The sexual theme was continued when a Baptist pastor in Weston-super-Mare claimed that the darkness and the close confinement of the shelters was leading to personal corruption. 'It has now become dangerous to a young man's moral reputation for him to be seen coming out of an air raid shelter at night', the report stated.[76]

The newspaper failed entirely to note the rising crime rates that were affecting young men far more profoundly than nights in shelters, although it did carry a report from Manchester, 'Sentries guard milk'. The report read: '"Milk watchers" have been organized in Manchester to break a racket that is robbing babies of their breakfast – the theft from doorsteps every morning in the blackout of bottles of milk.'[77] The report, the reference to babies' breakfasts designed to incur the reader's indignation, alleged that one supplier had counted 5,000 bottles missing in one week, yet, curiously no Manchester newspaper picked up the story. Whether that casts doubts on the veracity of the report is debatable, but the *Mirror*

---

[74] 'Mother To 500 Children', *Daily Mirror*, 17 December 1940, p. 7.
[75] Cudlipp, *Publish and Be Damned*, p. 69; Ruth Dudley Edwards, *Newspapermen: Hugh Cudlipp, Cecil Harmsworth King and the Glory Days of Fleet Street* (London: Secker and Warburg, 2003), p. 180.
[76] 'Vice Danger in Shelters', *Daily Mirror*, 17 December 1940, p. 2.
[77] 'Sentries Guard Milk', *Daily Mirror*, 21 December 1940, p. 11.

had several tales during the study period that provoke scepticism, most notably the crippled woman who had survived a night of extreme misfortune. It read: 'Tin hats off to a brave old lady who has been "bombed out" four times in a night.'[78] The report did not include the identity, the age or where this remarkable old lady lived but she was 'still smiling'.

The *Salford City Reporter*'s initial coverage of the Manchester Blitz almost certainly suffered because of the Christmas holiday. Published on 27 December 1940, the four-page edition suggested that many of its pages had been set before the first bomb had dropped and it was noticeable that a review of the year on page four amounted to more copy in terms of length than a report on page three, the main news page, on the air raids that had left more than 200 Salfordians dead and 900 injured. A further clue that the review had been compiled some time before publication was absence of any mention of the Blitz. The copy in the news report of the attacks was deferential to the censor in a manner even more pronounced than the Manchester newspapers and the introduction read: 'A town in the Manchester district had its most severe raid of the war on Sunday night. It lasted for many hours during which the sound of enemy bombers was heard at short intervals.'[79] Later the report went through the propaganda almost point by point: 'The public bore the indiscriminate attack with composure. In the morning they went to their occupations as normal. Morale was high.' There were just two reports on the raid and they amounted to less than two columns in a paper that contained 28, amounting to around seven per cent of the edition.

---

[78] 'Tin Hat Tales', *Daily Mirror*, 17 December 1940, p. 4.
[79] 'Blitz on N. W. Town', *Salford City Reporter*, 27 December 1940, p. 3.

This was not atypical. The *Reporter*, which cost three halfpence, did not ape the national and Manchester newspapers by moving its news focus to London, but it did not do justice to the very important story on its doorstep either. Apart from 27 December, the *Reporter* comprised six pages throughout the study period, with adverts on the front page and reports from the courts dominating every edition. The first newspaper of 1941 proved to be the high water mark in terms of coverage of the Christmas Blitz, comprising nearly 70 per cent of the main news page (although this still represented a surprisingly meagre amount in the context of the whole paper). The lead story maintained the anonymity of Salford but the adjoining report illustrated the balancing act newspapers had in trying to appease the censor because it carried a tribute from an un-named Mayor.[80] Given the parochial nature of the rest of the newspaper, it would have been inconceivable that he could come from anywhere other than Salford.

The following week's newspaper, 10 January 1941, gave explicit mention of the Blitz only twice, an editorial on firewatchers and another report on housing the homeless, but that could have been because of censorial pressure. Certainly the coverage expanded when the editorial on 17 January announced: 'It is now possible to mention that Salford has recently suffered from air attack by the enemy.'[81] This tacit acknowledgement of government control would not have been news to the readers of the *Reporter*, who not only could see the city had been attacked but had been reading about it in the *Manchester Evening News* and *Evening Chronicle* since 23 December. Nevertheless, the relaxation of the censorship restrictions allowed the *Reporter* to chronicle the visits of the Duke of Kent and Wendell Willkie and to print some human

---

[80] "Mayor's Message', *Salford City Reporter*, 3 January 1940, p. 3
[81] 'After The Raids', *Salford City Reporter*, 17 January 1941, p. 2.

interest stories even if they never strayed from an heroic narrative. Thus there was the driver who courageously saved a bus depot; the Salford man who was awarded the George Medal for rescuing a woman and three children from a bombed building; and the gas foreman who fought a blaze in perilous circumstances.[82] The less commendable were absent from the *Reporter*'s pages and by 7 February 1941 the Christmas Blitz was almost as scarce. There were just three mentions, and none was substantial.

---

[82] 'Drove Burning Bus into Street', *Salford City Reporter*, 24 January 1941, p. 3; 'Gallantry in Salford Air Raids', *Salford City Reporter*, 31 January 1941, p. 3; 'Fought Fire on Top of Gas Holder', *Salford City Reporter*, 31 January 1941, p. 3.

CHAPTER TEN

'USELESS TO BUY NEWSPAPERS'

1. The Front Line

While the *Daily Mirror* may have had an old lady smiling through the Blitz, the evidence suggests she was an exception. Just as the East End had been filled with plucky souls who could withstand the worst of the Luftwaffe, Mancunians were portrayed in the newspapers as a people unbowed by the Blitz of December 1940. This was a myth and, while many carried on bravely, a significant number were depressed and frightened. Calder wrote: 'Its [the myth's] construction involved putting together facts known or believed to be true, overlaying these with inspirational values and convincing rhetoric – and leaving out everything known or believed to be factual which didn't fit.'[1] Gardiner also noted:

> The Blitz has given the British – politicians in particular – a storehouse of images on which to draw at times of crisis ... There were thousands of examples of extreme bravery, fortitude and selflessness. There was also a pervasive sense of exhaustion, uncertainty and anxiety, and acts of selfishness, intransigence and contumely.[2]

The first civilian war-related deaths recorded in Britain in the Second World War were the result of a Heinkel bomber crashing into the home of Mr and Mrs W. Gill of Victoria Road, Clacton-on-Sea, killing husband and wife in May 1940; by its end 60,000 had perished.[3] Each death sent grief, fear and regret

---

[1] Calder, *The Myth of the Blitz*, p. 43.
[2] Gardiner, *The Blitz*, p. xv.
[3] Carol Harris, *Blitz Diary: Life Under Fire in World War II* (Stroud: History, 2010), p. 35.

'Useless to Buy Newspapers'

coursing through the community, but for most people, particularly those living away from the bombing, the war brought tedium. There was weariness with the rationing, frustration brought on by the restrictions and irritation caused by the disruption to lives. An ARP warden living in Leytonstone, London, in September 1940 summed up the terror and the boredom: 'I must confess that the long weary hours of waiting and listening through the night, quite alone in the house with not a soul to talk to, are very trying, but I am profoundly glad that Rube and the kiddies are away. This is no place for women and children.'[4]

Newspapers, undoubtedly, provided an escape. They entertained and informed, they maintained morale, provided a conduit for vital information and kept servicemen around the world in touch with events back home. The provincial and local press played a huge role in this despite newspaper offices being bombed, occasionally to destruction, the rationing of newsprint and ink, shortages of staff, and disruptions to transport infrastructure, and its contribution was acknowledged by Sir William Bailey, the president of the Newspaper Society, in 1946 when he wrote: 'Provincial newspapers overcame their difficulties, and, true to long established tradition, they always came out.'[5]

This claim was justified, but this book has challenged another of Bailey's assertions, namely:

> Now, after nearly six years of war – in which those newspapers have carried home-town news to men and women in every part of the world, and by their faithful reporting of local, national and international events have inspired new confidence in their readers – those newspapers

---

[4] Ibid., p. 65.
[5] Fletcher, *They Never Failed*, p. 5.

enjoy a prestige higher than at any other time in their long history.[6]

This was nonsense. By examining the three most influential provincial newspapers in Manchester in 1940 and 1941, this book has shown that the reporting was not faithful to the events, but chose instead to adopt a narrative that relentlessly stressed the positive and, as a consequence, confidence in the press did the opposite to Bailey's assertion and diminished. This was borne out by Home Intelligence inspectors, by Mass Observation diarists and by surveys that were commissioned by the Ministry of Information. More damningly, it led to reduced confidence in the press, as the British public, jaundiced by the reporting of the First World War, further questioned what they read in their newspapers. Mass Observation reported that, in the early weeks of the war, people said it was 'useless to buy newspapers since all the front pages were identical and could not be trusted', a sentiment underlined by Home Intelligence in May 1940 when it reported: 'The general curve of distrust of the news has been rising during the last year.'[7] Hylton wrote that the MOI tried to stem the flow of rumours but were not wholly successful and one explanation for their proliferation (and for the initial high audience figures for Lord Haw-Haw) was that 'the public did not believe what they were being told by the official media'.[8]

Much of this distrust was caused by censorship. Curran and Seaton have argued that the Second World War was different from previous conflicts in that the British public were in the front line for the first time. They wrote:

---

[6] Ibid.
[7] Hylton, *Their Darkest Hour*, p. 151; University of Sussex, Mass Observation Archive, FR 126.
[8] University of Sussex, Mass Observation Archive, FR 126.

'Useless to Buy Newspapers'

The strategic objective of the Blitz was to both physically impede war production and destroy psychologically the will of the civilian population to service the war effort. Extensive censorship controls were needed, it was claimed, in order to combat the new, deadly technology of aerial warfare.[9]

Newspapers, as the principal sources of news at the start of the war, became the focus of this censorship and the consequence was a shaping of content so that the press became an outlet for government propaganda. This applied to Manchester and other provincial newspapers as much as to the national press. Circulation figures underline the importance of local and regional newspapers in the Second World War in that, while the sales of national newspapers rose by 5.5 million to 15.4 million between 1937 and 1947, the corresponding figure for the provincial, weekly and bi-weekly publications was 10.2 million (13.5 million to 23.7 million).[10] This meant the British public were reading more provincial newspapers in comparison to the national press at a rate of between 36 and 54 per cent.

Bingham wrote that the rise in circulation showed that newspapers were satisfying a need, but with a qualification: 'The journalist did not necessarily believe what he or she wrote, just as the reader did not necessarily believe what he or she read.'[11] This echoed a contemporary report on the press by Home Intelligence that stated: 'In war-time when there is open censorship, everybody accepts that the government can choose what news about the war shall be published.'[12] Yet the numbers of newspapers being sold would suggest that the heroic narrative was what the readers wanted at times other

---

[9] Curran and Seaton, *Power Without Responsibility*, p. 56.
[10] Appendix 1.
[11] Bingham, *Gender, Modernity and the Popular Press,* p. 11.
[12] University of Sussex, Mass Observation Archive, FR 126.

than in the immediate aftermath of serious bombing raids. When they were victims of a Blitz, readers wanted the truth so that others could bear witness to their suffering; at other times reports of resilience and quiet courage were exactly what they required. Andina-Diaz, citing Lipset et al., argued: 'Most individuals expose themselves most of the time to the kind of material with which they agree to begin with.' [13]

A report by Mass Observation in May 1940 listed why people bought newspapers.[14] It stated that people looked to war news first, but had more permanent interests that overcame the scepticism provoked by the stream of propaganda. It

Table 5: Responses to Mass Observation survey on why people bought newspapers.

Items	Totals
News	30
Truth	20
Articles	19
Politics (The political attitude of the paper)	19
Sport	7
Format	7
Comics	7
Pictures	6
Stories	2
Astrology	1

---

[13] S. M. Lipset, P. F. Lazarsfeld, A. H. Barton and J. Linz, 'The Psychology of Voting: An Analysis of Political Behavior' in G. Lindzey, ed., *Handbook of Social Psychology*, II (Cambridge: Addison-Wesley, 1954), cited by Ascension Andina-Diaz, 'Reinforcement vs. Change: The Political Influence of the Media' in *Public Choice*, 131, 1–2 (2007), p. 67.

[14] University of Sussex, Mass Observation Archive, FR 126.

also included a table of responses from 118 interviewees in Fulham and Silvertown, London, to the question: what items do you like best in your daily newspaper? The answers are shown in Table 5.

This was a London survey, with a relatively low number of responses, but it nevertheless was an indicator of the motives behind newspaper buying. It is interesting that, at a time when newspapers felt it was important frequently to conceal the truth, 20 of the respondents chose that as their principal motive for reading the press.

2. Final Word

An indicator of the Manchester press's misjudgement of the mood of its readers, and its desire not to criticise the authorities was epitomised by a cameo that happened on the first anniversary of the city's Blitz, Christmas Eve 1941. Manchester's centre was full of shoppers, particularly in the Market Street and Deansgate areas, Dennis Wood, a retired Manchester policeman from the Heaton Park area of the city, among them. He recalled:

> Fresh in everyone's mind was the awful bombing of the previous year when the Blitz had taken such a toll. Following that horrendous period the bombing had eased and the people were beginning to relax.[15]

The festive mood disappeared at 3 pm, however, when three bombers appeared low over the roofs, the bomb doors opened, and objects were seen to be falling from the aircraft. Wood continued: 'Everyone dashed to find shelter fearing that bombs were falling. In the rush several people including some children were injured, some being run over by vehicles.' Only when it became apparent that there were no explosions and the objects were leaflets bearing a road safety message from

---

[15] Freethy, *Lancashire v Hitler*, p. 16.

the Chief Constable did the panic subside. The reaction to this insensitive act was one of suppressed anger, particularly as neither the Chairman of the Watch Committee nor the Lord Mayor, who was laying a wreath on the communal grave for the victims of 1940 as the incident happened, had been informed. The Mayor said: 'It might have been wise to have given some warning to the public before carrying out the leaflet drop.'[16] As Freethy noted:

> This was an understatement if ever there was one, but there must have been a great deal of pre-planning because photographs of the leaflet-dropping were taken, as were shots of civilians reading the leaflets. What had not been properly thought out was the insensitive disregard for the feelings of those who grieved for the dead or perhaps were injured themselves during the 1940 raid. No wonder there was a mini panic.[17]

The incident, with people so scared that they were injured fleeing, stripped bare the myth that had been peddled by newspapers of the phlegmatic British and 'we can take it', and perhaps that influenced the reaction of the press. Under normal circumstances, reporters would have berated official incompetence, particularly as the drop had happened because a police inspector had close friends in the RAF, but the *Manchester Guardian* instead nosed the story on road safety and then attacked the public. The reaction was so extraordinary the first four paragraphs of the report are reproduced in full:

> As part of a new campaign to reduce the number of road accidents in the Manchester area, three RAF bombers were employed to fly over the rooftops of the city on Wednesday afternoon and drop leaflets containing an appeal by the Chief Constable for more care on the part of drivers and

---

[16] Ibid., p. 18.
[17] Ibid.

pedestrians. The planes made several runs over the principal shopping streets, which were thronged with people doing last minute Christmas buying, and allowed what wind and air currents there were to carry the message below.

To the great majority of people the great roar of the aircraft and the sudden descent of the leaflets came as a surprise. The only notice given to the public was by means of a paragraph in a late edition of an evening newspaper.

Until the markings of the planes were distinguished there was some speculation as to whose machines they really were. When the leaflets came down many people, drawing the conclusion that they must have been sent in order to read them, went into the roadway to collect them. In doing so they paid little heed to the long lanes of Christmas traffic, and there were many narrow escapes from accident. Some other people, astonished by the unusual display, or interested in seeing a bomber at such close quarters, chose the roadway as a vantage-point from which to watch.

This foolishness on the part of the bewildered public was said by a police official amply to illustrate that the public is still unaware of the need to take infinite care, whatever their circumstances. He added that as all the other forms of propaganda seemed to have failed to educate the public sufficiently, it was decided to organise the air raid as a 'novel' way of attracting attention.[18]

The *Guardian*'s report is an extreme example, but the haranguing of people who had been scared by an act of insensitive official incompetence epitomises how far removed the reports appearing in Manchester newspapers were from what was happening on the streets of the city. It is not difficult to understand why readers lost trust in what they read, and why, if the self-appointed watchdogs of their society could

---

[18] 'R. A. F. Bombers Over Manchester', *Manchester Guardian*, 27 December 1941, p. 4.

misjudge and fabricate so readily, the press could also subscribe to an uncritical version of steadfastness under the fire of the Luftwaffe.

The above report was indicative of the gap that had been opened between newspapers and readers and helps answer the questions posed at the start of this book. Manchester's newspapers did exceed the demands of the censor and did so because of a number of reasons, the most potent of which was a desire to support the war effort. Paradoxically the effect was to damage the reputation of newspapers – Evans noted that people used to quote newspapers to establish fact: 'Oh, but it was in the papers' – while, at the same time, the narrative of the press has been so persuasive that it has become *the* history of the home front in the Second World War.[19] Such was the scale of the contribution made by journalism to the articulation and social negotiation of the myth of the Blitz. As this book has shown, the Manchester newspapers performed a significant role in the writing of that history.

---

[19] Harold Evans, *My Paper Chase: True Stories of Vanished Times* (London: Little, Brown, 2009), p. 7.

APPENDIX 1

NEWSPAPER CIRCULATIONS

The circulation of national daily newspapers in the UK (in thousands, to the nearest thousand). [1]

	1910	**1930**	**1939**	**1951**
Daily Express	400	1,603	2,486	4,193
Daily Herald	–	750	2,000	2,071
Daily Mail	900	1,968	1,510	2,245
Daily Mirror	630	1,071	1,367	4,567
Daily News	320	900	–	–
Daily Sketch	750	1,013	850	777
Daily Telegraph	230	222	640	976
Daily Worker/ Morning Star	–	–	100	115
Manchester Guardian	40	47	51	140
News Chronicle	800	967	1,317	1,583
The Times	45	187	213	254
TOTAL	**4,115**	**8,728**	**10,534**	**16,921**

---

[1] Butler and Sloman, *Political Facts*, p. 388.

Newspaper circulations in Great Britain, pre and post-war.[2]

Class of newspaper	Total circulation 1937 Average net circulation per issue	Total circulation 1947 Average net circulation for four weeks ending 29 June 1947
National morning	9,903, 427	15,449,410
London evening	1,806, 910	3,501,599
TOTAL	11,710,337	18,951,009
Provincial morning	1,600,000*	2,700,000*
Provincial evening	4,434,042	6,780,540
Other weeklies and bi-weeklies	7,420,000	14,241,692
TOTAL	13,454,042	23,722,232

* to the nearest 100,000, given to the Royal Commission of the Press in round figures to avoid disclosure of exact circulations.

---

[2] HMSO, *Royal Commission*, p. 195.

APPENDIX 2
NATIONAL NEWSPAPERS PRINTED IN MANCHESTER IN 1940

Daily Express
Daily Herald
Daily Mail
Daily Sketch
Daily Telegraph
News Chronicle
Manchester Guardian
The People
The Sunday Chronicle
Sunday Dispatch
Sunday Express
Sunday Graphic
Sunday Times

BIBLIOGRAPHY

Unprinted/Manuscript Sources

Churchill Archives Centre, Churchill College, University of Cambridge
Sir William John Haley. Diaries and correspondence 1922–86.

John Rylands Library, University of Manchester
The Guardian Archive. Papers and correspondence 1821–1970s.

Liverpool Central Library
E. Chambré Hardman Archive.

University of Sussex, Brighton
Mass Observation Archive
Diaries 1939–65.
SxMOA1/1/5/9, Box 1, *Propaganda and Morale 1939–42.*
SxMOA1/1/5/1/9, FR 24, *The Cinema in the First Three Months of the War*, January 1940.
SxMOA1/1/5/5/32, FR 126, *Report on the Press*, May 1940.
SxMOA1/1/5/11/17, FR 495, *Coventry*, November 1940.
SxMOA1/1/6/1/7, FR 538, *Liverpool and Manchester,* January 1941.
SxMOA1/1/6/2/3, FR 568, *Morale in 1941*, February 1941.
SxMOA1/1/6/3/26, FR 620, *Manchester Air Raids*, March 1941.
SxMOA1/1/6/5/26, FR 706, *Liverpool*, May 1941.
SxMOA1/1/6/8/28, FR 839, *Manchester Industrial Atmosphere*, August 1941.
SxMOA1/1/8/3/26, FR 1648, *Recent Trends in Anti-Semitism*, March 1943.

Bibliography

Published Primary Sources

Government Reports and Publications
Documents on British Foreign Policy 1919–1939 Third Series, VI and VII (London: HMSO, 1953).
Hansard, (London: HMSO).
House of Commons Debate, 10 November 1932, 270.
House of Commons Debate, 27 September 1939, 351.
House of Commons Debate, 11 October 1939, 352.
House of Commons Debate, 18 June 1940, 362.
House of Commons Debate, 31 July 1940, 363.
House of Commons Debate, 19 March 1942, 378.
House of Commons Debate, 30 June 1942, 381.
House of Lords Debate, 5 March 1940, 115.
House of Lords Debate, 8 August 1940, 117.
HMSO, *Royal Commission on the Press 1947–1949* (London: HMSO, 1949).
Library Association, *A Century of Public Libraries: 1850–1950* (London: Library Association 1950).
O'Brien, T. H., *Civil Defence* (London: HMSO, 1955).
Political and Economic Planning, *Report on the British Press: A Survey of its Current Operations and Problems with Special Reference to National Newspapers and their Part in Public Affairs* (London: Political and Economic Planning, 1938).
Political and Economic Planning, *The British Film Industry* (London: Political and Economic Planning, 1952).

Newspapers
Daily Express
Daily Mail
Daily Mirror
The Daily Telegraph
Evening Chronicle
The Independent

Manchester Evening News
Manchester Guardian
The Observer
The Times
(Copies in Manchester Central Library)

The Star
(Copies in British Library Newspaper Archive, Colindale.)

Secondary Sources

Adamthwaite, Anthony, 'The British Government and the Media, 1937–1938', *Journal of Contemporary History*, 18 (1983), 281–97.

Aldgate, Anthony and Richards, Jeffrey, *Britain Can Take It*, 2nd edn (Edinburgh: Edinburgh University Press, 1994).

Anderson, Benedict, *Imagined Communities*, 3rd edn (London: Verso, 2006).

Andina-Díaz, Ascension, 'Reinforcement vs. Change: The Political Influence of the Media', *Public Choice*, 131, 1–2, (2007), 65–81.

Andrew Marr's The Making of Modern Britain, episode 6, dir. by Roger Parsons (BBC2, broadcast on 4 December 2009).

Audit Bureau of Circulations <http://www.abc.org.uk>

Ayerst, David, *The Manchester Guardian: Biography of a Newspaper* (London: *The Guardian*, 1971).

Bandits of the Blitz, prod. by Liz Carney (BBC Radio 4, Broadcast, 8 September 2010).

Barthes, Roland, *Roland Barthes: Mythologies*, trans. by Annette Lavers (London: Vintage, 1993).

BBC, *People's War* <http://www.bbc.co.uk/ww2peopleswar>

Beaven, B. and Thoms, D., 'The Blitz and Civilian Morale in Three Northern Cities, 1940–1942', *Northern History*, 32 (1996), 195–203.

Bibliography

Bell, Amy Helen, *London Was Ours: Diaries and Memoirs of the London Blitz* (London: Tauris, 2011)

Bell, P. M. H., *The Origins of the Second World War in Europe*, 2nd edn (London: Longman, 1997).

Bernays, E. L., *Propaganda* (New York: Liveright, 1928), republished (New York: Ig Publishing, 2005).

Billig, Michael, *Banal Nationalism* (London: Sage, 2008).

Bingham, Adrian, *Gender, Modernity and the Popular Press in Inter-War Britain* (Oxford: Clarendon, 2004).

Bingham, Adrian and Conboy, Martin, 'The *Daily Mirror* and the Creation of a Commercial Popular Language', *Journalism Studies*, 10, 5 (2009), 639–54.

Blundy, A., *The Bad News Bible* (London: Review, 2004).

Box, Kathleen, and Thomas, Geoffrey, 'The Wartime Social Survey', *Journal of the Royal Statistical Society*, 107 (1944), 151–89.

Boyd-Barrett, Oliver, 'Understanding the Second Casualty', in ed. by S. Allan and B. Zelizer, eds., *Reporting War: Journalism in Wartime* (London: Routledge, 2004), pp. 25–42.

Bradley, Henry J., ed., *Fifty Great Years: Through the Eyes of the Evening Chronicle, 1897–1947* (Manchester: Kemsley, 1997).

Briggs, A., *The War of Words, 1939–45* (Oxford: Oxford University Press, 1995).

Broad, Lewis, *Winston Churchill* (London: Hutchinson, 1956)

Bryan, Tony, *Everlasting Words: Childhood Memories During War*, (BBC, People's War, 2003) <http://www.bbc.co.uk/ww2peopleswar/stories/90/a2009990.shtml>

Burnham, Lord, *Peterborough Court: The Story of The Daily Telegraph* (London: Cassell, 1955).

Butler, David and Sloman, Anne, eds., *British Political Facts 1900–1975*, 5th edn (London: Macmillan, 1975).

Calder, Angus, *The People's War: Britain 1939–45* (London: Jonathan Cape, 1969).

Calder, Angus, *The Myth of the Blitz* (London: Jonathan Cape, 1991).

Calder, Angus and Sheridan, Dorothy, eds., *Speak for Yourself: A Mass-Observation Anthology 1937–1949* (Oxford: Oxford University Press, 1985).

Camrose, Viscount, *British Newspapers and their Controllers* (London: Cassell, 1947).

Carruthers, Susan L., *The Media At War* (London: Macmillan, 2000).

Churchill, Winston S., *The Second World War*, III, *The Grand Alliance* (London: Cassell, 1952).

Clarke, Peter, *Hope and Glory: Britain 1900–1990* (London: Penguin, 1997).

Cockett, Richard, *Twilight of Truth: Chamberlain, Appeasement and the Manipulation of the Press.* (London: Palgrave Macmillan, 1989).

Cole, Hugh M., *The Ardennes: The Official History of the Battle of the Bulge* (St Petersburg, FL: Red and Black Publishers, 2011).

Conan Doyle, Arthur, *Memories and Adventures* (Cambridge, Cambridge University Press, 2012).

Conboy, Martin, 'The Print Industry – Yesterday, Today, Tomorrow', in Richard Keeble, ed., *Print Journalism: A Critical Introduction* (London: Routledge, 2005), pp. 4–20.

Conboy, Martin, *Journalism in Britain: A Historical Introduction* (London: Sage, 2011).

Cook, Andrew, *Jack the Ripper: Case Closed* (Stroud: Amberley, 2009).

Co-operative Wholesale Society, *The Manchester Blitz: Manchester Took it Too* (Imperial War Museum) <http://www.youtube.com/watch?v=Fte9DpZRfwo> [accessed 3 January 2012].

Cottle, Simon, *Mediatized Conflict* (Maidenhead, Open University Press, 2006).

Bibliography

Crozier, W. P., *Off The Record, Political Interviews 1939–45* (London: Hutchinson, 1973).

Cudlipp, Hugh, *Publish and Be Damned* (London: Dakers, 1953).

Curran, James, 'Press Reformism 1918–98: A Study of Failure', in H. Tumber ed., *Media Power, Professionals and Policies* (London: Routledge, 2000), pp. 35–55.

Curran, J. and Seaton, J., *Power Without Responsibility: Press, Broadcasting and the Internet in Britain*, 6th edn (London: Routledge, 2003).

Di Felice, Paul, 'Reconstructing Manchester's Little Italy', *Manchester Region History Review*, 12 (1998), 54–65.

Demm, Eberhard, 'Propaganda and Caricature in the First World War', *Journal of Contemporary History*, 28, 1 (1993), 163–92.

Demographia <http://www.demographia.com> [accessed 19 November 2012].

Dilks, D., 'The Unnecessary War? Military Advice and Foreign Policy in Great Britain, 1931–1939', in Adrian Preston, ed., *General Staffs and Diplomacy before the Second World War* (London: Croom Helm, 1978), pp. 98–132.

Dorril, Stephen, *Black Shirt: Sir Oswald Mosley and British Fascism* (London: Penguin, 2007).

Dudley Edwards, Ruth, *Newspapermen: Hugh Cudlipp, Cecil Harmsworth King and the Glory Days of Fleet Street* (London: Secker and Warburg, 2003).

Eatwell, Roger, 'Munich, Public Opinion and Popular Front', *Journal of Contemporary History,* 6, 4 (1971), 122–39.

Edelman, Maurice, *The Mirror: A Political History* (London: Hamish Hamilton, 1966).

Evans, Harold, *My Paper Chase: True Stories of Vanished Times* (London: Little, Brown, 2009).

Ferguson, Niall, *The Pity of War* (London: Penguin, 1998).

Fielding, Steven J., 'The Irish Catholics of Manchester and Salford: Aspects of Their Religious and Political History,

1890-1939' (unpublished doctoral thesis, University of Warwick, 1988).

Fleischer, Wolfgang, *German Air-Dropped Weapons to 1945*. (Hinckley: Midland, 2004).

Fletcher, Leonard, *They Never Failed: The Story of the Provincial Press in Wartime* (London: Newspaper Society, 1946).

Fox, Kathleen, *Manchester Blitz 1940: The Worst Night*, (BBC, People's War, 2004) <http://www.bbc.co.uk/ ww2peoples war/stories/90/a2396090.shtml>

Frankland, Noble and Webster, Charles, *The Strategic Air Offensive Against Germany, 1939–1945*, II, *Endeavour* (London, HMSO, 1961).

Franklin, Bob, Hamer, Martin, Hanna, Mark, Kinsey, Marie and Richardson, John E., *Key Concepts in Journalism Studies*, (London: Sage, 2005).

Freethy, Ron, *Lancashire 1939–1945: The Secret War* (Newbury: Countryside, 2005).

Freethy, Ron, *Lancashire v Hitler: Civilians at War* (Newbury: Countryside, 2006).

Fuller, Jack, *News Values* (Chicago, IL: University of Chicago Press, 1997).

Fussell, Paul, *Wartime: Understanding and Behaviour in the Second World War* (Oxford: Oxford University Press, 1989).

Galtung, Johan and Ruge, Mari, 'The Structure of Foreign News: The Presentation of the Congo, Cuba and Cyprus in Four Norwegian Newspapers, *Journal of International Peace Research*, 1 (1965), 64–91.

Gannon, Franklin R., *The British Press and Germany 1936–9* (Oxford: Clarendon, 1971).

Gardiner, Juliet, *The Blitz: The British Under Attack* (London: Harper, 2010).

Garfield, Simon, ed., *We Are at War: The Diaries of Five Ordinary People in Extraordinary Times* (London: Random House, 2005).

Bibliography

Gaskin, M. J., *Blitz: The Story of 29th December 1940* (London: Faber and Faber, 2005).

Gillespie, Marie, 'Transnational Communications and Diaspora Communities' in Simon Cottle, ed., *Ethnic Minorities and the Media* (Buckingham: Open University Press, 2000), pp. 164–78.

Gittins, Margaret, *The Day the Telegram Came* (BBC, *People's War*, 2005) <http://www.bbc.co.uk/ww2peopleswar/stories/92/a3607292.shtml>

Goldfarb Marquis, Alice, 'Words as Weapons: Propaganda in Britain and Germany during the First World War', *Journal of Contemporary History*, 13, 3 (1978), 467–98.

Goodman, Phil, '"Patriotic Femininity": Women's Morals and Men's Morale During the Second World War', *Gender and History*, 10, 2 (1998), 278–93.

Greenslade, Roy, *Press Gang: How Newspapers Make Profits from Propaganda* (London: Pan, 2004).

Greenslade, Roy, 'The Sun Publishes on Christmas Day' (*Guardian*, 2010) <http://www.guardian.co.uk/media/greenslade/2010/dec/23/sun-christmas>

Hadley, W. W., *Munich: Before and After* (London: Cassell, 1944).

Haldane, J. B. S., *ARP* (London: Gollancz, 1938).

Haley, Sir William, Hammond, J. L., Nichols, H. D. and Scott, C. P., *C. P. Scott 1846–1932: The Making of The Manchester Guardian* (London: Muller, 1946).

Hall, Stuart, 'Encoding/Decoding', in Paul Marris and Sue Thornham, eds, *Media Studies: A Reader*, 2nd edn (New York: New York University Press, 2000), pp. 51–61.

Hamilton, Denis, *Editor-in-Chief: Fleet Street Memoirs* (London: Hamish Hamilton, 1989).

Harcup, Tony and O'Neill Deirdre, 'What is News? Galtung and Ruge Revisited', *Journalism Studies,* 2, 2 (2001), 261–80.

Hardy, Clive, Cooper, Ian, and Hochland, Henry, *Manchester at War* (Bowdon: Archive, 1986).

Harris, Carol, *Blitz Diary: Life Under Fire in World War II* (Stroud: History, 2010).

Harrison, Stanley, *Poor Men's Guardians: A Survey of the Struggle for a Democratic Newspaper Press 1763–1973* (Southampton: Camelot, 1974).

Harrisson, Tom. *Living Through the Blitz*, 2nd edn (London: Penguin, 1990).

Hastings, Max, *All Hell Let Loose: The World At War 1939–45* (London: Harper, 2011).

Hayes, Cliff, ed., *Our Blitz: Red Skies over Manchester* (Bolton: Aurora, 1995).

Herman, Edward S. and Chomsky, Noam, *Manufacturing Consent: The Political Economy of the Mass Media* (New York: Pantheon, 1988).

Hodgson, F. W., *New Subediting* (Oxford: Butterworth-Heinemann, 1998).

Hodgson, Guy, 'Sir Nevile Henderson, Appeasement and the Press' (unpublished Master's dissertation, Open University, 2005).

Hutt, Allen and James Bob, *Newspaper Design Today* (London: Lund Humphries, 1989).

Hylton, Stuart, *Their Darkest Hour: The Hidden History of the Home Front 1939–1945* (Stroud: Sutton, 2001).

Hylton, Stuart, *A History of Manchester*, 2nd edn (Andover: Phillimore, 2010).

Imperial War Museum North, *Manchester Blitz* <http://www.iwm.org.uk/server/show/ConWebDoc.2790>

Ingles, George Harold, *When the War Came to Leicester: The Account of the Air Raids on this Great Midland City*, (Leicester: Brooks, 1945).

Bibliography

Jones, Benjamin, 'Mass Observation 75 Years On: The Extraordinary in the Everyday' (*Guardian*, 2012) <http://www.guardian.co.uk/commentisfree/2012/apr/19/mass-observation-75-years> [accessed 1 April 2013]

Jones, R. V., *Most Secret War: British Scientific Intelligence, 1939-1945* (London: Coronet, 1979).

Jowett, Garth S., and O'Donnell, Victoria, *Propaganda and Persuasion*, 5th edn (London: Sage, 2012).

Keeble, Richard, *Ethics for Journalists* (London: Routledge, 2001).

Keeble, Richard, *The Newspapers Handbook*, 3rd edn (London: Routledge, 2005).

King, Ian, 'The Press at War: The *Manchester Evening News* 1939-1945' (unpublished undergraduate dissertation, University of Manchester, 1989).

Knightley, Phillip, *The First Casualty: The War Correspondent as Hero and Myth-Maker from the Crimea to Iraq*, 5th edn (Baltimore, MD: Johns Hopkins University Press, 2004).

Koss, Stephen, *The Rise and Fall of the Political Press in Britain* (London: Hamilton, 1984).

Lang, Kurt, and Lang, Gladys Engel, 'Personal Influence and the New Paradigm: Some Inadvertent Consequences' in *The Annals of the American Academy of Political and Social Science*, 608, 1 (2006), 157-78.

Lasswell, Harold D., *Propaganda Technique in the World War* (London: Kegan, 1927).

Lasswell, Harold D., *Power and Personality* (New York: Norton, 1948).

Lawton, Richard and Cunningham, Catherine M., eds, *Merseyside: Social and Economic Studies* (Harlow: Longman, 1970).

Lees, Brenda, *Letter to my Husband Christmas 1940*, (BBC, *People's War*, 2004) <http://www.bbc.co.uk/ww2peopleswar/stories/96/a2875296.shtml>

L'Etang, Jacquie, *Public Relations in Britain: A History of Professional Practice in the Twentieth Century* (Mahwah, NJ: Lawrence Erlbaum Associates, 2004).

Levine, Joshua, ed., *Forgotten Voices of the Blitz and the Battle of Britain* (London: Ebury, 2006).

Longmate, Norman, ed., *The Home Front: An Anthology 1938–1945* (London: Chatto and Windus, 1981).

Lukowitz, David C., 'British Pacifists and Appeasement: The Peace Pledge Union', *Journal of Contemporary History*, 9, 1 (1974), 115–27.

Maconie, Stuart, *Pies and Prejudice: In Search of the North* (London: Ebury, 2007).

Madge, Charles, and Harrisson, Tom, *Britain by Mass-Observation* (London: Penguin, 1939).

Margach, James, *The Abuse of Power: The War Between Downing Street and the Media* (London: Allen, 1978).

Marr, Andrew, *My Trade* (London: Macmillan, 2004).

Masterton, Vicki and Cliff, Karen, *Stretford: An Illustrated History* (Derby: Breedon, 2002).

McNair, Brian, *News and Journalism in the UK*, 4th edn (London: Routledge, 2003).

Merseyside Maritime Museum, *Spirit of the Blitz* (2003) <http://www.liverpoolmuseums.org.uk/maritime/exhibitions/blitz/blitz.asp>

National WW2 Museum <http://www.nationalww2museum.org/history/pearlharbor.html> [accessed 11 March 2013]

Nicholas, S., *The Echo of War: Home Front Propaganda and Wartime BBC* (Manchester: Manchester University Press, 1996).

Nicolson, Harold, *Diaries and Letters 1939–1945* (London: Fontana, 1970).

Nohrstedt, S. A., Kaitatzi-Witlock, S., Ottosen R. and Riegert, K., 'From the Persian Gulf to Kosovo – War Journalism and

Bibliography

Propaganda', *European Journal of Communication*, 15, 3 (2000), 383–404.

Oxford English Dictionary <http://www.oed.com>

Perkins, Chris, and Dodge, Martin, 'Mapping the Imagined Future: The Roles of Visual Representation in the 1945 City of Manchester Plan', *Professional Geographer* 59, 1 (2007): 22–34.

Ponting, Clive, *1940: Myth and Reality* (London: Sphere, 1990).

Price, Lance, *Where Power Lies: Prime Ministers v the Media* (London: Simon & Schuster, 2010).

Pronay, N., 'The News Media at War', in N. Pronay and D. W. Spring, eds, *Propaganda, Politics and Film, 1918–45* (London: Macmillan, 1982), pp. 173–208.

Pronay, Nicholas, and Croft, Jeremy 'British Film Censorship and Propaganda Policy in the Second World War' in James Curran and Vincent Porter, eds, *British Cinema History* (London: Weidenfeld and Nicolson, 1983), pp. 144–163.

Ramsey, Winston, ed., *The Blitz Then And Now*, II (London: Battle of Britain, 1988).

Randall, David, *The Universal Journalist*, 2nd edn (London: Pluto, 2000).

Read, Donald, *A Manchester Boyhood in the Thirties and Forties: Growing up in War and Peace* (Lampeter: Edwin Mellen Press, 2003).

Reisigl, M., and Wodak R., *Discourse and Discrimination: Rhetorics of Racism and Anti-Semitism* (London: Routledge, 2001).

Richardson, John E., *Analysing Newspapers: An Approach from Critical Discourse Analysis* (Basingstoke: Palgrave, 2007).

Richardson, John, 'Readers' Letters' in Bob Franklin, ed., *Pulling Newspapers Apart: Analysing Print Journalism* (London, Routledge, 2008), pp. 56–66.

Sansom, William, *The Blitz: Westminster at War,* 3rd edn (London: Faber and Faber, 2010).

Schopflin, George, 'The Functions of Myth and a Taxonomy of Myths' in Geoffrey Hosking and George Schopflin, eds, *Myths and Nationhood*, (London: Hurst, 1997), pp. 19–35.

Secrets of the Blitz, dir. by Steve Humphries (Channel 5, broadcast on 20 January 2011).

Seymour-Ure, Colin, *The British Press and Broadcasting Since 1945*, 2nd edn (Oxford: Blackwell, 1997).

Sharf, Andrew, *The British Press and Jews under Nazi Rule* (London: Oxford University Press, 1964).

Slater, Jean, *My Memories: A Childhood in Manchester* (BBC, People's War, 2003) <http://www.bbc.co.uk/ww2peopleswar/stories/99/a2062199.shtml>

Smith, Anthony D., *Nationalism and Modernism* (Abingdon: Routledge, 2000).

Smith, J. Richard, and Creek, Eddie J., *Kampfflieger*, II (Hersham: Ian Allan Publishing, 2004).

Stansky, Peter, *The First Day of the Blitz* (London: Yale University Press, 2007).

Summerfield, Penny, 'Mass Observation: Social Research or Social Movement', *Journal of Contemporary History*, 20, 3 (1985), 439–52.

Taylor, A. J. P., *English History 1914–1945*, 2nd edn (Oxford: Oxford University Press, 1988).

Taylor, A. J. P., *The Origins of the Second World War*, 2nd edn (London: Penguin, 1991).

Taylor, Philip M., *Munitions of the Mind. A History of Propaganda from the Ancient World to the Present Era*, 2nd edn (Manchester: Manchester University Press, 1995).

Taylor, Philip M., *British Propaganda in the Twentieth Century*, 2nd edn (Edinburgh: Edinburgh University Press, 1999).

Temple, M., *The British Press* (Maidenhead: Open University Press, 2008).

Terraine, John, *The Right of the Line: The Royal Air Force in the European War 1939–1945* (Ware: Wordsworth, 1997).

Bibliography

Thomson, George P., *The Blue Pencil Admiral: The Inside Story of Press Censorship* (London: Sampson Low, Marston, 1947).

Thornburn Muirhead, J., *Air Attack on Cities: The Broader Aspects of the Problem* (London: Allen and Unwin, 1938).

Thorpe, Denis, ed., *A Long Exposure: Pictures from 100 Years of Guardian Photography in Manchester 1908–2008* (Manchester: Axis, 2008).

Times, The, History of The Times, Part 2. 1921–1948 (London: *The Times*, 1952).

Tomalin, Claire, *Charles Dickens: A Life* (London: Viking, 2011).

Turner, E. S. 'Snooping', *London Review of Books,* 3, 18 (1981), 23–24.

Van Dijk, T. A., 'Opinions and Ideologies in the Press', in Allan Bell and Peter Garrett, eds., *Approaches to Media Discourse* (Oxford: Blackwell, 2000), pp. 21–63.

Wahl-Jorgensen, Karin, 'Understanding the Conditions for Public Discourse: Four Rules for Selecting Letters to the Editor', *Journalism Studies*, 3, 1 (2002), 69–81.

Wahl-Jorgensen, Karin, 'Op-ed Pages', in Bob Franklin, ed., *Pulling Newspapers Apart: Analysing Print Journalism*, (London, Routledge, 2008), pp. 67–74.

Waterhouse, Robert, *The Other Fleet Street* (Altrincham: First Edition, 2004).

Watson, Sheila Elizabeth Rosemary, 'The Ministry of Information and the Home Front in Britain, 1939-1942' (unpublished doctoral thesis, University of London, 1980).

Weatherworld, <http://www.ukweatherworld.co.uk/forum/index.php?/topic/49321-the-severe-winter-of-1939-40-a-special-report/>

Webster, Frank, 'Information Warfare in an Age of Globalization', in Daya Kishan Thussu and Des Freedman, eds., *War and the Media,* (London: Sage, 2003), pp. 57–69.

Wells, H. G., *The War in the Air* (Whitefish, MT: Kessinger, 2004).

White, H., 'The Value of Narrativity in the Representation of Reality', in W. J. T. Mitchell, ed., *On Narrative* (Chicago, IL: Chicago University Press, 1981), pp. 5–27.

Williams, Bill, *Jews and other Foreigners: Manchester and the Rescue of the Victims of European Fascism, 1933-40* (Manchester: Manchester University Press, 2011).

Williams, F., *Dangerous Estate: The Anatomy of New Papers* (London: Arrow, 1959).

Williams, Kevin, *Get Me a Murder a Day!: A History of Media and Communication in Britain*, 2nd edn (London: Bloomsbury, 2010).

Wodak, Ruth and Meyer, Michael, eds., *Methods of Critical Discourse Analysis* (London: Sage, 2009).

Wood, D. and Dempster, D., *The Narrow Margin: The Definitive Story of the Battle of Britain* (London: Arrow, 1969).

Woods, Oliver and Bishop, James, *The Story of The Times* (London: Michael Joseph, 1985).

Wright, Simon, *Memories of the Salford Blitz. Christmas 1940* (Manchester: Richardson, 1987).